THE GESTAPO

CARSTEN DAMS AND MICHAEL STOLLE

THE GESTAPO

Power and Terror in the Third Reich

TRANSLATED BY CHARLOTTE RYLAND

OXFORD
UNIVERSITY PRESS

OXFORD
UNIVERSITY PRESS

Great Clarendon Street, Oxford, OX2 6DP,
United Kingdom

Oxford University Press is a department of the University of Oxford.
It furthers the University's objective of excellence in research, scholarship,
and education by publishing worldwide. Oxford is a registered trade mark of
Oxford University Press in the UK and in certain other countries

First Edition published in 2014
Impression: 1

Published in the United States of America by Oxford University Press
198 Madison Avenue, New York, NY 10016, United States of America

British Library Cataloguing in Publication Data
Data available

Library of Congress Control Number: 2013950536

ISBN 978–0–19–966921–9

Printed in Italy by
L.E.G.O. S.p.A.—Lavis TN

CONTENTS

CONTENTS

CONTENTS

LIST OF PLATES

PREFACE

The Secret State Police (*Geheime Staatspolizei*, 'Gestapo' for short) has come to stand for National Socialist rule and the terror of the 'Third Reich'. As the central executive organ of the Nazi state, its authority was far-reaching. It was capable of instilling a 'mixture of fear and horror' even in its contemporaries, as its head Reinhard Heydrich remarked with satisfaction on the Day of the German Police in 1941. The Day of the German Police was a propaganda event, intended to champion the work of the police in the National Socialist state. The Gestapo were also showcased, and Reinhard Heydrich announced in gratified tones that the secret police force was 'enveloped in the murmured and whispered secrecy of the political crime novel'.

Yet the Secret State Police was anything but secret. Its methods were publicized very early on in the Nazi-controlled press, the idea being that all 'opponents' of the Nazi state should be perfectly aware of whom they would be dealing with if they did not adapt to the new conditions. Nor did the Gestapo hide its workforce behind a veil of silence. Anybody who wished to could look up the names of its leading officials in one of the many calendars issued by the public authorities, or in one of the officer rank lists, which were far from secret. Indeed there was even an approachable side to the Gestapo: on the Day of the German Police Gestapo officers stood on street corners and took part in the Winter Relief collections. The aura of omniscience and omnipotence that surrounded the Gestapo was summed up by Heydrich, albeit in ironic tones, when he stated: 'And so, to put it jokingly, we are everything from "maid-of-all-work" to "rubbish bin of the Reich".'[1]

How do you approach an institution like this, which is interlaced with myth and apparent omnipotence? If you investigate the Gestapo's organization and personnel, its extraordinary dynamism immediately jumps out: in just a few years the Gestapo increased its ranks several-fold, which meant that its personnel structures were constantly evolving. The structure of the organization was also repeatedly altered. This was not the result of inadequate planning, but a conscious decision. For as Alfred Schweder, later head of the Bremen Gestapo office, outlined in his doctoral thesis in law in 1937, the Nazi state 'required a broadly dynamic police force'.[2] The force's tasks continued to evolve and expand: at first the Gestapo was only active in the German Reich, but later in the whole of Europe. This change also transformed state police practice. Many Nazi institutions went through processes of transformation, but the defining feature of the Gestapo was its state of permanent metamorphosis or, more precisely, adaptation. In other words, the Gestapo of 1933 was a different beast from that of 1936, 1939, 1942, or 1945.

A further striking feature is the close connection between the Gestapo and the SS. Franz Neumann, a German lawyer and emigrant, drew an apt conclusion as early as 1944 in his ground-breaking work *Behemoth*. Following his description of the Gestapo and its unlimited powers, he stated: 'This is the Police System in Germany. Its soul is that of the SS.'[3] Like the Gestapo, the SS is far more intertwined with National Socialist terror than all other NSDAP organizations. The symbiosis of Gestapo and SS was also evident in its leading figures: Heinrich Himmler was at once 'Reichsführer-SS and Chief of the German Police'; and Reinhard Heydrich headed the Reich Security Main Office (RSHA), which brought the state organizations of the Gestapo and the Criminal Police together under one roof with the party's SS security service (SD). This fusion of different police and party affiliations blurs the boundaries between the various agents and their competencies. It is not always clear who did what, and whether a particular deed was carried out by a Gestapo officer, a member of the criminal police, or an SD man. The question of who or what the

Gestapo was, in the final analysis, may well have been of little relevance for its victims, but it is nonetheless important to correct our understanding of it. For the Secret State Police amounted to more than just the individuals that bore its name.

Ernst Fraenkel, another lawyer who fled Germany, published a book entitled *The Dual State* in 1941, in which he differentiated between a 'Normative State' (*Normenstaat*) and a 'Prerogative State' (*Maßnahmenstaat*). He argued that both forms co-existed in the 'Third Reich', intermingling at certain points. The Normative State produced rules and legislation for the non-persecuted majority of the population. The Prerogative State, on the contrary, was able to take measures against the groups that it defined as enemies, without legal obligation, in wholly arbitrary ways and by means of brutal terror. According to Fraenkel, the Gestapo had the power 'to transfer entire spheres of life from the jurisdiction of the Normative State to the Prerogative State'.[4] In other words, the Gestapo was *the* core institution of the National Socialist Prerogative state.

More recent research into the Gestapo caused quite a stir, including in the media, when it announced that the Gestapo's success within 'state police practice' was essentially due to the fact that much of the population was prepared to support the persecution through denunciations; indeed, that these interventions even made that success possible. Although the broad scale of denunciations certainly played its part in the innumerable misfortunes of the Nazi state's victims, the active participation of organized state and party units and apparatus was more decisive. From the simple SS man to the block warden, from the security police through the officers of the Gendarmerie to the administrative clerk and the postman: all belonged to the Gestapo in their deeds, whenever they gave energetic assistance in the persecution of the 'Third Reich's' stigmatized minorities. According to one of the dictums of Werner Best, who made his inglorious mark as chief ideologue of the security police and SD, the Gestapo was to be 'doctor to the German national body', a role which permitted and required it to eradicate disease from that body—and this is how the political and above all racial 'enemies' of the Nazi regime soon came to be viewed. Yet there can be no doctor without assistants, no operation without a hospital: anyone wishing to understand the workings of the Gestapo has to consider the infrastructure of this self-appointed 'doctor'. In the case of occupied Europe it has become self-evident that the broader context in which the crack troops of mass murder were operating must be taken into account. The groups of perpetrators involved in the Holocaust were too many and varied, the institutions that took part in the crimes were too complex. Within this mass of agents it was difficult to make out the individual apparatus of the Gestapo. However, in the future a sharper focus should rest on the fact that the Gestapo functioned as part of a network *within* the Reich as well.

After 1945 the Gestapo quickly became a target for projection: all the atrocities of National Socialism were attributed to the Gestapo and/or the SS. In this way the full scope of the persecution and extermination network was suppressed. And consequently, for a long time neither the army nor the 'normal' police were made the object of prosecution, which helped millions of former soldiers, policemen, administrators, and 'simple' National Socialists to integrate into the young West German democracy or the socialist GDR state. Historical research also echoed this basic tenor at first, viewing the Gestapo as an omnipotent secret police force. It was only in the 1990s that this viewpoint changed. The image of the Gestapo then occasionally slipped into that of a rather weak political police. Although the former view did need rectifying, we believe that this new analysis was at times exaggerated: the Gestapo was by no means omniscient and omnipotent, but it was nonetheless an effective instrument of terror which, along with others, committed murder on a massive scale.

This book is not intended to provide a comprehensive account, shedding light on all aspects of the subject. This would require a far broader and more detailed study. Rather, we wish to provide a concise overview, underpinned by the authors' own research and the now considerable number of scholarly studies.[5] We intend this synthesis to close a gap in the *writing* of history. Until now, anybody who wished to find out about the Gestapo had to consult incomplete, outdated, or sensational accounts, or to work independently through the ever-growing mass of research works.[6]

The first two chapters describe the founding, organizational development, and self-image of the Gestapo, which are understood as being closely connected to state police practice. In the third chapter, by contrast, the agents step into the foreground. Starting with the leadership ranks, all the employee groups from leaders to simple civil servants are examined. The fourth chapter is devoted to the Gestapo's concrete mode of operation, which is elucidated by way of individual examples. General frameworks are explored alongside the role of informants and denunciations. The Gestapo's success, however, was rooted far more in their subsequent co-operation with other police departments and party apparatus. To reiterate: persecution through division of labour was an essential feature of the Gestapo and ultimately of the whole Nazi system.

Chapter 5 turns to the practice of persecution within the German Reich in its various phases. Here, the persecuted groups move to the foreground. At first the Gestapo's sights were set on political opponents of the regime, thus mainly communists and Social Democrats. The Gestapo also put into practice the National Socialists' hostility towards the church and religion. It held a similarly central function in the persecution of the Jews. The fact that, in addition, homosexuals and the so-called 'work-shy' and 'asocials' were persecuted makes it clear how comprehensive the Gestapo's surveillance was. This chapter closes with a section on the control of 'foreign national' (*fremdvölkisch**) forced labourers, who became the Gestapo's principal target in the final years of the war on the 'home front'. In the sixth chapter, we follow the bloody footprints that the Gestapo left across the whole of Europe. Their murderous trail moved from Poland across northern and western

---

* Translator's note: The adjective 'fremdvölkisch' literally means 'of a foreign people', whereby 'fremd' also suggests 'alien' and 'strange'. The term was used by the Nazis to mark a clear contrast with *das deutsche Volk*, the racial ideal of a 'German people'.

Europe, to south-eastern and eastern Europe. The Gestapo also played an important role in the initiation and implementation of the Holocaust. The methods practised in Europe began to be applied within the German Reich around the middle of 1944: at the last, the destructive energies hit back at the very country that had unleashed them.

The seventh and last chapter tells the post-war story of the Gestapo. What became of the perpetrators, what criminal proceedings were brought against them? Did they manage to integrate into post-war society and what form did their careers take? Finally we end where we began with Reinhard Heydrich's words: the Gestapo as myth and metaphor.

1

FOUNDATION AND EARLY YEARS

The backstory: state security in the Weimar Republic

In March 1931 the National Socialist Gauleiter for Berlin, Joseph Goebbels, wrote in his diary: 'The police are absolutely scrupulous. You can barely cough.'[1] Goebbels was particularly affected by the actions of the Prussian political police, who placed nineteen temporary bans on *Der Angriff*, the newspaper that he edited, between November 1930 and July 1932. The financial losses were significant and bans like this forced several Nazi newspapers into bankruptcy. Goebbels himself and over eighty other prominent Nazi orators were temporarily prohibited from making speeches in Prussia. The party was also closely observed by the intelligence services, which further affected Goebbels, who complained numerous times that he was plagued by spies.[2]

The information obtained through these observations and surveillance was impressive, as were the conclusions subsequently drawn, which were formulated as early as 1930 in a memorandum: 'It is further noted that the Party's participation in government and thus its influence on the allocation of government offices poses the great danger that the state itself will ultimately assist in the dismantling of the state and its powers. If the National Socialists achieve this aim, to which they are already very close, then the path to the achievement of their second aim is all the shorter: to overthrow the state through violent means and to establish a "Third Reich" in the form of a

National Socialist dictatorship, with all its damaging and pernicious repercussions in both domestic and foreign policy.'[3] This assessment makes it perfectly clear that the Prussian political police were aware of the dangers represented by the NSDAP. In other federal states, too, such as in Baden, the political police seemed competent and were above all well informed in intelligence matters.[4] It was particularly in Prussia, however, that the state security services actively intervened against the National Socialists. The Weimar Republic was not defenceless: there was a legal basis for an energetic opposition to the NSDAP, which runs counter to many current assumptions.[5] The institution charged with protecting the state was traditionally called the 'political police'. Its basic duties included surveillance, the combat of right- and left-wing extremism, and counterespionage. In other words, the duties that are today the responsibility of the regional government offices (*Landesämter für Verfassungschutz*) and the Federal Office for the Protection of the Constitution (*Bundesamt für Verfassungsschutz*) were at this time carried out by the police.

In 1930 the political police in Prussia had around 1,000 employees. It was established as Department I of the police administration in each of Prussia's forty-four administrative districts. In Berlin the political police numbered 300 employees, while other large cities such as Aachen, Dortmund, or Kiel had only a dozen.[6] The majority were trained criminal police, who had in the main volunteered for this particular role. The Prussian political police were by and large a loyal instrument of the social democratic police leadership, which was evident in the equal attention that they gave to the surveillance and combat of both KPD and NSDAP. The Prussian police were certainly not blind to the fascist threat. Nonetheless, large swathes of them were later instrumentalized by the new powers, as will be seen.

Outside Prussia, the Gestapo took even more of its recruits from the regional political police forces, on both an individual and an institutional level. Bavaria was particularly prominent in this respect: here, police officers tended already to be involved in far-right organizations and to have supported the political murders during the early years of the Weimar Republic.[7] Later, those same officers failed to take adequate action against the burgeoning National Socialist movement, which distinguished them clearly from the energetic opposition to Nazism in Prussia. In the smaller federal states, such as in Oldenburg, there was often no separate political department within the police force.[8] In other states, on the contrary, the NSDAP had already taken on some local government responsibilities before they came to power in 1933, and were thus able to exercise their influence over the police. This was the case with Wilhelm Frick, who was Minister of the Interior in Thuringia from January 1930 onwards. A survey of the state security services in the Weimar Republic thus shows that the situation differs greatly from state to state. This was due to the traditionally federal nature of the German police system. And it makes it all the more astonishing that a Gestapo which was initially organized regionally could be so successful across the whole country.

In Prussia, the crackdown on the NSDAP came to an end during the Weimar Republic. On 20 July 1932 the Prussian government was toppled, coup-like, by the chancellor Franz von Papen. This 'Papen Putsch' resulted directly in the dismissal of eleven police chiefs along with several other political police officers, amongst them Berlin's police chief, Albert Grzesinski, his deputy Bernhard Weiß, and the state secretary in the Prussian interior ministry, Wilhelm Abegg. These measures only affected the political leadership, and there were no redundancies amongst the normal rank and file. Nonetheless, this so-called 'Prussian Coup' (Preußenschlag) in the police apparatus of 20 July 1932 was the decisive breach on the path towards the 'Third Reich'.

Other personnel changes within the Berlin political police followed: convinced republicans were not dismissed, but were redeployed in administrative roles or in the criminal police, and replaced by more politically acceptable officers. At first, these were not National Socialists. In the autumn of 1932, however, individual officers began to approach the NSDAP and to make initial contacts. At this stage there was also a marked change of style in the practice of the political

3

police: in the summer of 1932, co-operation with the Central Association of German Citizens of Jewish Faith (*Centralverein deutscher Staatsbürger jüdischen Glaubens*) was halted and surveillance of the NSDAP was minimized. At the same time, communists and now Social Democrats became the almost exclusive targets of the Prussian political police. Thus, even in the months prior to the so-called 'seizure of power', the Gestapo began increasingly to crack down on the opponents of National Socialism.[9]

The Gestapo is formed

After 30 January 1933, one of the National Socialists' prime goals was to gain control of the police apparatus. However, the different conditions in each federal state meant that power could not be taken in one fell swoop. Prussia was the priority, owing to its size and the number of inhabitants, as well as the strength of its police force. National Socialist strategy was therefore aimed at this region: after Adolf Hitler as Chancellor and Wilhelm Frick as Reich Minister of the Interior, Hermann Göring ranked third amongst the National Socialist leadership. Although as Minister without Portfolio he seemed to hold a minor position, as Reich Commissioner for the Interior Ministry of Prussia he in fact played a central role in the National Socialist campaign for power. Göring was intent on turning the Prussian police into a pliable instrument for power, and on using them ruthlessly to extinguish opposition at home.

As early as 30 January 1933 Göring gave the order that all communist functionaries should be registered, so that they might be arrested as soon as the opportunity arose. The substantial material gathered by the political police of the Weimar Republic came in useful at this stage, since they were extremely well informed about both the NSDAP and the KPD. The measures taken to further transform the political police from an instrument of republican state security into a National Socialist tool were intense, as was the enforced conformity of the Schutzpolizei (the uniformed police in the cities). For a long time historians assumed that the widespread 'purging' of police personnel was triggered by the National Socialists, since they had, after all, loudly and wholeheartedly declared that they would do so. More recent investigations have suggested, however, that there was on the whole a good deal of continuity amongst personnel. How did it work in Prussia, then? By 1 February 1934 over 1,000 officials had been discharged from the Prussian police force, but this number was relatively small, comprising only 7.3 per cent of Schutzpolizei officers and 1.7 per cent of sergeants (*Wachtmeister*). Within the criminal department it amounted to 1.5 per cent, albeit over 10 per cent of the higher ranks.[10]

Within the political police the situation was different. There were no mass dismissals here, either, but a good number of redeployments and clear instances of personnel restructuring. The first to be removed from their duties were those officers who were obviously of a democratic mindset. In the main, this affected exposed officers in higher leadership positions, such as Johannes Stumm, the Chief of the Inspectorate for Right Wing Extremist Parties (*Inspektionsleiter für rechtsextreme Parteien*), who became chief of the West Berlin police after 1945. The heads of the political police executive in Bochum, Duisburg, and Frankfurt am Main were also replaced. Of a total of fifty-nine known higher-ranking criminal police officers in the Prussian police, fourteen were discharged, twenty-eight redeployed in the criminal police, eleven transferred to the Gestapo, and four posted to the Police Institute in Berlin-Charlottenburg within two years of the seizure of power.[11] In other words, there was a clear tendency towards discharge and redeployment in the higher ranks of the political police. Karl Schäfer, head of the counter-espionage department of the Frankfurt political police, confirms this in his memoirs: 'If I recall which of the criminal commissars of my acquaintance moved from the former Department I A in Prussia [...] to the Stapo, then they were either pure Defence Commissars or pure KPD specialists from the greater authorities, or those who were already clandestine NSDAP supporters.'[12]

5

Unfortunately, there are no extant statistics about the continuity of personnel within the Prussian political police as a whole. Nonetheless, it is possible to make clear assessments of certain precincts.

In Bochum, eleven of the twenty police officers active in December 1932 had been redeployed or dismissed by April 1933. By June 1935, seven of those twenty Bochum officers were working for the Gestapo.[13] Continuity was also limited in Aachen, Cologne, and Frankfurt am Main.[14] An investigation of the Prussian province of Schleswig-Holstein showed that only eighteen of its forty-three officers were transferred to the Gestapo.[15] In other words, there is much to suggest that around half of the Prussian police force was not transferred to the Gestapo.

This assertion runs contrary to mainstream research on the Gestapo—although most of those examples stem not from Prussia but from Hamburg, Bremen, or Bavaria, where the continuity of personnel was significantly greater.[16] It is also correct to say that there was constancy throughout the police apparatus as a whole. And in some respects this is true of the Gestapo, as criminal police officers were transferred into the Gestapo to replace dismissed or redeployed colleagues and to deal with the increasing need for personnel. Aside from a few exceptions, however, at first scarcely any National Socialists were recruited unless they already had the relevant professional background.

It was not only the composition of the police force that underwent change; the institution itself was also fundamentally restructured. A central feature of this process was the detachment of the political police from the interior administration. In Prussia this began as early as 9 March 1933, when the political police moved into its new home in the Karl Liebknecht Haus, the occupied KPD headquarters. The Secret State Police (Gestapo) was then officially founded in the Law on the Secret State Police of 26 April 1933.[17]

The Gestapo, as they quickly came to be known colloquially, also remained spatially separate from the police headquarters. In May 1933 the Secret State Police Office (*Geheimes Staatspolizeiamt* = Gestapa), the

Gestapo headquarters, moved into the former arts school at 8 Prinz Albrecht Straße, and stayed there until the end of the war. The later Reich Security Main Office (*Reichssicherheitshauptamt* = RSHA) was based there, too, although as the apparatus of the security services developed, their offices were spread out across more than thirty buildings.[18]

The first Gestapo Law of 26 April 1933 formed the basis for the further development of the political police and defined its extensive remit in the National Socialist context. Yet the Gestapa was not solely responsible for the remit of the political police, but only 'alongside or in place of the usual police authorities', as stated in the law.[19] In a decree of 26 April 1933, which laid out the conditions for implementing the law, Hermann Göring (recently made Prime Minister of Prussia) made the following statement about the Secret State Police: 'Its task is to investigate all political activities in the entire state that pose a danger to the state, and to gather and evaluate the results of these enquiries. This will be carried out by its own enforcement officers, with the help of regional state police offices (*Staatspolizeistellen*) and with the support of the usual police authorities [...]. Further, within its jurisdiction, the Secret State Police headquarters is authorized to request police measures from other police authorities and to issue directives.'[20]

These definitions immediately broadened the Gestapo's operational scope. The concept of 'posing a danger to the state' as opposed to being an 'enemy of the state' allowed for a broad scale when defining one's opponents.[21] And this definition of endangering the state was used solely by the Gestapo. At this early stage, then, the Gestapo was already in a special position. The Gestapa continued to hold the power to command other authorities, of which the Berlin headquarters made full use. There was one particularly significant innovation, which was not part of the law: alongside the headquarters, regional Gestapo offices (*Staatspolizeistellen* or *Stapostellen*) were founded as field offices. At their core, these were the Departments I (political police) that had been phased out, having once existed in all regional police administrations in Prussia.

Yet these regional offices had a dual function: on the one hand they were subordinate to the Gestapa, and on the other, as regional police authorities for the political police, they came under the command of the district governor (*Regierungspräsident*). This led to almost inevitable conflict over the status of the new regional Gestapo offices.

The first Gestapo Law and the changes that it brought about meant that the Gestapo was largely detached from the interior administration. Its move towards independence was then furthered by the second Gestapo Law of 30 November 1933 and the attendant regulatory statutes of 8 and 14 March 1934. The Gestapa and the regional Gestapo offices were removed from the portfolio of the interior ministry and the local police administration and put under the direct command of the Prussian Prime Minister Hermann Göring as 'Chief of the Secret State Police'. The Gestapo was now headed by the 'Inspector of the Secret State Police', Rudolf Diels, who had previously been the first head of the Gestapa. This was therefore only a change of title, although Diels did now hold significantly greater powers over the subordinate offices. Both the new official titles as well as the formal structure were firsts in the history of the Prussian administration.

This restructuring was principally Göring's reaction to the fact that the interior ministries of Prussia and the Reich were about to be combined. To prevent the Gestapo falling into the hands of Reich interior minister Frick, it had to be declared a special branch of the administration and separated off completely from the general interior administration. In view of this, Diels also restructured the Gestapa internally, so that it now consisted of five departments: I: Organization and Administration; II: Judicial Department; III: Movement Department; IV: Treason and Espionage; V: Alliance leaders (to the SA, SS, the Reichsführer-SS, and the Schutzpolizei).[22] Locally, the regional Gestapo offices were organized in a similar way: in Düsseldorf Departments I and II were identical to those in the Berlin headquarters, while the remaining roles were gathered into Department III (Executive Department).[23]

In the other Reich states the Gestapo developed along similar lines, if not under the centralized control of Berlin or Prussia. On the contrary, the example of Baden shows that the foundation, establishment, and development of the National Socialist instrument of repression in the German states was by no means an act of Prussian paternalism. Instead, it was a local response to the feared centralization of the police apparatus, as well as to the imminent reduction of the federal states' powers within the unitary state. Key positions here were initially held by Gauleiters, who as Hitler's sentinels took a strong position within the character-driven power union of the Nazi state; albeit—and this will become clear in individual cases—only until Heinrich Himmler began his rise to power out of Bavaria and raced up the career ladder within the police apparatus.

In spring 1934 the Prussian Gestapo could look back upon its first year of existence. Viewed as a whole, its development had been extraordinarily dynamic: two laws and several regulatory statutes and decrees in just one year were the expression of this rapid transformation. As a result the Gestapo had—at least on paper—been fully detached from the interior administration, and had been well stocked with additional personnel. After only one year it represented a significant force within the National Socialist power structure and aroused various forms of covetousness and jealousy.

2

ORGANIZATIONAL DEVELOPMENT

'Verreichlichung': Himmler and Heydrich take over leadership of the Gestapo*

The political police developed differently in most other states than it did in Prussia. On 9 March 1933 Heinrich Himmler was made Chief of the Munich Police. In his wake, Reinhard Heydrich became head of Department VI in the Bavarian police force—the political police. On 1 April 1933 Himmler gained the title 'Commander of the Bavarian Political Police' and an office in the Bavarian interior ministry. At the same time the Bavarian Political Police itself, BPP for short, came into being and was immediately withdrawn from the authority of Munich's police department. The BPP thus gained independence much more quickly than the Prussian Gestapo. Since Heinrich Himmler was head of the SS, the Bavarian police was associated with the SS from a very early stage, albeit at first solely on informal grounds.[1] Nonetheless, this gave a taste of things to come.

Himmler succeeded in gaining control of the political police in various other Reich states between autumn 1933 and spring 1934.[2] He was made political police commander almost everywhere, at least formally. But this should not disguise the fact that the political police in the federal states, such as in Baden or Hamburg, were initially

---

* The term *Verreichlichung* refers to the process during the 'Third Reich' by which all state structures were gradually brought together under the dominant Nazi ideology.

able to operate with significant autonomy.[3] For the time being the Gauleiters and the individual chiefs of the political police remained the main players to be reckoned with. Nonetheless Himmler and Heydrich had clearly made good progress in centralizing the political police in Germany. The only states missing in their collection were Prussia and the insignificant state of Schaumburg-Lippe. The takeover of the Prussian Gestapo, which would control well over 60 per cent of the population and surface area of the German Reich, was therefore of prime importance for Himmler and Heydrich.

They had two opponents in this aim: Prussian Prime Minister Hermann Göring and the Reich interior minister Wilhelm Frick. Göring wanted to retain control of the Prussian Gestapo because it was such a powerhouse, and Frick's motivations were the same. So what spoke in favour of handing over control of the Gestapo to Himmler and Heydrich? As Prussian Prime Minister and Minister of Aviation, Göring was powerful enough in Hitler's eyes and could deal with this loss without losing face. For Frick to take over the Gestapa would have made more sense in terms of the basic plans for centralization, but would have strengthened the civil service apparatus of the ministry, which Hitler viewed with suspicion.

In order to retain equilibrium in the Nazi leadership, it was therefore an obvious step to assign the Prussian Gestapo to Himmler and Heydrich, especially considering the need to keep the whole of the SA under surveillance, as it threatened to slip out of Hitler's control. Long negotiations in the spring of 1934 resulted in a solution that at least appeared to maintain all the reputations involved. Göring remained the official Chief of the Gestapo, Himmler became Inspector of the Gestapo, and Reinhard Heydrich took over the official business itself as Director of the Gestapo. Rudolf Diels, meanwhile, was made District Governor of Cologne, de jure a promotion, but meaning that de facto he was driven out of the central power of the Nazi state. With this, however, Himmler had not yet reached the high point of his career, although he had already made a meteoric rise.

Son of a schoolteacher, Heinrich Himmler was born on 7 October 1900.[4] His godfather and namesake was Prince Heinrich of Bavaria, who had for a period been tutored by Himmler's father. Himmler by no means came from poor stock. Towards the end of the First World War he completed his military service as an officer candidate without ever seeing action at the front. In November 1918 he was released from the military, completed his school-leaving exams (*Abitur*), and joined a Free Corps before beginning to study agriculture. During his studies he developed a world view that would be dominated by two topics until the end of his life: anti-Semitism and German settlement in the East.[5] Even if in this respect Himmler showed himself open to romantic tendencies, he was by no means an esoteric dreamer. Rather, he possessed the necessary intellectual armoury to pursue his goals with a clear awareness of power.

Through Ernst Röhm he later joined the NSDAP—taking part in the Hitler putsch of November 1923. He thus belonged to the few who were permitted to wear the Blood Order (*Blut-Orden*), which made him one of the 'old fighters' elite.[†] In 1925 he became secretary to Gregor Strasser and deputy Gauleiter of Lower Bavaria-Upper Palatinate (Niederbayern-Oberpfalz), in 1926 deputy Reich propaganda chief and a year later deputy Reichsführer-SS, until he was made Reichsführer-SS in January 1929.This was the turning point in his life: with single-minded ambition he set about building up an SS that at that point numbered only 280 men. In contrast to the SA thugs, the SS was considered a disciplined troop and was initially responsible for Hitler's personal protection. Himmler conceived the SS as a National Socialist elite, distinguishing itself through unconditional loyalty and devotion to the 'Führer'. He wanted to make of them a political and ideological order, founded on racial ideas. The growth in membership of his organization was extremely impressive: one year after taking the reins, the number of members had risen to 1,000, and by 1931 it was

---

[†] The so-called 'Alte Kämpfer' ('old fighters') were those who had joined the Nazi Party before 1930.

close to 3,000. By the beginning of 1932 the SS had increased its membership to 25,000, and when the Nazis seized power it had reached 50,000. Just a few months later there were 100,000 members.[6]

Himmler took a decisive step closer to his career goal when he was named Inspector of the Prussian Gestapo. He had strengthened the position of the SS and had largely neutralized Göring in the internal wrangling for control over the political police. They now joined forces to confront a troublesome antagonist within the National Socialist movement: as head of the SA, Ernst Röhm had become a significant force in the new state, and at the same time a constant cause of unrest.[7] Although his SA men had been indispensable as auxiliary police during the brutal consolidation of National Socialist power in 1933, Röhm's view was that the restructuring of the state should continue. He therefore sought to develop a militia whose core would be the SA, and as a result came into conflict with the leadership of the German army (the Reichswehr, the armed force of the Weimar Republic). Elements of the NSDAP around Hermann Göring and Rudolf Heß also perceived a growing danger in the SA. Yet the central figures and go-betweens in the battle against Röhm and the SA were Heinrich Himmler and Reinhard Heydrich. Together they held both the leadership of the Gestapo and the SS, including the party's own intelligence service (SD). They thus had the means at their disposal to extinguish the SA leadership. Finally, Hitler was persuaded that it was time to act.[8]

It was not only Ernst Röhm and high-ranking SA officials who fell victim to the so-called 'Night of Long Knives' of 30 June 1934. Conservative opponents to the regime and former antagonists of Hitler were also murdered, reaching a total of over 100 people. Although the Gestapo were not directly responsible for the murders, as these were carried out by SS commandos, it was involved in preparing the action, such as gathering incriminating evidence against the SA. For the SS, 30 June 1934 amounted to an increase in power: on 20 July 1934 Hitler raised them to the status of an autonomous organization within the NSDAP. By the summer of 1934, Himmler and Heydrich had not only succeeded in taking over all the political police forces in the Reich, but had also achieved complete emancipation from the SA.

The two years that followed, up to the summer of 1936, were defined by behind-the-scenes political wrangling over policing. Just as Himmler had further centralized the Gestapo, so Wilhelm Frick, who as of November 1934 was both Reich interior minister and Prussian interior minister, wished to do away with the federal structure of the police. During 1935 plans were therefore still being laid out in the interior ministry for a Verreichlichung that had already been under way for some time.[9] According to these plans, the political police would be re-integrated into the general police. This was set out in a memo by Kurt Daluege, who at the time headed the police department in the interior ministry.[10] But in a discussion with Hitler on 18 October 1935, Himmler not only succeeded in forcing his hand on the question of the anatomy of the political police but managed to have the whole police force placed under his own jurisdiction. Frick and the interior ministry were unable to make any headway against this major decision. In everything that followed, the question was simply how Himmler and the state police could be incorporated into the apparatus of state administration.

At the beginning of June 1936 the interior ministry proposed that Himmler be made head of the interior ministry's police department, at the rank of Ministerial Director, and that he be given the title 'Inspector of the German Police'. Heydrich countered this proposal and on the following day conveyed the SS view: Himmler should be given the rank of Minister and made Chief of the German Police. The disagreement could only be settled by Hitler, who refused to make Himmler a minister. Instead he followed Heydrich's suggestion and on 17 June 1936 brought together the roles of Reichsführer-SS into one title: 'Chief of the German Police in the Reich Interior Ministry'. As a result, Himmler was nominally subordinate to Frick, but was *de facto* only responsible to Hitler. Himmler refused his appointment to a civil service role, remaining a functionary in the National Socialist movement.[11] Himmler had become the most significant figure for the police as well as for the Gestapo. As Werner Best fittingly noted: 'Under the leadership of the Reichsführer-SS, the German police has become the point at which the movement and the state intersect.'[12]

The phase of relative independence came to an end in the federal states, too. In many ways the regional Gestapo offices resembled their Prussian or Bavarian predecessors, in that they had been transformed into instruments of persecution that functioned according to totalitarian principles. However, these other states had not been so quick to develop their police forces into special authorities with such wide-ranging powers. This was about to change. In a nationwide goosestep, the Gestapo gathered speed.

The construction of a *völkisch* police force: police and SS systems in the Reich and the occupied territories

The decision to appoint Himmler as 'Chief of the German Police' on 17 June 1936 was a major step in the organization of the police in the National Socialist state.[13] The SS and the police could now be merged. And by subordinating the state police to the Reichsführer-SS, the stage was set for the police finally to be restructured according to National Socialist principles. New main offices for the order police (*Ordnungspolizei*) and the security police (*Sicherheitspolizei*) were instituted on 26 June 1936, which corresponded to the existing SS headquarters. Naming these new institutions 'main offices' (*Hauptämter*) put them nominally on an equal footing with the top-ranking departments of the SS, which expressly demonstrated Himmler's desire to fuse party and state institutions. While the order police comprised the Schutzpolizei (the uniformed police in the cities), the Gendarmerie (the equivalent formation in the rural districts), and the local police (*Gemeindepolizei*), as well as the technical emergency service (*Technische Nothilfe*) and the fire guard (*Feuerschutzpolizei*), the Security Police Main Office included both the criminal police and the Gestapo. This structural consolidation makes it clear that in the Nazi state the criminal police were by no means apolitical.[14] SS-Obergruppenführer Kurt Daluege became head of the order police main office, and Reinhard Heydrich took over the main office of the security police.

In August 1936 the organization of the Gestapo was standardized across the Reich. From this point on, all political police forces were known as the 'Secret State Police'.[15] Until that point there had been no less than seventeen different terms for the political police and the Gestapo respectively.[16] In September 1936 the Gestapa in Berlin was instructed to define the duties of the political police commanders in the federal states. This was an essential step towards centralization. The third Gestapo Law, which had been signed on 10 February 1936, also contributed to this development. At first glance it was a direct continuation of its predecessor and codified the existing legal status: the Gestapo maintained the monopoly over protective detention, which had been the subject of long-standing conflict between the justice and the interior ministries on one side and the Gestapo on the other. In practice the Gestapo had already got its way, and this was now enshrined in law.[17] Furthermore, the law contained a general enabling clause which defined the role of the Gestapo as follows: 'The Secret State Police is to investigate and combat all activities throughout the entire state that pose a danger to the state, to gather and evaluate the results of these inquiries, to report to the state government and to keep the relevant authorities informed about important observations and provide them with incentives. The detail of which particular activities are to be transferred to the Secret State Police will be decided by the Chief of the Secret State Police together with the Minister for the Interior.'[18]

The Gestapo leadership still saw one disadvantage, however: the regional Gestapo offices came under the control of the district governor (*Regierungspräsident*), which initially torpedoed attempts to centralize the whole force. But only two weeks later Göring issued a decree that turned the right to issue directives upside down by instructing that, where there was doubt, a district governor had to seek a decision from the Gestapa. With this, the Gestapo had gained the highest possible level of autonomy in relation to the state administration. In the meantime, however, they faced competition from another angle: a further agent in the field of political intelligence was the Security Service (*Sicherheitsdienst*) of the SS, abbreviated to SD. Created in 1931, it was developed by Reinhard Heydrich with the aim of gaining information about political opponents and rivals in one's own ranks. Initially, the numbers in the SD were not overwhelming. In 1932 it had only thirty-three members, and although by 1936 this number had increased to 269, it was still not a large-scale organization.[19] Nonetheless, its significance should not be underestimated: as of June 1934, the SD was the only intelligence service in the NSDAP and Himmler raised it to the status of an SS Main Office on 25 January 1935.[20]

When Himmler took over the entire political police it initially seemed that, as an intelligence service, the SD was superfluous to requirement. But its role was newly defined, and it was now conceived of as an arm of the Gestapo with a more advanced ideological grounding.[21] At a closer look, it is clear that the work of Gestapo and SD overlapped significantly. Consequently, an internal document stated: 'The closest co-operation between the two organs is necessary, since they are both basically pursuing the same goal.'[22]

A first measure to intermesh the Gestapo, criminal police, and SD was the institution of the 'Inspectors of the Security Police' (IdS). All the inspectors were at the same time SD chiefs in their own districts, and none of them came from the criminal police. Although their role was initially just supervisory, and they were outranked by the higher SS and police chiefs who were instituted after them, the inspectors nonetheless played an important role in the efforts to fuse the security police and SS. These moves towards integration were strengthened by the shared training guidelines for both security police and SD, which Himmler decreed in February 1938.[23] In June 1938 there followed a further step towards amalgamation.[24] In a new decree, Himmler set out the conditions for appointing security police functionaries to the SS and determined how their ranks should be compared: all members of the security police who joined the SS were automatically made members of the SD. They were required to fulfil the standard SS conditions as well as further criteria: the individual should either have been a member of the NSDAP or one of its sub-departments before the seizure of power, or have been active in the security police for at least three years. Himmler's and Heydrich's intentions were plain: they were aiming to merge the police and SS under the leadership of the SD. But these lofty goals could not be realized without more work. Although many security police officers joined the SS, and therefore the SD at the same time, there were still scores of SD members who did not belong to the police, and who were therefore not state civil servants.

It was only the attack on Poland and the occupation that quickened the integration and led at last to the foundation of the Reich Security Main Office (RSHA) on 27 September 1939, which brought together the Main Offices of the security police and SD.[25] Predictably, its first head was Richard Heydrich, who had previously headed up both the main offices. The RSHA represented a new kind of structure, enjoying the double status of ministerial authority and SS Main Office. Although this was also nominally the case for the Main Office of the Security Police, the integration of the party's own intelligence service (SD) meant that the RSHA really did represent 'a completely new creation in political and institutional terms'.[26]

Perhaps the most important sub-department of the RSHA was Office IV: Investigating and Combating Opponents, which comprised large parts of the former Main Office of the Security Police and Departments II and III of the Prussian Gestapa. At first it was only one office of six, and as of 1941 of seven: I: Personnel; II: Organization, Administration, Law; III: German Lands; IV: Investigating and Combating Opponents; V: Crime Fighting; VI: SD—Foreign Intelligence Service; VII: Ideological Research and Evaluation. Offices I and II were responsible for the other five and formed the bureaucratic spine of the RSHA. As Reich Criminal Police Office (*Reichskriminalpolizeiamt*), Office V was the headquarters of the German criminal police, while Offices III, VI, and VII were former SD agencies.

Office IV had a special position, both in terms of content and personnel. Although it changed over time, the Gestapo always had around five times more personnel than the SD and almost three times as many as the criminal police. Furthermore, the Gestapo was the central executive organ of National Socialist terror, regardless of the powers of the criminal police. In addition, Office IV succeeded in absorbing increasing numbers of SD offices. This was above all the achievement of Gestapo chief Heinrich Müller, who was particularly trusted by both Heydrich and Himmler.

Office IV was flexible and dynamic in terms of its internal organization and development, and was frequently restructured in order to adapt to changing demands. It is consequently difficult to describe the office, and clearly any consideration or analysis can rely only on snapshots. Until its restructuring in 1943/44, Office IV was made up of six groups: IV A: Persecution of Political Opposition; IV B: Persecution of Churches and Jews; IV C: Protective Custody and Registry, Press, and NSDAP; IV D: Occupied Zones; IV E: Counterintelligence; IV F: Passports and Policing of Foreigners. Each group was then divided into up to six sections (*Referate*). Section IV B 4, for example, was responsible for Jewish matters and headed by Adolf Eichmann, while Section IV C 2 took care of 'protective custody' matters. In the restructure, Office IV was divided into just two groups: Group IV A encompassed all the specialist departments and had nineteen sections, while IV B formed the so-called Regional Divisions (*Gebietsabteilungen*) with fifteen sections.[27]

As the headquarters, Office IV was responsible for all regional Gestapo offices in the German Reich and occupied zones. It exercised extensive influence through its targeted personnel policies: Heinrich Müller had sole responsibility, in consultation with Office I of the RSHA, for appointing the heads of the regional Gestapo offices. In addition he was able to direct the regional offices through his targeted policy of information dissemination: from May 1940 the 'Command Sheet from the Security Police and SD Chief' (*Befehlsblatt des Chefs der Sipo und des SD*) appeared weekly, and was used by Office IV to instruct

The structure of Office IV of the RSHA

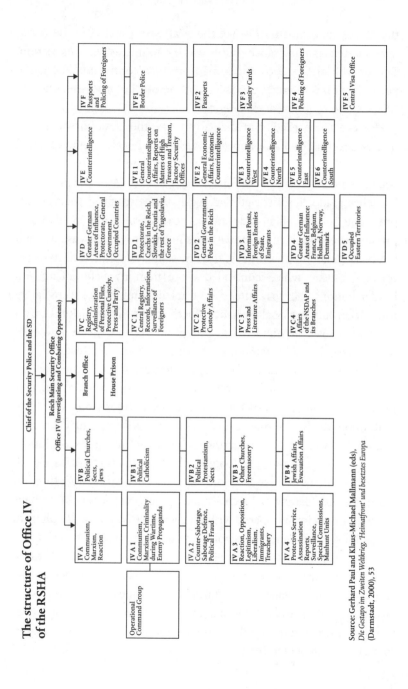

Source: Gerhard Paul and Klaus-Michael Mallmann (eds),
Die Gestapo im Zweiten Weltkrieg. 'Heimatfront' und besetztes Europa
(Darmstadt, 2000), 53

the offices subordinate to it. Yet the relationship between the Berlin headquarters and its branch offices was by no means without friction. The provincial Gestapo offices made regular complaints about the patronizing bureaucracy, the length of the official processes, and the RSHA's lack of practical experience.

However, in particular in the early years, the Gestapo was by no means as centralized as it appeared on paper. Local potentates could continue to exercise significant influence. In the last months of the Nazi regime the chain of command from the RSHA to the provincial branches gradually dissolved and local offices regained their autonomy. The Gestapo, then, had a strong headquarters only in its middle phase. Moreover, its institutional basis in the provinces was anything but broad and complex: in 1935 the Prussian Gestapo had thirty-three regional offices, which controlled more than 117 field offices and border stations.[28] In 1937, after the Verreichlichung, there were barely more than fifty regional Gestapo offices in the German Reich. By 1 September 1939 the number had grown to sixty-four, although only eleven were situated beyond the former borders of the Reich.[29]

The files of the Düsseldorf Gestapo office are some of the few that have survived. Taking this office as an example, we gain a clearer picture of the internal structure and the Gestapo's regional and local infiltration of the German population. The government district of Düsseldorf covered 5,498 square kilometres and had 4,183,235 inhabitants (in 1939), and in 1938, alongside the headquarters in Düsseldorf, there were plans for six field offices and four subsidiary offices in Duisburg with Hamborn, Essen, Krefeld, Mönchengladbach, Oberhausen with Mülheim, Wuppertal with Barmen, Remscheid, and Solingen. In addition there were three border police commissariats and three border police stations in Emmerich with Emmerich-Bahnhof, Kleve with Kranenburg, and Kaldenkirchen with Straelen-Herongen. This shows that the Gestapo's own stations and branch offices were situated above all in urban locations and border zones. The Düsseldorf Gestapo office and its sub-departments had 291 employees in March 1937 and 349 in September 1941.[30]

Few new branches were added to the sixty-four regional Gestapo offices that were already in place at the beginning of the war. By September 1941 there were sixty-seven, of which twenty-six were located outside the 1937 Reich borders. Within the Old Reich, however, regional Gestapo offices were merged and so the overall number reduced. The only separate regional Gestapo offices to be set up were those in the so-called General Government (German-occupied Polish territories not annexed by Germany) and in the areas that had been incorporated into the German Reich. In the other occupied zones the Gestapo was subordinate to the commanding officer of the security police and of the SD (BdS) or to their ancillaries the commanders (KdS).

These commanders and the aforementioned inspectors of the security police and the SD (IdS) were wholly new creations of the National Socialist 'Prerogative State'. On 20 September 1936, the day on which Himmler vested the Prussian Gestapa with the duties of the federal political police commanders, the office of 'Inspector of the Security Police' was decreed for the first time. Nonetheless it took over a year for the first inspector to be appointed. In the course of 1937 the SS and the police force were restructured and brought into line with the military districts (*Wehrkreisen*). By September 1937 seven inspectors had been appointed, all in border zones. Their primary task was initially to secure the centralization of the security police at a regional level, which meant that their first activities involved amalgamating various existing departments and sections. In addition, preparations for mobilizing the Gestapo, the Criminal Police Department (*Kripo*), and the SD were now co-ordinated by the IdS.[31] Reinhard Heydrich wanted to turn the IdS into an institution that would eventually replace traditional state police structures.[32] For a long time, however, they were rather to be seen as the ambassadors of a future National Socialist administration.

After the outbreak of the war the powers of the IdS were expanded. Although they were granted very few institutional powers, their new position resulted rather from their capacity to assert themselves personally. Their principal task was to complete the fusion of security police and SD into a National Socialist state security force. The IdS were not integrated into the bureaucratic structures of the security police apparatus until 1941/42: initially, on 12 June 1941, they took over the functions of the main Gestapo offices in the regions (*Stapoleitstellen*), and on 22 January 1942 those of the main Kripo offices (*Kripoleitstellen*).[33] In the last months of the war, after the attack on Hitler of 20 July 1944 and in the face of advancing allied troops, attempts to fuse the security police and the SD were intensified. To this purpose the office of Commander of the Security Police and the SD (*Kommandeur der Sicherheitspolizei und des SD*) was also created within the German Reich, and subordinated to the IdS. At the same time, from mid-1944, some inspectorates were turned into Commanding Officer stations (*Befehlshaber-Dienststellen*), in particular in border zones, in order to increase the active capacity of the security police. Total war had brought about an exceptional situation. Only now was it possible to establish the new police structure that Heydrich had planned years previously.

Inspectors of the security police were not appointed in the zones that were occupied from 1939 onwards, although this had been initially planned for Warsaw. Instead, the new office of Commanding Officer of the Security Police (BdS) was instituted, first in Poland, based in Cracow with the General Governor. Unlike the IdS, the BdS's role was more than supervisory; they also assumed permanent command over the Gestapo, Kripo, and SD. Moreover, they were to represent the concerns of the security police and SD and thereby to take an active role in the development of occupation policy. The BdS took over all the tasks that were carried out by the RSHA within the Reich. Its office was therefore structured in a similar way to the RSHA. The BdS also supervised all SD members and all members of the Gestapo and Kripo.

Further BdS were established in The Hague and Oslo in 1940, in other words in the countries with a civilian administration. Commanding Officers for Alsace Lorraine followed in Strasbourg and Metz, the parts of France that were later to be incorporated into the Reich. The Commanders of the Security Police and SD (KdS) were created as subordinate entities to the BdS. Poland was once again the forerunner and model for this development. Further KdS were established in the occupied areas of the Soviet Union as of 1941, and later in France, Italy, and Hungary. Compared to the commanders in the German Reich, the KdS in Europe had much more room for manoeuvre.

The Higher SS and Police Leaders (HSSPF) had far greater powers, earning them the nickname 'Himmler's long arm'.[34] This new office was created on 13 November 1937. Just like the IdS, the HSSPF were each responsible for a single military district. As an institution, they embodied the connection between the SS and the police, just as Himmler himself did—it was no coincidence that were they later known as 'little Himmlers'. Initially the HSSPF's role was solely to amalgamate and to direct, and they had only a small administrative apparatus. Even though they were neither a Gestapo nor security police organization, the inspectors and commanding officers of the order and security police were subordinate to them, as were the large SS districts (SS-Oberabschnitte) together with their districts (Abschnitte), regiments (Standarten), battalions (Sturmbannen), and units (Stürmen). Depending on the military district over 200,000 men came under the command of an HSSPF. Yet they did not have completely free rein; the state administration and the SS Main Offices kept a wary eye on them.

The HSSPFs' powers were significantly greater in the occupied zones, where from the beginning of the war in 1939 they commanded the shared operations of the police and SS. There was considerably less state observation here, which they made use of in autocratic fashion. After the invasion of the Soviet Union, the SS enjoyed greater room for manoeuvre and so the HSSPFs' powers also increased. Depending on the time and place, they operated between the conflicting priorities of the civil administration, the army, and the foreign office. In deploying their own units, the HSSPFs took a central role in the extermination of the European Jews.[35]

The Holocaust reached its climax in the concentration and extermination camps throughout Eastern Europe. There, too, the Gestapo and the political departments had a number of branches, although the

The structure of the security police
after 1939

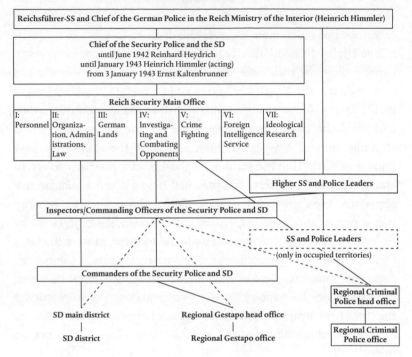

Reichsführer-SS and Chief of the German Police in the Reich Ministry of the Interior (Heinrich Himmler)

Chief of the Security Police and the SD
until June 1942 Reinhard Heydrich
until January 1943 Heinrich Himmler (acting)
from 3 January 1943 Ernst Kaltenbrunner

Reich Security Main Office

I: Personnel	II: Organization, Administrations, Law	III: German Lands	IV: Investigating and Combating Opponents	V: Crime Fighting	VI: Foreign Intelligence Service	VII: Ideological Research

Higher SS and Police Leaders

Inspectors/Commanding Officers of the Security Police and SD

SS and Police Leaders
(only in occupied territories)

Commanders of the Security Police and SD

Regional Criminal Police head office

SD main district	Regional Gestapo head office
SD district	Regional Gestapo office

Regional Criminal Police office

concentration camps were run by the SS Business and Administration Main Office.[36] Nonetheless, a political department was established in the concentration camp at Dachau as early as 1933, tasked with overseeing the instructions given by police when prisoners were detained and released. The new department was also firmly anchored in the camp, keeping records of the prisoners and interrogating the detainees. Its sub-departments corresponded to its various areas of responsibility: records, admission/release, registry, identification, and interrogation.[37] In 1934 and 1935 political departments were also established in the camps on Prussian soil, which were under the control of the Inspector of Concentration Camps, Theodor Eicke.[38]

The political departments were an integral element of the camp structure. However, usually only the head came from the Gestapo or criminal police, while his subordinates were generally SS men. The relatively low rank is striking: the long-term head of the political department in Auschwitz, Maximilian Grabner, was a *Kriminalsekretär* when he took on the position, while his successor Hans Schurz was merely a *Kriminalassistent*.[‡][39] The position of the political departments was at first glance far from simple: they were subordinate on the one hand to the RSHA and the regional Gestapo offices, on the other to the Concentration Camp Inspectorate and the camp commandants.[40] Nonetheless, this rarely caused friction. The various agents involved in the systematic destruction that took place in the concentration camps generally collaborated well.

Alongside the political departments in the concentration camps, the Gestapo had their own detention centres within the National Socialist camp system—the *Arbeitserziehungslager* ('work education camps', abbreviated to AEL). Unlike the concentration camps, which came under the control of the SS Main Office for Economy and Administration, they were subordinate to the local Gestapo offices.[41] The first AEL were established in 1939/40 on the back of local initiatives and were only tolerated by Himmler for the duration of the war, since in effect they ran against the centralized KZ system which he controlled.

Several different groupings contributed to the genesis of the AEL, including agricultural businesses, local authorities, and other institutions that used them as a source of cheap or free labour. At first domestic and foreign 'shirkers' ('Arbeitsvereigerer') or 'slackers' ('Bummelanten') were sent to an AEL for three weeks. Later all manner of infringements were punished by the responsible Gestapo office with a temporary transfer to an AEL. The short-term but brutal terror that the inmates underwent was intended to 'educate' them—the cruel living and working conditions sometimes exceeded those in

---

[‡] Both 'Kriminalassistent' and 'Kriminalsekretär' were relatively low-ranking positions within the criminal police and Gestapo from the late 1930s onwards.

concentration camps. They were hugely important for the Gestapo: 'The AEL rapidly developed in importance within the Nazi system of terror, until they established themselves, beyond justice and independent of the concentration camps, as the security police's third level of repression.'[42]

During the Second World War there were approximately 200 AEL in the German Reich. They were staffed exclusively by the police: while the guards were recruited from the reservists of the order police, the camp commandants and their deputies came from the security police. They were all mid-ranking civil servants. Taking over the leadership of a camp was more a sideways step than a promotion. But the establishment of an AEL in the locality greatly enhanced the significance of the regional Gestapo office. The fact that local units enjoyed this degree of independence shows that, in practice, the state police was by no means a centralized force.

The fact that 'normal' prisons were also part of the Nazi state, and therefore an integral part of the system of repression, was disregarded for a long time by historians. The fact that they belonged neither to the Gestapo nor the SS meant that they were ignored in both these areas of research.[43] Nonetheless, there were also so-called extended police prisons (erweiterte Polizeigefängnisse), which—like the AEL—were subordinate to the Gestapo. They were also similar to the AEL in their structure and administration, lacking only the 'educating' principle. Any prisoner in police custody could be sent to an extended police prison. Both the AEL and these prisons were simply Gestapo detention centres and therefore—from a purely organizational point of view—not part of the concentration camp system. For the regional Gestapo offices these detention centres were a welcome addition to the repertoire of persecution, since there they could pursue their usual harassment with unusual methods, completely unsupervised and free of regulation.[44] This shows that the Gestapo was at its core a centralist organization, but that its institutional framework meant that it could develop differently at a local level, in order to permit specific forms of persecution. All this was grounded in the Gestapo's self-image which, both engine and vanishing point, was directly conceived on the ideological bases of National Socialism. This mixture of centralized guidelines and local self-will initially appears paradoxical. However, it did not weaken the organization, but rather increased its potential for repression. In sum, the Gestapo developed into a multi-faceted and complex institution within the National Socialist Prerogative State. Along with its extraordinary dynamism, its most striking feature was its amalgamation with the SS and particularly the SD.

The Gestapo's self-understanding and ideology

When the National Socialists came to power, the political police were still bound by existing legislation. Most of their staff were trained criminal investigators who had generally joined voluntarily. There was no ideological coherence except for a widespread anti-communism, which the new ruling powers were able to exploit. The rapid expansion of powers from February 1933 onwards changed the way that the state police functioned, but it did not initially succeed in producing a new and coherent understanding of its own identity. In addition, the Gestapo's early development was moulded by several different forces. It was only with Himmler's and Heydrich's takeover of the Prussian Gestapo in April 1934 that a process of ideological transformation began, which then had widespread effects.

It was Reinhard Heydrich who brought this development to public attention in 1935 under the label 'Transformations of our Struggle', giving it concrete form a few weeks later in the journal *Deutsches Recht* ('German Law'). In an article entitled 'Combating the Enemies of the State' ('Die Bekämpfung der Staatsfeinde'), Heydrich explained that National Socialism no longer developed 'out of the state, but out of the people. The Führer has already laid this out in *Mein Kampf*. He defined the state as the "means to an end", as "an institution for the people of each age", designed for the maintenance and promotion of a "community of physically and psychologically homogenous beings".' 'Accordingly, we National Socialists recognize only the enemy of the people (*Volksfeind*). He is always the same, he never changes. He is the enemy of the racial, *völkisch* and spiritual substance of our people.'[45] Here Heydrich formulated a central concept that became decisive for the practice of the Gestapo: thought and action no longer revolved around the state, but around the people. Heydrich's remarks may have remained general, but they marked a crucial turning point. Moreover, the reference to the Führer made them practically sacrosanct.

Werner Best, for a long time legal counsel to the Gestapo, put it in yet more concrete terms. Best had invested his ideas in the third Gestapo Law as early as April 1936, and he also took a leading role in the ongoing formulation and formation of Gestapo ideology.[46] There is no doubt of his significance as the theoretical mind behind the security police. His writings also considerably influenced developments in the study of police law.[47] He articulated the Gestapo's self-understanding in biological metaphors: 'An institution that keeps a careful eye on the political health of the German national body (*Volks-körper*), identifies each symptom in good time and locates the destructive germs—whether they have arisen through internal corruption or have been carried in from outside by deliberate poisoning—before using all appropriate means to get rid of them. That is the idea and the ethos of the political police in the *völkisch* Führer-state of our era.'[48] The Gestapo thus became 'doctor to the German national body', keeping watch over its health and compelled—as well as willing—to combat all pathogens and diseases ruthlessly. The causes of this 'disease' of the National Socialist national body were quickly ascertained: they were communists, Freemasons, and the churches—and above and behind all these stood the Jews.

Heinrich Himmler, who despite his significant intellect was not versed in legal theory, borrowed this line of argument and conceptual framework from the accomplished expert Werner Best when, in May 1937, he stated of the duties of the National Socialist police in general: '(a) The police is to fulfil the will of the state leadership and to create and maintain the order required by the same. (b) The police is to defend the German people as an organic being, and to protect its life force and institutions against destruction and subversion. The competencies of a police force faced with these tasks cannot be restricted.'[49]

Reinhard Heydrich also made use of Best's wording at the beginning of 1937: 'The overall task of the security police is to defend the German people as a whole being, to protect its life force and its institutions against all kinds of destruction and subversion. This task is therefore naturally both defensive and offensive. Defensively, it has to repel the attacks of those forces that can weaken and destroy the health, life-force and capacity of the people and of the state that is organized by the people. And offensively, it has to research and thereby combat all antagonistic forces, so that they do not have the opportunity to exercise their destructive and subversive influence.'[50] This statement laid down all the essential features of Gestapo ideology: first, thinking in terms of biological concepts and metaphors, which had not been invented by the National Socialists;[51] secondly, emphasizing the primacy of the people over the state; and thirdly, using the resulting self-empowerment for prevention and not imposing any restrictions on this endeavour.

The formulation of such central ideas was one thing, but how did these thoughts make their way into the heads of the Gestapo officers? In this, the National Socialists left nothing to chance. Himmler himself was convinced that his men had to be ideologically instructed—in Nazi jargon this was called 'ideological schooling' ('weltanschauliche Schulung'). This was not dallying in pedagogy, nor a temporary whim; the leadership of the National Socialist police accorded the topic significant importance. To this end Himmler considered it particularly important that the material was conveyed coherently: 'I will under no circumstances tolerate ideological digressions.'[52] Alongside Himmler, Best and Heydrich also took this issue very seriously.[53]

Himmler had a series of training establishments set up, including the 'Security Police Leadership College' in the Charlottenburg district of Berlin, which had until 1937 been known as the Police Institute, and the Border Police College in Pretzsch, which from the summer of 1941 continued its work as the Security Police College in Fürstenberg.[54]

This 'ideological training' was valued even more highly after the outbreak of war, since ideological coherence was of the greatest importance in the war of extermination, ensuring the smooth functioning of the security police's Einsatzgruppen. Anti-Semitic indoctrination was the top priority here; the Jews were 'enemy number one'.[55] Various training materials were compiled and the trainers had to be able to ground the theory in practice: for the leadership of the security police it was not only about conveying knowledge; rather, examples of this ideological attitude were to be set. Consequently, a majority of the instructors had themselves played an active part in the 'Final Solution to the Jewish Question'.

It is hard to make a detailed assessment of how much this ideological training impacted on operations or legitimized actions. A consideration of the extent of the indoctrination and of the forms that it took, however, suggests that it was not without effect. Surviving letters from the field, written by members of the SS and the police reporting on their operations in Eastern Europe, indicate a broad internalization of the anti-Semitic enemy stereotype.[56] But who were the officers who received this training and were required to give life to this Nazi ideology?

3

GESTAPO EMPLOYEES

Developments in personnel

When it was founded, the Gestapo was a relatively small unit. Its core, the Prussian political police, had nearly 1,000 employees.[1] By January 1934 it employed 1,700 and this rapid increase continued: in June 1935 the Prussian Gestapo had close to 2,500 employees, and in March 1937 it was 3,500—not including the female clerical staff and secretaries.[2] The political police massively expanded in the other German states, too. In Hamburg it was initially a sub-department of the criminal police and in March 1933 had over fifty officers and twelve auxiliary staff. By the beginning of 1934 it had been detached from the criminal police department and increased to 151 officers—at a cost to the criminal police, who had to transfer some of their own staff. By the summer of 1935, the Gestapo in Hamburg had 260 employees, including 150 criminal police officers. But the growth in personnel did not end there. At Himmler's command, the regional Gestapo office in Hamburg recruited a further fifty criminal police officers by October 1936, bringing the total to 200.[3]

In another small state in northern Germany the number of Gestapo employees did not rise quite so rapidly: the Brunswick Gestapo grew from sixteen officers at the beginning of 1933 to thirty-three by the end of 1936.[4] The Gestapo ranks also swelled in the southern German states: when the Baden Gestapo began official operations on 1 September 1933 they numbered seventy-five officers, which rose to 165 by March 1937.[5] The Bavarian Political Police (BPP) in Munich also hugely increased its numbers in an incredibly short time: 115 employees in March 1933 rose to 200 by the summer, plus thirty Schutzpolizei officers working exclusively for the BPP. But the need for personnel was still not met, and in May 1934 a further 174 positions were requested.[6]

The increase in staff is also evident at the level of individual Gestapo offices. In Leipzig the political police had fifteen officers at the beginning of 1933. By April of the same year it had thirty-one and two years later around 100.[7] In Erfurt, at the time part of Prussia, there were also huge increases in staff. From sixteen employees in 1934, the number had increased to seventy-one by 1937, including forty criminal police officers.[8]

It thus becomes clear that, with mild regional variations, the Verreichlichung of the Gestapo in 1936–37 was preceded by a significant expansion in staff in the regional offices. Many new recruits were appointed, but this growth in personnel occurred largely at the cost of the criminal police and Schutzpolizei. By March 1937 there were an estimated 6,500 Gestapo employees across the Reich, in the Berlin headquarters and in the fifty-four regional offices.[9] From 1938 onwards the expansion of National Socialist Germany beyond its original borders meant that the personnel requirements rose more rapidly. Staff were required from March 1938 for the six new Gestapo offices in Austria and from October 1938 for the three additional offices in the Sudetenland. Two further offices were set up in the Protectorate of Bohemia and Moravia in March 1939.[10]

With the outbreak of war, the Gestapo's duties and field of operation increased further. The recruitment process could barely keep up. Although the Gestapo had around 15,000 officers in September 1941, redeployments outside the Reich meant that there were barely more active employees in the Old Reich than there had been four years previously. New Gestapo offices were set up in the occupied territories, but staff also had to be redeployed to the Einsatzgruppen. By January 1944 the Gestapo had over 31,000 employees. And although it was consequently the largest unit in RSHA operations—the Kripo had 12,792 and the SD 6,482 members—in view of the task at hand it certainly wasn't overstaffed. The ratio of Gestapo employees to inhabitants was still relatively low, and the capacity for surveillance consequently quite limited. This is put into perspective, however, if you consider that the average 'national comrade' (*Volksgenosse*) was not the focus of the Gestapo's activities. Statistical ratios of Gestapo employees to inhabitants are thus largely worthless and of little significance.

The regional Gestapo offices varied greatly in staffing terms. In the main, offices in the more densely populated industrial regions were better staffed than in sparsely populated areas. Regional Gestapo offices in the interior had fewer staff than those along the Reich borders. It is possible that political traditions played a role, too: heartlands of political Catholicism and of the workers' movement such as the Saarland, the administrative districts of Düsseldorf or Hamburg were notably very well staffed. Admittedly, these were also industrial regions and border or port areas.[11] But who were these Gestapo employees? Numerous media representations have imprinted the image of the brutal and fanatical National Socialist, preferably clothed in a long leather coat, deep into the memory. But even a glance at the leadership of the Gestapo shows that this image is misleading.

The Gestapo leadership: Diels, Heydrich, Best, Müller

In its twelve-year history the Gestapo had three heads, who differed significantly in background, character, and fate. The first chief of the Prussian Gestapo was Rudolf Diels, who was born in 1900 in Berghausen in Taunus.[12] After his Abitur (grammar-school leaving examination) and military service towards the end of the First World War, he joined a Free Corps and then studied Law. He subsequently worked as an administrative lawyer in several provincial administrations. In 1930 Diels became department head for left-wing extremism in the police department of the Prussian Interior Ministry and therefore at an interface with the political police. He chose the right moment to transfer to the reactionary forces around Chancellor von Papen and provided evidence that led to the coup-like deposition of the Prussian government on 20 July 1932. He was rewarded for his treachery and promoted to Senior Government Councillor (*Oberregierungsrat*). At this stage Diels had a good sense of what was on the horizon: he established contact with Hermann Göring at the end of 1932 and began to provide him with confidential information from his professional sphere. As a reward, Göring named him first chief of the Prussian Gestapo in April 1933. In October of that year, following a series of intrigues that are difficult to unravel, Diels had to leave Berlin briefly, but he returned soon after and was promoted to ministerial councillor (*Ministerialrat*). Later he was made Vice-President of the Police and in March 1934 Inspector of the Prussian Gestapo. Just one month later, however, his career in the Gestapo was over: Diels was made District Governor in Cologne, which was nominally a promotion but in fact sidelined him from the regime leadership.

Diels was of little significance for the development of the Gestapo outside Prussia. But he still played a central role: it was Diels who initiated the process of detaching the Gestapo from the interior state administration, even though as a traditionally trained administrative lawyer he cleaved to old ways of thinking. Diels was portrayed as a contradictory character by his contemporaries: intelligent, with administrative capabilities and a charming manner, he was primarily an opportunist, concerned with his own career. Indeed, it has been proved that he used his powers to warn opponents of the Nazi regime and so helped them to escape arrest.

His career in Cologne and then Hamburg was not without conflict and in 1943 and 1944 he once again had much contact with the Gestapo—although this time not as its head but its victim. He was arrested by the Gestapo twice, apparently because of remarks he had made that amounted to high treason. The spirits that he had conjured up now caught up with him. Hermann Göring, once his supporter, again held a protective hand over him and made sure that he was released. After the attempt to assassinate Hitler on 20 July 1944 he found himself in the claws of the Gestapo again, was thrown out of the SS and spent the time until the end of the war in a series of Gestapo prisons and penal divisions (*Strafkompanien*). After 1945 he wrote his memoirs under the sensational title 'Lucifer ante portas: Here Speaks the First Chief of the Gestapo', in which he sketched a positively biased image of his activities. Diels survived denazification and the Spruch-gericht* and lived a relatively quiet life until his death. He died in a hunting accident on 18 November 1957, in circumstances that remain unexplained.

Diels' successor as Chief of the Gestapo was Reinhard Tristan Eugen Heydrich, four years his junior.[13] For many he represented the proto-type of the National Socialist: the apparently perfect symbiosis of high intelligence, athletic masculinity, ideological conviction, and cool, objective ruthlessness. Heydrich was more than Himmler's right-hand man, and one of Hitler's absolute favourites. He owed his career to a misunderstanding. Coming from a well-respected family of musi-cians, he joined the Navy in 1922 against the will of his parents, who had hoped that their talented son would pursue a career in music. He was dishonourably discharged from the Navy in 1931, and his mother arranged for him to meet Himmler, who was looking to build up an intelligence service for the SS. Heydrich, who had been a communi-cations officer in the Navy, seemed to be the right candidate. Himmler did not know that a communications officer was a radio officer and had nothing to do with intelligence activities.

Irrespective of this misunderstanding, the Reichsführer-SS was impressed by Heydrich's demeanour and by a sketch in which he demonstrated to Himmler how the intelligence services should be organized. He began to build up the SS Intelligence Service, 'SD' for short, in the summer of 1931. After the seizure of power Himmler was

---

* *Translator's note*—The 'Spruchgericht' or 'Spruchkammer' was a type of lay court established in West Germany after the Second World War to try crimes committed during the 'Third Reich' that were not the subject of the major war crime trials. As such it was a core instrument of denazification.

made chief of the political police in Bavaria, and Heydrich became his deputy and later his successor. As Himmler gradually took control of all political police forces in the Reich, the power of his subordinate Heydrich increased accordingly, until finally in April 1934 Heydrich was made Chief of the Prussian Gestapo, while remaining head of the SD. His power constantly increased: in 1936 he became head of the Security Police Main Office, which brought together the Gestapo and the criminal police. Consequently he became the first head of the RSHA in September 1939. But this was not yet the climax of his career: in recognition of his achievements he was made Deputy Reich Protector of the Protectorate of Bohemia and Moravia on 27 September 1941. Heydrich stood the test of this task, too, crushing resistance groups, having the Czech Jews deported, and increasing the productivity of the local arms industry. For the exiled Czech government, then, Heydrich was enemy number one. They opted for assassination, which was finally successful in May 1942.

His early death turned Heydrich into a myth. He died at the peak of his power and was spared the downfall of the 'Third Reich' and its RSHA. Thus Reinhard Heydrich was remembered as the 'ideal National Socialist'.[14] This idealization during the 'Third Reich' was followed by demonization after 1945, the likes of which barely any other National Socialist was subjected to. Even today, over seventy years after his death, it is difficult to separate the image of the historical Heydrich from the myth. Nonetheless, Reinhard Heydrich was beyond doubt of central importance for the development of the Gestapo.

The same can be said of his temporary deputy Werner Best. Born on 10 July 1903, he was barely eight months older than Heydrich.[15] Rooted in a nationalist milieu since his youth, he gained a doctorate in law before joining the NSDAP on 1 November 1930. His path led by way of various party and SD offices into the Gestapa in September 1934, where he progressed to become Heydrich's closest colleague. He took over the main department I (Administration and Law) and also built up the defence department. As a lawyer, in charge of personnel and Heydrich's deputy, Best played a decisive part in the theoretical and practical shaping of the Nazi police state.

Until 1936 his work consisted mainly of legal investigations into competing state and party institutions. In these investigations, key issues were always resolved in the Gestapo's interests, and subsequently Best moved into the foreground as theoretician, organizer, and head of personnel of the Gestapo. However, his attempts to professionalize the Gestapo and, above all, its personnel only saw limited success, at best with the leadership functions in the RSHA and with the provincial Gestapo offices.

Nonetheless there were divergent interests in the Gestapo's top positions: Heinrich Müller tended to favour officers with police training and experience. Himmler and Heydrich, on the contrary, preferred the officers to have undergone SS socialization; and Best prioritized the capacity to make legal judgments, as proven by a university qualification. In short, each favoured the model which reflected his own *curriculum vitae.* The tensions that arose as a result led to Best's departure from the RSHA, although his theoretical writings and organizational achievements had made him practically irreplaceable. Yet the question of how the future leadership would look turned in the summer of 1939 into a 'War of Memoranda' between Best on one side and Heydrich, Müller, and the ambitious SD chief Schellenberg on the other.[16] After Best publicized his demands in a specialist journal, the break with Heydrich could no longer be patched up and finally led—albeit a year later—to Best's resignation.

The career of the third and final Chief of the Gestapo was different again from the previous two. Neither a sparkling figure like Diels, nor a charismatic character like Heydrich, he was to a certain extent an average civil servant and he had the name to fit: Heinrich Müller.[17] Müller, born in 1900, attended a college of further education (*Volkshochschule*) and then completed an apprenticeship as an aircraft mechanic. Towards the end of the First World War he served in an air force division, acquitted himself well, and was awarded the Iron Cross, First Class. On 1 December 1919 he joined the police headquarters in Munich as an auxiliary worker. He was transferred into the political police relatively quickly, charged with the surveillance of communists, and remained in this role until 1933. In May 1929 he passed the exam for the middle grade of the civil service. Heinrich Müller was hard-working and ambitious, but nobody would have expected his career to be above average.

After the National Socialists took power, Müller's knowledge of communist activities was much in demand and he was promoted twice in 1933: in May to Polizeiobersekretär and in November to the rank of Criminal Inspector. There was no inevitability to this career success: Müller was regarded with suspicion by the NSDAP because he had not joined the party until 1939. He did not look like a committed National Socialist. But his new boss, Reinhard Heydrich, relied on his expert knowledge. Moreover, Müller's ruthlessness and great diligence quickly impressed both Heydrich and Himmler. In April 1934 they took him with them to Berlin, where he was rapidly promoted up the ranks of the Gestapa. Along with combating communism, he was also responsible for the surveillance of the NSDAP and its organizations. On 1 November 1934 he was promoted to Senior Criminal Inspector.

Heydrich's great trust in Müller was displayed when, on 1 July 1936, he made him head of Department II (Interior Political Affairs), which Heydrich had headed until that point. In December 1936 Müller leapt three levels in the police hierarchy and was made Senior Government and Criminal Councillor. In the SS, too, which he had joined in 1934, he made quick progress: on 20 April 1939, the Führer's fiftieth birth-day, he was made SS-Oberführer. But this was not the peak of his career: in December 1940 he became Major General of the Police and at the same time SS-Brigadeführer. Finally, in November 1941, Müller rose to the position of SS-Gruppenführer and General Lieutenant of the police. Müller often deputized for his boss Heydrich, and later for Heydrich's successor Ernst Kaltenbrunner.[18] Whether he himself har-boured hopes of becoming Heydrich's successor is unclear. Above all in the time between Heydrich's death in May 1942 and Kaltenbrunner taking office on 30 January 1943, Müller played a central role in the organization of the Holocaust. Until the end of the war he remained a fanatical bureaucrat and servant of the National Socialist state. Heinrich Müller disappeared during the battle for Berlin in 1945. It is assumed that he was killed or committed suicide, yet there is no evidence for it.

Despite all the differences in character of these three Gestapo chiefs, one feature is striking: they all owed their positions to a powerful patron. Diels was Hermann Göring's protégé, Reinhard Heydrich was supported by Himmler, and Heinrich Müller was Reinhard Heydrich's favourite. All three of them were absolutely loyal in their duties. This power based on personal relationships was a typical feature of the Nazi system of rule. And all three of them, despite all the differences in their professional development, functioned well in their office and did justice to the tasks set them.

It is further notable that neither Diels nor Müller were committed National Socialists. They were not so-called 'old fighters' nor did they excel in any particular ideological mindset. The basis of their careers was anti-communism, a bureaucratic sense of duty, and a marked ambition and will to power. In other words, they had not thrown themselves at the National Socialist movement, but the National Socialist movement had come to them. They not only kept office during the regime change of 1933 but—above all in Heinrich Müller's case—exploited this change to forge a career that would probably not have been possible otherwise.

The leadership of the Gestapa and the Reich Security Main Office

The level below Diels, Heydrich, Best, and Müller was not populated solely by veteran Nazi functionaries either. There were a range of different career paths in the Gestapa and in the later Office IV of the RSHA.[19] In the early phase of the 'Third Reich' the priority for the National Socialist rulers was the persecution of political opponents, that is to say Social Democrats and communists. Consequently, all employees who had previous experience of these activities were deployed. Before 1933, these figures had generally not been notably committed to the NSDAP, but their anti-communist attitudes brought them close to the new rulers. Reinhold Heller was one such figure. He had been active in the political police since the beginning of the Weimar Republic, having failed a law degree and served as an officer on the frontline during the First World War. From 1931, as criminal councillor, he was in charge of the Field Inspectorate of the Berlin unit responsible for the KPD. As an expert on communism he was indispensable to the new rulers and did valuable work for them. By 1939 he had been promoted to Senior Government and Criminal Councillor and then made chief of the Potsdam Gestapo office.[20] Born in 1885, he was significantly older than his superiors. Rudolf Braschwitz, on the other hand, was born in 1900 and qualified as a dentist, but a lack of jobs in that field during the 1920s led him to train as a criminal commissar. From 1928 he worked for the political police in Berlin and then transferred into the Gestapa. In May 1934, when the consolidation phase of the 'Third Reich' was almost complete, he was transferred into the criminal police and made his career there. The move from the criminal police to the political police and back was—above all in those early years—in no way unusual.

The later Office IV of the RSHA also housed officers with similar backgrounds. The veteran criminal police officers, who had begun their careers in the Weimar Republic, were found particularly in Group IV A—Persecution of Political Opponents. Not all of them came from the political police, some having gained their spurs in the criminal police. Josef Vogt, for example, who succeeded Reinhold Heller in 1939 to become head of Section IV A 1 (Communism, Marxism, United Front, Enemy Propaganda), had worked in the central homicide division in the Ruhr district. The core of Group IV A was remarkably homogenous: all the officers had been born between 1894 and 1903 and had joined the police before 1933. They operated according to established criminal police standards, yet at the same time they welcomed their expanded scope and the lapse of constitutional constraints. Their principal motivation lay in their anti-communism. It was only during the Second World War that this group was clearly radicalized further, as is shown by their actions within and beyond the Reich. Their career development mirrored that of their boss, Heinrich Müller. Only Horst Kopkow, who played a leading role in the manhunt for the 'Red Orchestra' resistance group (*Rote Kapelle*), had joined the Gestapo in August 1934 as a relative newcomer. He had been an active member of the NSDAP since 1931.

Section IV C 2, Protective Detention, was also made up predominantly of officers from the Weimar police. Group IV C, which was largely made up of the protective detention section, was the largest group in Office IV. During the Second World War it had more than 800 employees. From 1934 until the end of the war the section was run by Emil Berndorff, who had joined the Berlin criminal police in 1920 following a doctorate in law. The defence group (IV E) had a similar leadership structure. The young lawyer and SD member Walter Schellenberg was its chief until 1942. But the core of personnel around the section heads were officers from the criminal police of the Weimar Republic.

Group IV D, responsible for the occupied territories, was composed completely differently. A department like this was not necessary until the invasions that began in September 1939. At the outbreak of war, none of the department's employees was over 40 years old: they all came from the generation of the so-called war youth, which appeared to be open to radical life decisions and paid little heed to bourgeois norms of behaviour. Apart from one exception, none of them had a background in the criminal police. All of them had studied, and more than half had completed doctorates. They had either joined the Gestapo in 1937 or 1938 as Referendars or Assessors,[†] or had come from the SD. And they were by no means just bureaucratic perpetrators: almost all of them had been active in the occupied

---

[†] *Translator's note*—'Referendar' and 'Assessor' are the titles given to students of law who have passed the first and second state examinations respectively—i.e. they are part of the way through their legal training.

territories in Einsatzgruppen or as the chief of a regional Gestapo office. To some extent, they were a symbiosis of Best's demand for legal qualifications and Heydrich's idea of a 'fighting administration'.[21]

The final group in the RSHA's Gestapo headquarters was IV B, responsible for the Christian churches and the Jews. Section IV B 4—Jewish and Evacuation Affairs—played above all a major role in the operation of the Holocaust. It was run by Adolf Eichmann, probably the most prominent of all the Gestapo's officers.

While Heydrich's historical image has been distorted by demonization, the distortion of Eichmann's image is down partly to banalization. Although he was a third-ranking functionary within the Nazi state and his actual power was somewhat limited, there are numerous publications about him.[22] Hannah Arendt has contributed the most to his historical image, projecting onto him her theory of totalitarianism and subtitling her study of the Eichmann trial 'A Report on the Banality of Evil'. According to Arendt, Eichmann was a lacklustre bureaucrat who served the Nazi state out of obedience and a blind faith in authority. Born in 1906 in Solingen, he grew up in Linz, Austria, joined the Austrian NSDAP and SS in 1932, and moved to Germany in August 1933. In September 1934 his application to join the SD was accepted and his career gained momentum. Until this point there was little to suggest that Eichmann would become a central figure in the persecution and extermination of the Jews. It was only in the SD that Eichmann began to deal with anti-Semitism in any meaningful way, and he finally made a career of it. Initially he dealt with low-level activities, but with great zeal, and this found its reward: in January 1938 Eichmann was promoted to Untersturmführer.

Eichmann had passed his first test after the so-called 'annexation' of Austria in 1938. As head of the newly created Central Agency for Jewish Emigration, he profited above all from the fact that Zionist organizations co-operated with the agency. As a result, when Eichmann left Vienna in May 1939 he was able to boast that he had caused over 100,000 Jews to emigrate 'legally'. When the National Socialist police apparatus was restructured, Eichmann's post was integrated into the

RSHA and allocated to the Gestapo, an appropriate move given that the Gestapo was being granted more and more executive functions. As a result, more SD men with no specific police experience joined the Gestapo, including Theodor Dannecker, who later became an enforcer and 'travelling salesman' of the 'Final Solution' in France, Bulgaria, Italy, and Hungary.[23]

The leadership of the Gestapo in the RSHA, then, comprised three very different groups: first, the veteran criminal police, who had been active during the Weimar Republic and generally did not have a National Socialist background; secondly, the young legal administrators, who had proceeded directly to the Gestapo, mostly out of a mixture of conviction and professional ambition; and thirdly the SD employees, whose National Socialist sympathies were beyond doubt. There were constant tensions and conflicts between these groups, such as in the question of how SD members and security police officers should be remunerated and ranked when the RSHA was being constructed. However, the results of the RSHA's activities suggest that these conflicts tended to improve efficiency and were in no way a hindrance, as each group took pains to prove its worth. This was particularly the case during the Second World War, when internal competition led to a radicalization of the leadership. Of all the different types of Nazi perpetrators, the leadership of the Gestapo was clearly the administrative and executive core of the Holocaust. As we have seen, it was by no means so-called drop-outs who were responsible here. On the contrary: 'The Reich Security Main Office was an institution of social climbers.'[24]

The governors in the provinces

The RSHA in Berlin rose to prominence as an agency of terror. But without subordinate authorities in the provinces, the Gestapo would have been a secret police without foundations. So who were these provincial governors? We turn first to the heads of the regional Gestapo offices.

It is necessary to differentiate here between two phases: the early phase until around 1936/37, when there were numerous regional and local differences; and the phase after the Verreichlichung. In the first years of the 'Third Reich' the regional Gestapo offices were usually run by trained criminal police officers. They came from the political police departments of the federal states or from the ranks of the criminal police, and were taken on by the Gestapo or redeployed there. Gustav Pitz, the first chief of the Cologne Gestapo, is one such example: 44 years old at the time, he was head of the 4th criminal commissariat before being promoted to Criminal Councillor on 1 April 1933.[25] Theodor Bilo, two years Pitz's junior, headed both the criminal and political police forces in Wilhelmshaven. He had held this dual post since March 1931.[26] Bilo was an experienced police practitioner, who had started out as a Kriminalassistent in 1920 and worked for the criminal police in the Ruhr district during the twenties. Further, there were Nazi functionaries who were granted this office despite having no specialist knowledge. The first chief of the Lübeck Gestapo, Wilhelm Bock (b. 1903), is one such example: he had joined the NSDAP and SA in 1929, and then left the SA in 1931 in order to join the SS. This sufficed for the former sales clerk to be appointed to serve the state after the Nazis came to power.[27] Nonetheless, careers of this kind remained the exception.

By 1938, however, the leadership in the provinces had changed considerably and become remarkably homogenous: the chiefs of the regional Gestapo offices were extraordinarily young.[28] In the main they had been born after the turn of the century and were not yet 30 years old when they joined the Gestapo. Although they had been aware of the First World War, none of them had frontline experience. Three years previously, the situation had looked very different: of the thirty-three Prussian Gestapo chiefs, only ten had been born after 1900.[29] But within a very short time, redeployments had made the leadership significantly younger and brought in a whole new generation.[30]

Family background was astonishingly uniform at this stage, too: the majority came from reasonably well-off civil service families. A good third of the fathers, though, were self-employed, and most of the families had nationalist sympathies. The level of education reflected the social environment: 95 per cent of the Gestapo chiefs in 1938 had completed their school leaving exams, 87 per cent had then studied law, and half of them had doctorates. So while the leadership of the RSHA shows clear differences, the Gestapo chiefs in the provinces were in the main young lawyers. In this way they differed from their bosses Heydrich and Müller, but were similar to Werner Best, Gestapo head of personnel, who also held a doctorate in law. At least on this level, then, Best's personnel policy had seen widespread success.

What motivated these young lawyers to join the Gestapo? The first thing to note is that, for lawyers living in Germany, the state was one of the biggest employers, and that applying to the Gestapo was therefore not unusual. Furthermore, many must have been professionally ambitious, since there were more opportunities for rapid promotion in the fast-growing Gestapo than in the justice system. While many of them did share some ideological sympathies with National Socialism, very few were particularly involved in the party. The chief of the Gestapo in Frankfurt am Main, Dr Joachim Boes, only joined the NSDAP in 1940, after he had been in his position for four years.

Regardless of their commitment to the party, almost all of them achieved the career to which they aspired: rapid promotions were common in the Gestapo and the chiefs of the regional Gestapo offices particularly benefited from them.[31] Moreover, the need for personnel grew steadily from the beginning of the war, as the new offices in occupied Europe required new chiefs. Many of the Gestapo chiefs were made Inspectors (IdS), Commanders (KdS), or Commanding Officers (BdS) of the Security Police. The headquarters in the RSHA was also always in need of new leaders, as a result of the numerous transfers and secondments, and a total of eleven Gestapo chiefs moved into the RSHA as heads of sections, groups, or offices. Here the policy of rotating personnel made itself felt, too, since each post lasted less than two years. The Gestapo career of the doctor of law Werner

47

Braune shows this policy in action: in September 1938 he became deputy chief of the Gestapo in Münster, and then in Koblenz. By spring 1940 he was chief of the Gestapo office in Wesermünde, and in May 1941 held the same post in Halle. From October 1941 until September 1942 he was in charge of an Einsatzkommando in the Soviet Union. From January 1943 until the end of 1944 he headed the German Academic Foreign Service, finally becoming Commander of the Security Police and the SD in Norway.[32]

Around a third of the Gestapo chiefs had taken part in the campaign in Poland in 1939, as leaders of Einsatzgruppen or Einsatzkommandos. Behind the front lines they carried out the mass liquidation of the Polish ruling class. In the Soviet Union, too, fifteen Stapo chiefs including Werner Braune were deployed in 'special mobile units'. This high proportion of secondments was by no means restricted to the Gestapo, but common amongst the other police departments. In March 1934 the Berlin criminal police had an average age of 56, since all the younger officers had been seconded elsewhere.[33] Most of the Schutzpolizei leaders were also seconded to external service: at the end of the war, 90 per cent of the officers in Düsseldorf's Schutzpolizei were not in service at home.[34] Heydrich personally urged all members of the security police and SD under 40 years of age to be suggested for 'external assignment', in order to 'prevent the depressing feeling that they have not actively participated in the great events of our age, and to dispel the fear of being mocked at the end of the war as a "home warrior" or "shirker" ...'.[35]

Closely interlinked with the chiefs of the regional Gestapo offices were the Inspectors, Commanding Officers, and Commanders of the Security Police. The great majority of them were born after 1900, came from a high-class milieu, and found their way to National Socialism early: around half of them had joined the NSDAP before the 'seizure of power'. Most of the inspectors were drawn from the SD Main Office, in particular when the position was newly founded. A further, somewhat smaller, group were the career policemen, who had previously held top positions in the Gestapo, often as chiefs of regional Gestapo offices.

Gradually a new generation then took over. In line with Werner Best's personnel policies, the young lawyers born after 1905 were the largest group—just as with the Gestapo chiefs after 1938. There were also similarities to the RSHA leadership, which was partly because there were a number of exchanges between the Gestapo chiefs, the RSHA, and the Inspectors, Commanding Officers, and Commanders of the Security Police. The youngest members were particularly favoured towards the end of the war, and they replaced the older ones who—despite their qualifications—were thought to be past their best. The ideal type for a leadership position in the security police is thus a young, career-oriented lawyer, ideologically wedded to National Socialism.[36]

The variety of Gestapo officers

The leadership ranks described above accounted for an extremely small proportion of the total officers. The majority of the staff were at the rank of Kriminalassistent or Kriminalsekretär. But in this category we can also include those criminal commissars who did not hold a direct leadership position in the Gestapo or RSHA—all of these characters formed a very heterogeneous group. The Gestapo's backbone, above all in its early stages, were the career policemen, experienced in service and qualified in their field, who had either been transferred from the political police, the criminal police, or the Schutzpolizei. At first, they accounted for the majority of Gestapo employees. Transfers from the political police were by no means par for the course, in particular if, prior to 1933, the employee had been especially zealous in the crackdown on the NSDAP or particularly committed to democracy. But even this did not necessarily spell the end of a career. Franz Josef Huber, who later became chief of the Viennese Gestapo, had once been responsible for surveillance of the NSDAP. Like his friend Heinrich Müller, he nonetheless raced up the career ladder within the security apparatus of the Nazi state, finally making it to Inspector of the Security Police and the SD in Military District XVII (Vienna, Lower and Upper Danube).[37]

Numerous Gestapo employees had been active members of the SPD before 1933. Whether and how these careers continued often depended on local idiosyncrasies and relationships. In the main, however, it can be said that in the early years qualifications were more important than ideological commitment. Those who joined the Gestapo later, however, were generally loyal to the new regime. Most had joined the SA and NSDAP during the Weimar Republic and were much younger than the career policemen. They were in the main middle class, and many had been affected by the unemployment of the early thirties. This may have provided their main motivation for joining the NSDAP. The number of such figures that joined the Gestapo varied a lot depending on the region: while in Prussia the newcomers only made up 21.6 per cent of the staff—with much local variation—in Baden it was 37 per cent. In Hamburg, the newcomers were in the majority.[38] As so often, local and regional factors made all the difference.

The need for additional staff meant that, above all in 1938 and 1939, new recruits were transferred from other branches of the police. These officers had rarely served more than ten years before their transfer. The vast majority came from the region in which they would later serve. Three-quarters of them had been born after 1900 and most were from working-class or lower-middle-class backgrounds. Many of them had volunteered for the Gestapo, hoping for faster career progress or at least to benefit from the 'Stapozulage', a bonus paid to Gestapo employees. Indeed, officers were often promoted shortly after their deployment, although great careers were rare.

At the end of the thirties more newcomers joined the ranks of the Gestapo. They were at the beginning of their careers, with no training, and, above all, they were young. The key characteristics were: 'Reich citizenship, German bloodline, adequate general education, suitability for police service and physical fitness, membership of the NSDAP or one of its sub-organizations, having completed labour service and military service unless a dispensation was provided, good leadership skills, political reliability, shorthand and typing skills, minimum age 23, maximum age 30.'[39] The appointment of these untrained and inexperienced employees inevitably reduced the professional standards, as it was hardly possible to train the newcomers systematically overnight.

A further group to join the Gestapo in the few years leading up to the Second World War were the border police candidates. All border police candidates began their two-year training at the border police college in Pretzsch an der Elbe. There, in just two months, they were expected to take on board the theoretical foundations that would underpin their future activities, before being deployed to one of the Reich's seventy-two border police commissariats or 282 border police stations. A total of nineteen cohorts, each with up to 150 participants, were trained at Pretzsch.[40] When the war began and the Gestapo's tasks multiplied, the need for staff increased too, and the ongoing deprofessionalization of the employees stepped up a gear. Retired officers were re-employed, although before their retirement very few of them had served in the field, mainly working instead in the general administration. Supplementary forces were also taken on. This group of newcomers was thoroughly heterogeneous, ranging from those who were more or less press-ganged into joining the Gestapo by the labour exchanges to those who were living out their ideological fanaticism. Towards the end of the war, the urgent need for staff resulted in truly bizarre appointments: in Frankfurt am Main some of the opera cast were called up.[41] In addition there were the women who worked for the Gestapo, mainly as shorthand typists or telephone operators. But the staffing shortfall also meant that women were employed in other fields, from head of administration to investigative work. In all, towards the end of the war around a quarter of Gestapo staff were women.

To sum up: there was no such thing as the Gestapo employee. Rather, there were several different groups who did not always work together in harmony. But the tensions did not necessarily lead to dips in quality, tending instead to increase efficiency and effectiveness. Where some brought professional qualifications, others provided ideological conviction, which was often expressed in ruthless brutality. The Gestapo was certainly not a perfectly oiled machine, but it was far more than a rag-bag of unqualified thugs unable to function in civilian life. In the course of the war, the deprofessionalization continued and the staff got even younger. This probably sped up the process of radicalization in the Gestapo. Another factor was the deployment of the security police in occupied Europe. This measure was not likely to have a civilizing influence, but resulted on the contrary in a further deterioration of civil behaviour.

After 1945 the Gestapo officers, in particular those in the lower ranks, tried to exculpate themselves of any individual guilt: they had only followed orders and were only active in subordinate positions. This exculpatory mechanism misrepresents the considerable powers that even subaltern officers had. This is made clear in the case of Gestapo man Christian Heinrichsmeier from Hannover. Initially responsible for churches and sects, he later organized the deportation of Jews from Hannover. Many attested to the fact that he conducted this task with a 'human' attitude. Furthermore, he made good use of his influence and had Jews who were marked for deportation to work camps registered as unfit for work by doctors. In this way, he helped numerous individuals to survive.[42] Such cases, in which Gestapo officers became rescuers, were nonetheless extremely rare. However, it is impossible to divide the officers up into a black-and-white schema of rescuers and perpetrators. As they say, the basic colour of history is grey: often it was one and the same person who behaved with both brutality and thoughtfulness.

A look at the officers in the Düsseldorf Gestapo's Jewish section shows the full range of persecution. Several officers treated their victims and their victims' relatives with cynicism, some in particularly remarkable ways. Hermann Waldbillig, for example, who had joined the Gestapo in autumn 1939 without relevant experience or qualifications, seemed to use his service to live out his craving for recognition. His appearance reflected the clichéd image of the Gestapo man: he wore a leather coat and a hat, and had a 'Führer'-style moustache. Waldbillig was extremely verbally aggressive, constantly threatening to shoot his victims dead, despite apparently never going through with it.[43] To an extent, he was the epitome of a Gestapo man.

However, much more typical was the officer who neither screamed nor bullied, who did not use physical violence, but who took pains to fulfil the tasks set him. Here the 'consequences of the hierarchical and functional division of labour'[44] become clear: the fact that only part of the persecution and extermination had to be carried out by each individual officer made it run more smoothly. Furthermore, the case workers in the Jewish sections, for example, generally did not see the results of their activities. The individual became a number or a formula, which could be handled with minimal sympathy. The National Socialist use of language supported this tendency, too: 'special treatment' ('Sonderbehandlung') or 'resettlement' ('Umsiedlung') sounded harmless but meant nothing less than murder.[45] In other words, many Gestapo officers administrated the terror for a long time without becoming direct perpetrators themselves. This changed significantly as the war went on. It was above all the deployment of the security police in South-Eastern and Eastern Europe that turned the officers into active enforcers of the National Socialist war of extermination. These collective experiences of violence then became perceptible in their service on the 'home front'.

We are therefore dealing with multiple types of perpetrators who must be differentiated according to their position, role, commitment, background, and training. There was no predominant perpetrator type, but just different agents and institutions, a will to persecute on the one hand and structural conditions on the other. We see acts of individual malice and the dynamics of violence that change according to the situation.[46] Experienced police and young newcomers from the Nazi movement work together in one and the same administration. And the experienced officers were confronted with a job description that clearly seemed to favour the 'new blood'. In addition to hard work, achievement, and immaculate conduct inside and outside of service, a firm grounding in National Socialist ideology was required, along with so-called Aryan descent and a fit, athletic appearance.

The traditional career ladder was replaced by promotions for notable National Socialists, and core tasks were no longer allocated according to rank but to ideological conviction. There was no need to reach a high position in order to carry out these core tasks and direct activities. It is barely possible to overlook the results of this uprooted structure: tensions between colleagues were rife, experienced policemen felt challenged by National Socialist fanatics, and 'old fighters' felt derided by young SS leaders.

After the Verreichlichung these employee groups became yet more diverse, which raised the levels of competition within the service. As a result, internal conflicts tended more often to be dealt with externally, through violence. Even long-serving employees with professional interrogation methods, who had initially been taken on to secure the decent functioning of the Gestapo, were transformed from apolitical career policemen into Gestapo men.[47] Internally, the individual employee groups of the Gestapo were linked by a web of sympathies and antipathies, of good and bad co-operation, of conformity and autonomy, and of competition and egotistical ambition. This complex network largely defined the mechanisms of the Gestapo, differing from case to case and varying in combination and intensity. The competition within the Gestapo as to who proved to be more efficient, more ideologically reliable and single-minded in the eyes of the state, party, or police, triggered a 'pressure to radicalize',[48] which rendered their methods ever more brutal. Disciplinary punishments for extreme misconduct or excessive brutality were not on the cards; ultimately, the security police leadership gave all Gestapo officers free rein.

Within the parameters of bureaucratic persecution, various factors— individual initiative and group discipline, careerism, obedience, and blind faith in authority—thus coalesced into a blend of motivations and sensitivities. This blend permitted the Gestapo officers to disregard traditional values and to participate in the comprehensive persecution of the opposition. The door for brutal behaviour was therefore kicked wide open. The lack of any disciplinary monitoring system, which might have been able to prevent this development, was intentional.

Furthermore, many Gestapo officers were convinced that their activities were reasonable. Only by taking the National Socialists' anti-Semitism and racism seriously is it possible to gain a real sense of the attitude of those who took part in these acts of murder. Marxists, Jews, 'gypsies', and Slavs were not viewed as human beings but as 'vermin' or 'subhumans', who needed to be eradicated, since they were threatening the National Socialist national body. The perpetrators, then, did not view themselves as murderers or sadists, but as having a serious task to fulfil. Heinrich Himmler had formulated this attitude particularly clearly in his speech to the SS-Gruppenführer in Poznań on 4 October 1943: 'Most of you will know what it is like to see 100 corpses lying side by side or 500 or 1,000 of them. To have coped with this and—except for cases of human weakness—to have remained decent, that has made us tough.'[49]

This may sound cynical here, but Himmler did not mean it in this way: the task at hand is hard, and it must be carried out objectively and coolly. These men believed that their actions were morally sound.[50] Himmler referred to this, too: 'We were morally in the right, we had a duty to our people—to kill these people who wanted to kill us. [...] But ultimately we can say that we carried out this hardest of tasks out of love for our people. And inside ourselves, in our souls, we have come to no harm because of this.'[51]

4

THE MODUS OPERANDI

Frameworks

Himmler's Poznań speech of 1943 set out the guidelines which, as Chief of the German Police, he also expected the Gestapo to follow. For him, it was about objectivity, decency, and a sense of duty—all in view of a task that had to be fulfilled and that ultimately ended in the verbally euphemistic mass murder of the Jews. The goals were one thing; but what about the strategic implementation, in other words the state police practice? Could the Gestapo really achieve all it set out to do? Was it a perfect, all-knowing, all-powerful or at least effective and efficient authority?[1]

Recent research has produced clear areas of doubt here: arrests based on printed material often had to be reversed, because Gestapo officers had misunderstood the documents. House searches regularly produced no tangible evidence. Border controls and raids were only partially effective, and it proved hard to prevent illegal propaganda from being smuggled. The Gestapo were aware that many citizens listened to banned radio programmes, but they never uncovered most of the 'radio crimes' (*Rundfunkverbrechen*). Nor did political jokes always reach the ears of the Gestapo. The Gestapo only discovered the night before that the papal encyclical 'With burning concern' ('Mit brennender Sorge') was to be read out on Palm Sunday 1937, and this was too late to prevent it from being made public. The manhunt for Karl Goerdeler, sentenced to protective detention, took four weeks, and would have failed completely had Goerdeler not been denounced. The RSHA knew nothing about Stauffenberg and his group of conspirators before 20 July 1944. Claus Schenk Graf von Stauffenberg was even one of Himmler's favourites. Four days after the failed assassination, Ernst Kaltenbrunner still believed that the attack had been carried out by 'a small clique'. Only in the weeks that followed did the special commission set up by the RSHA realize how extensive the opposition really was.[2]

Do such failures mean that the Gestapo was a weak, ineffective, and inefficient authority? Far from it. If a house search was not successful, then the Gestapo arrested the suspects anyway, precisely to show their power and to intimidate them through interrogation. Even if the matter then ended with merely a fine or just the threat of punishment, they had achieved their goal because they had influenced the future behaviour of the individuals involved. It was always assumed that the Gestapo could at any time turn to harsher measures. The basic right to personal freedom ('Freiheit und Unverletzbarkeit der Person'), the right to free speech including freedom of the press, and the confidentiality of the postal and telegraph services had already been suspended in the Reichstag Fire Decree of 28 February 1933. Since then there had been no guaranteed protection against despotism and arbitrary sanctions. Letters could be opened and meetings tapped. The Gestapo was not bound by any legal or administrative accountability or burden of proof, it was thereby possible for them to create their own laws of persecution and to make use even of chance information for their own ends. Terror could be seeded without a scrap of evidence. This terror that the Gestapo spread, the fear of its methods, was based in reality: the complete abrogation of all constitutional principles in the National Socialist Prerogative State.

One of the most important instruments available to the Gestapo was 'protective detention', which was 'implemented' in state concentration camps.[3] There was no legal defence against it. It is impossible to ascertain the total number of people who were detained in this way. From 1934 the Gestapo recorded protective detention orders using an official code that contained both the initial of the prisoner and a serial number. One of the last detention orders was given in 1945 and marked: 'M 34591'.[4] The Gestapo could not be held accountable for whether and how long the person remained interned in the concentration camp. 'Protective detention' was consequently an important feeder for the concentration camp system, which was gradually developed by Heinrich Himmler from the mid-1930s onwards, according to his own ideas.[5] From that point on, the number of prisoners in the concentration camps increased very quickly, from 3,500 inmates in 1935 to 24,000 before the 'Night of Broken Glass' on 9 November 1938 and 56,000 after the pogrom.

The Gestapo was particularly notorious for its brutal interrogation methods, torturing prisoners into making incriminating statements. The victims were insulted and degraded, threatened with shooting or beaten with rubber truncheons, cattle prods, whips, sticks, or other objects. The abuse was silently tolerated by the Gestapo leadership, as long as it was kept off the record. However, since the effects of the abuse could not be concealed during court appearances, the Gestapo modified their torture during the course of the Nazi regime: in so-called 'intensified interrogation', police interrogators were allowed to deal out a maximum of twenty-five blows to the delinquent's behind. If it was more than ten blows, a doctor had to be present.[6] This 'intensified interrogation' was initially limited to 'Communist and Marxist functionaries, Jehovah's Witnesses and saboteurs', but as of 1941 intensified examinations were permitted particularly with Poles and Russians. One year later this means of coercion could also be used on 'terrorists, members of resistance organizations, parachute agents*, asocials, Polish or Russian work-shirkers or slackers.'[7]

A further increase in brutality can be observed at the beginning of the Second World War. Reinhard Heydrich ordered all Gestapo offices to punish particularly harshly those who doubted the victory of the German people, who questioned the war, or who sabotaged armament facilities. As Heydrich put it, 'special treatment' was intended for

---

* Translator's note—'parachute agent' (Fallschirmagent) was the Nazi term for intelligence agents who parachuted into targeted zones.

these 'elements'.[8] On 7 September 1939 the communist Johann Heinen became the first victim of this 'special treatment'. For refusing to participate in the measures taken at his factory to protect against bombing raids, and because he already had a criminal conviction, he was executed in the concentration camp at Sachsenhausen. By 31 July 1942 a further ninety-five such cases were recorded.[9] Soon increasing numbers of Russian and Polish forced labourers, along with British and American pilots held as prisoners of war, were subjected to 'special treatment'. A detailed plan dictated that the Gestapo office responsible had to make all the preparations for the execution: they were to select the place of execution and were usually required to attend the macabre performance in force. Polish forced labourers, too, who were persecuted because of so-called 'GV Crimes' (prohibited sexual intercourse with German women), were usually executed very close to the 'scene of the crime'—under the Gestapo's surveillance.

However bloodthirsty individual cases of persecution might have been, the day-to-day business in Gestapo offices was generally less brutal. As long as there were no organizations to be uncovered or outright 'race enemies' to be persecuted, the daily toil was characterized by routine police work: interrogations, identification parades, highlighting contradictions and yet more interrogation were the standard methods of investigation employed by the Gestapo.[10] Nonetheless, the dominant mode was to follow guidelines sent from above—in a manner that showed indifference to the victims, that was formally correct and ultimately ruthless. The investigators strove to establish in detail how a suspect was involved in certain activities and whether they had been connected to others in the process. This procedure was also in evidence when the members of the student resistance organization 'The White Rose' fell into the Gestapo's clutches in February 1943. Robert Mohr, the investigator responsible for the case, employed harsh and meticulous criminal interrogation techniques, but avoided physical violence. Sophie Scholl, however, sidestepped the questions and harassment with great panache and remained unharmed for a long time. It was only after Mohr's colleagues found incriminating documents in the Scholls' apartment that the situation changed. The film *Sophie Scholl*, directed by Marc Rothemund, vividly represents this interrogation.

Most Gestapo officers carried out their work at a desk, not in the field. They were busy producing or updating index cards, working through the flood of instructions and regulations, filing documents, and preparing to support the endeavours of other state, police, or party institutions. Collecting and working through information was the normal state of affairs, even when it came to the persecution of the Jews.

The Gestapo's various index systems formed the bureaucratic linch-pin of the persecution, documenting information about the opponents of the Nazi state. At its core were the personal records: pre-printed fields were filled with the individual's personal data, political views, and information about existing police records. In 1934 Himmler decreed that the following information should be registered: 'covert or officially produced photographs, (b) criminal records, [...] (d) notifications of internment, (e) instructions regarding the imposition or termination of protective detention, (f) copies of the record of interrogation, [...] (o) other information of any kind, providing that it is relevant to the judgement of the individual, gives information about their connections, the results of interrogation etc.'[11] At the beginning of 1939, the central records office of the Gestapo is said to have comprised around two million personal index cards and more than 600,000 personal files.

The personal records were supplemented by a protective detention index, which contained essential data about protective detainees and samples for comparing handwriting. In addition there were the so-called A Cards for 'enemies of the state to be taken into protective detention in case of war'. Other special index systems were also developed, such as civil servant cards, Jew cards, company cards, and factory cards, which recorded those who had been dismissed from armament works for political or racial reasons. The spectrum of cards varied depending on the Gestapo office. Yet the fact that a card index like this could not be compiled without problems and friction is proven by the A Index, initiated by Heydrich, which took more than a year to be built up by the Gestapo offices throughout the Reich. To Heydrich's displeasure the card index initially comprised 46,000 names and was consequently not usable. After it had been edited, this index provided the basis for the arrest of between 2,000 and 4,000 people in early September 1939. Buchenwald alone took more than 2,000 prisoners. Another wave of arrests, similarly systematic, began towards the end of the war, more precisely in the late summer of 1944 after the assassination attempt of 20 July. Known as 'Action Thunderstorm' (*Aktion Gewitter*), it ordered the arrests of all former members of the Reichstag and regional governments, as well as city councillors from the KPD, SPD, and Centre Party (*Zentrumspartei*), 'regardless [...] of whether there is currently any evidence against them or not'.[12] As a result, well over 5,000 former representatives of the people were detained in concentration camps, and several thousand more men and women were arrested but not detained. Even in the agony of downfall, the Gestapo asserted its will to exercise systematic terror.

The formation of so-called 'Special Commissions' was proof of the Gestapo's willingness to provide a large number of staff, significant commitment, criminological skill, but also unqualified brutality when dealing with particularly serious political events. These commissions were not invented by the National Socialists, but during the 'Third Reich' they were deployed frequently by the Gestapo and RSHA in particularly significant cases. While the Reichstag fire at the end of February 1933 was still investigated by the political department of the Berlin police headquarters, the assassination of Reinhard Heydrich on 27 May 1942 saw around 1,200 officers from the entire Reich brought together for the commission. The largest special commission was established after the failed assassination of Hitler on 20 July 1944: between then and winter 1944 it is thought that the commission ordered more than 600 arrests, of which over 100 led to death sentences at the People's Court (*Volksgerichthof*). The 'Red Orchestra

Special Commission' was also of historical significance, formed in the summer of 1942 after decoded radio messages from Soviet military intelligence drew attention to the resistance activities of the group around Harro Schulze-Boysen, Senior Lieutenant in the Reich Air Force Ministry, and Alfred Harnack, Senior Government Councillor in the Finance Ministry. The Gestapo named the group 'Red Orchestra' to imply that they were a communist organization and part of a wider Soviet espionage network. In fact, the 'Red Orchestra' was one of the largest resistance groups working against the Nazis, and was composed of friends and acquaintances with various intellectual and political allegiances. In practice, this special commission was run by the Gestapo commissar Horst Kopkow, who had developed a specialism in the persecution of political resistance fighters. The commission comprised at least thirty Gestapo officers, and there were daily meetings in Kopkow's office. The Gestapo made rigorous attempts to uncover the network, making use of the full range of interrogation methods: threats, blackmail, flattery, torture, producing genuine or fake evidence, confronting suspects with genuine or fake statements from other prisoners. The interrogations mainly took place in the Gestapo's own prison in Berlin's Prinz Albrecht Straße. At the end of 1942, 130 members of the group were arrested, of whom four committed suicide, five were murdered before it came to trial, and forty-nine were executed, including nineteen women.[13]

The case of Georg Elser is further proof that the Gestapo worked effectively in special commissions and that these commissions functioned as part of a network. After Elser had attacked Adolf Hitler in the Munich Bürgerbräukeller on 9 November 1939, a major alarm was raised and the border controls were tightened. From the RSHA headquarters in Berlin, Himmler immediately deployed a 'Special Commission Bürgerbräu Attack' (*Sonderkommission Bürgerbräuattentat*) in Munich, including two sub-commissions, one for the perpetrators and one for the scene of the crime. At the same time the Berlin headquarters started to monitor reports of arrests from police and border stations, and sought to identify potential links to the attack.

Elser had been arrested on the Swiss border near Lake Constance before the bomb even went off, because the contents of his luggage were deemed suspicious. He was brought before the commission for perpetrators on 12 November 1939, having already been interrogated, beaten, and tortured a number of times. Clues at the scene of the crime indicated that the perpetrator had prepared the bomb while kneeling, and a Gestapo officer noticed that Elser suffered from knee troubles and confronted him with this connection. During the night of 13 November Elser confessed his sole responsibility, and was brought to the Gestapo prison in Prinz Albrecht Straße. The Gestapo chiefs continued to interrogate him, refusing to believe that he had operated alone. Himmler and Gestapo chief Müller took great personal pains in their abuse of Elser, attempting to extort a full confession. In the search for his co-conspirators, even relatives and several neighbours from Elser's most recent home in Königsbronn were arrested. But in the end no evidence could be found to support the Gestapo's conspiracy theories. Elser was delivered to Sachsenhausen concentration camp as a 'special prisoner' (*Sonderhäftling*), but he was not executed by firing squad until 9 April 1945, in Dachau. The Elser case further increased the significance of the Gestapo within Nazi power structures, and from that point on it was also responsible for security at events where leading Nazi functionaries were present. But while the Gestapo could boast of successful investigations, they were unable to prevent the assault of a man working alone.[14]

The rather more bureaucratic activities of Gestapo officers included writing field reports and daily updates, many of which are still extant and in the public domain.[15] Here, Gestapo officers made regular reports about general police matters and individual events, as well as about the economic and social state of the population and the local mood. In addition there were daily updates about particular political offences. The field reports were intended to paint a faithful picture of the state and disposition of the population. In the course of the Verreichlichung, Himmler and Heydrich increasingly delegated this reporting to the SD. Instead of just providing general reports on disposition, the Gestapo were from now on to report on resistant behaviour, and to give as much detail as possible about the individuals involved. They were to compile information on communist and Social Democratic workers' movements, on churches and sects, on Jewish and conservative organizations, on the NSDAP and the press, and only occasionally on the economic situation. Moreover, they began to produce special summary reports, such as on strikes, assassination attempts on leading figures, arrests, and confiscated leaflets. In 1937 the Gestapo put together its first large synoptic report on the 'illegal Marxist and communist movement'. Similarly, it later provided overviews of the investigation into the 'Red Orchestra'.

There has been repeated criticism of the use of these field reports as historical sources, in that they always also reflect the personal and structural shortcomings of the Gestapo. Nonetheless, as a whole they represent a valuable source for historical research, because they give ongoing and systematic information about the various forms of resistance as well as commenting on misunderstandings and dissatisfaction within the dictatorship.[16] These reports tell us little about state police practice, however. It is therefore necessary to take a look at further persecution practices.

Gestapo informants

The Gestapo's informants played an important role in the gathering of information. The Gestapo used them to gather information in areas of resistance or amongst groups of people who were under state police surveillance. The informants were particularly valuable to the Gestapo because the targets remained unaware that they were being observed in their immediate vicinity. The informants' core tasks were to observe incognito, to inform on illegal activities, and to report punishable offences. Informants were civilian moles, whose activities directly paved the way for the Gestapo's repressive measures. It is important to note that the informants were not nominal Gestapo officers, deployed as undercover agents or spies, but mostly 'co-opted illegals, enlisted or blackmailed deviants, who were made to feel at home in the investigative environment, and enjoyed respect there'.[17] In other words, informers were denouncers under contract to the state police, who mixed with the population and informed the Gestapo of their findings. According to the Karlsruhe Gestapo officer Adolf Gerst, the following types were above all suited to informant work: 'Idealists, committed National Socialists who chose this way of taking up arms against the state enemy; those who were obliged by their position or profession to pass on remarks that had been addressed to them more or less privately; those who wanted to earn some extra money on the side or who, particularly in wartime, wanted to get hold of scarce goods—this was mainly the case with foreigners.'[18] The Gestapo officer failed to mention that the informants included both volunteers and the victims of blackmail, 'turned' by the Gestapo's psychological and physical pressure. And those who were recruited after being released from detention (protective or otherwise) can hardly be considered to have 'volunteered' for the role.

Reflections on the work of the informants have been ambivalent in literature on the topic. Assessments and projections of their strengths are divided, and their effectiveness is both exaggerated and played down. The files of the Düsseldorf Gestapo tell us that the Gestapo in the Rhine and Ruhr region deployed around 300 informants with a communist background, while 600–800 spies were taken on in Vienna.[19] These figures do not suggest an 'army of spies', with a broad and comprehensive impact on the Gestapo's complete surveillance network. Nonetheless, the informants did have considerable success. Several successful Gestapo investigations can be ascribed to evidence from informants.

Informants from other sections of the NSDAP also contributed to this success, however. The SD above all ran a comprehensive persecution network. SD informants aimed to penetrate the widest range of social structures, with full coverage and with preventative aims. It is thought that the SD maintained around 30,000 informants, and while their reports rarely led to state police investigations, they certainly facilitated the specialized surveillance of society in the Nazi state, and enhanced the capacities of the Gestapo.[20] The network of block- and cell-leaders (*Block- und Zellenleiter*) should also be added to the list of Gestapo informants. These characters functioned as a point of contact for denouncers, and made their own observations or gathered information, which they then passed on to the Gestapo.

Although the Gestapo tended to be able to recruit informants in all sectors of society that were critical of the Nazi regime, it does seem that, as a result of their organizational structure, left-wing political groups were particularly susceptible to this form of betrayal. The Gestapa in Berlin decreed early on that all Gestapo offices in the Reich should establish a state police intelligence service to combat communism and Marxism. At the same time, the Gestapa recommended that those released from concentration camps should be recruited and employed long-term. Yet some police spies were already active in communist circles even before the Nazis took control. There were spectacular successes soon after the seizure of power: on 3 March 1933 Ernst Thälmann, head of the Central Committee (ZK) of the German Communist Party (KPD), was betrayed by a spy and arrested by the political police. His successor, John Schehr, also fell victim to the spies and was arrested on 9 November 1933. The Gestapo recruited informants in order to gain information about the illegal structures of the KPD. Their principal aim was then to destroy these structures as quickly as possible, so that informants were often recruited with short-term goals in mind and then abandoned soon after. Once their betrayal had been successful, these informants were then 'burnt' and discarded, in some cases even arrested.

The systematic deployment of informants produced significant gaps within the organized political resistance.[21] At certain times in Vienna, half of all the arrests of illegal communists could be attributed to 'Konfidenten', as the informants were known in Austria. Eugen Wicker was one of the most efficient Gestapo informants, coming from a communist milieu but 'turned' after his internment in 1933 at the Oberer Kuhberg concentration camp near Ulm.[22] After his release he was active for the Gestapo under the cover name of 'Hans', spying on illegal KPD structures in Württemberg—with the help of his brother Alfons Wicker, whom he was able to persuade to join the ranks of informants. Once the Wicker brothers had been made members of the Württemberg KPD district leadership in 1936, they were able to all but decapitate the communist structures known to them. Similarly, the 'Red Aid' (*Rothe Hilfe*) group in southern Bavaria were uncovered by an informant. It was an informant, too, who had a fatal impact on the case of the resistance group around Georg Lechleiter: the traitor gave the Gestapo the names of several members of the illegal group, which had amongst other things distributed the document 'Der Vorbote' ('The Herald'). As a result, Lechleiter and his co-conspirators were arrested by the Gestapo at the end of February 1942, interrogated non-stop for two days and nights, and handed over to the criminal justice department. The apartments of those arrested were searched and suspicious material was seized. The Gestapo made more and more arrests on the basis of the admissions under interrogation, and in total fifty to sixty people were arrested. On 15 May 1942 Lechleiter was sentenced to death by the People's Court in Mannheim, and shortly afterwards his nineteen co-conspirators were executed, while three others died in custody.[23]

Not even the Catholic Church was immune to informants. In the diocese of Aachen alone, information about what was happening at a pastoral and decanal level was passed to the Gestapo by a priest, two chaplains, two monks, and several laypersons.[24] In Freiburg, too, the Gestapo had spies in the religious arena, including a member of the head office of the Catholic Charitable Services (Caritas), Franz Xaver Rappenecker, who ran the Seminary for Public Welfare and offered the Gestapo his services for the surveillance of Gertrud Luckner and her initiatives to help Jews to flee. Rappenecker's statements helped the Gestapo to build a detailed picture of Gertrud Luckner's 'Juden-hilfe' (Jewish Aid).[25]

At first the informants were supervised by the individual Gestapo offices. But from around 1941 the RSHA ordered that the deployment of informants be systematized and professionalized. The Gestapo offices were ordered to create their own 'Section N', in order to recruit further contacts—separate from the existing informants—and to consolidate their activities. The SD's informants and those from the church were also to be slotted into the Gestapo structure.[26] In all field offices and border police stations, one officer was made the 'N Worker'. The recruitment and supervision of the informants was on the whole dealt with by individual case workers, while the superior Section N took over the central planning. It directed the informants towards areas of industry, economy, and transport that were at risk of sabotage and espionage, and also towards illegal political groups.

The use of informants was dependent on how successful they were likely to be. It only made sense to have spies if they were going to expose whole clandestine networks and uncover illegal structures. Thus informants were not required for the persecution of the Jews, since the structures and named composition of the communities and associations was known to the Gestapo. Gestapo informants only rarely became involved in Jewish activities or in the emigrant scene. Yet there was an important exception: the search for Jews who had gone into hiding, attempting to avoid deportation.

The Gestapo's recruitment of Jewish spies in large cities such as Vienna or Berlin took a particularly perfidious form, in that they took advantage of the Jews' extremely desperate situation. They attempted to corrupt potential spies by promising to treat Jewish collaborators and their relatives favourably, and in particular not to deport them to Auschwitz. Many rejected the offer, and some withdrew from the pressure altogether by committing suicide. However, in Berlin twenty-nine so-called Jewish 'Graspers' (*Greifer*) took up the offer and hoped through this 'forced betrayal' to improve their own situation and that of their relatives—often, however, in vain.[27] For spies who fell out of favour were deported just as often as promises of leniency were broken. Some spies did nonetheless survive until the end of the war under the Gestapo's protection.

Following the so-called 'Factory Action' (*Fabrik-Aktion*) of 27 March 1943, when the last of the Berlin Jews who were not subject to any privilege and were obliged to perform slave labour were arrested and deported, the capital of the Reich was considered 'clean of Jews' (*judenrein*). Despite this, between 5,000 and 7,000 Jews had still eluded arrest. It was the Gestapo's task to catch these 'illegals'. For this purpose a 'Manhunt Commission' (*Fahndungsdienst*) composed of Jewish spies was founded. The Gestapo received information about illegals from a variety of sources: they extorted information from Jews detained in transit camps, responded to denunciations, and developed an index of those in hiding. The Gestapo attempted to ascertain the location of Jews in hiding from those who had already been arrested. In exchange for this betrayal, the prisoners were usually offered an improvement of their own situation. The Gestapo attempted to recruit to the man-hunt commission Jews who they expected to deliver a particularly large number of 'illegals'. These 'Graspers' were to locate and arrest Jews in hiding. In Vienna the Central Agency for Jewish Emigration had already created a 'Special Commission' which had a similar remit. Here, too, 'unearthers' (*Ausheber*) or 'grabbers' (*Packer*) were deployed to search for and apprehend so-called 'illegal Jews'. The head of this department, Alois Brunner, was transferred to Berlin in 1942, in order to introduce the successful 'Viennese Methods' there—further evidence of the fact that the persecution of the Jews followed a number of examples in its development. Vienna, where actions against the Jews were often faster and more radical, consequently played an important role.

The headquarters of the Berlin manhunt commission was initially the transit camp for deportations on Große Hamburger Straße in the Mitte district of Berlin, once the old people's home for the Jewish community. The head of the transit camp was Walter Dobberke, who was also in charge of the manhunt commission. His role was to prepare and implement the deportation of Berlin's Jews. Under his direction, Jews were taken from their homes and brought to the camp. There Dobberke and his colleagues interrogated them, to help them to track down other Jews in hiding. Dobberke then instructed the

'Graspers' that he had recruited to arrest those in hiding. They were supported in this work by Jewish marshals, who helped the unprepared families to pack and ensured that nobody escaped.

The best-known 'Graspers' were Stella Kübler and Rolf Isaakson, who often worked together to locate Jews in hiding and hand them over to the Gestapo. They were allowed to leave the transit camp at any time and did not have to wear the yellow star. They were paid in money, ration cards, accommodation, and valid papers. In order to carry out their orders, the searchers even invented their own seizure methods. 'Stella', soon notorious, not only followed clues from Gestapo officers. She and the other Graspers also checked the ID cards of passers-by, preferably in busy public places where 'illegals' were known to linger. They addressed people they thought to be illegal and promised to get them food and accommodation, but then delivered them to the Gestapo's knife. Stella Kübler alone is responsible for the fates of several hundred Jews.

To survive as an 'illegal' was in the end only possible through a series of coincidences and the support of helpers. Of the estimated 5,000–7,000 Berlin Jews in hiding, it is thought that only 1,400 survived underground in the capital.[28] The Gestapo did not set up its own manhunt commission in any other cities in the Reich. But it did inform the Jewish communities there and forced them to cooperate in the location of those in hiding. If family members appeared to know where the fugitive was hiding, the Gestapo were able to put pressure on them through threats, taking away ration cards, or even internment. Tailing relatives, on the other hand, was rare. Instead the criminal police was usually notified and search warrants for the Jews were issued internally. But the life of an illegal, in particular getting hold of food, was so difficult that the Gestapo banked on those in hiding giving themselves up of their own accord.[29] For it was often not specially recruited informants who posed a problem for the persecuted, but quite simply the fellow German next door.

The role of denunciations

When a few years ago research into the Gestapo indicated that denunciations happened on a massive scale in the 'Third Reich', and concluded that the Gestapo could not have functioned at all without them, it caused a sensation in both scholarship and the media.[30] However, if you consider denunciations to be nothing more than some members of the population openly showing their willingness to inform the official and semi-official authorities of activities that they consider unlawful or possibly hostile to the state, then you have to concede that denunciations can occur at any time in any state: in democratic states as much as in pre-democratic or dictatorial systems. As long as they are not exploited to criminal ends, denunciations represent to a certain extent the normal condition of any political intervention.[31] Denunciations, then, were not a purely German phenomenon. They were by no means rare in occupied Poland or in France, either.[32] Likewise, denunciations were part and parcel of the Stalinist regime's attempts to extend and secure rule.[33]

But what is a denunciation? How does it differ from a normal report to the police? And who were the denouncers? Unlike with the informants, there was no compulsion involved in the cases of denunciation. It was not enforced betrayal. Like reports, denunciations were made voluntarily. It was colleagues, neighbours, relatives, and acquaintances who 'dished the dirt on' their peers to the party, police, or Gestapo. Both the denouncers and the denounced came from all strata of German society—with one exception: Jews were generally only to be found amongst the denunciated. The notion that women and the lower classes had a particular affinity to denunciation has not been conclusively proven by more recent research. Rather, it is men from the lower and middle classes who make up a disproportionately large percentage of the denouncers.[34] Most people denounced others because of private interests and base motives such as envy, revenge, anger, hatred, or malevolence. Furthermore, the typical denouncer remained anonymous—out of cowardice or fear. It was not usually easy to differentiate between private and political motives, because the aims were often similar and private denunciations could therefore also be categorized as political. There is much to suggest that traditional conceptions of morality and order, such as in terms of gender relations and the roles expected of them, linked up with elements of National Socialist politics and ideology. Anything that seemed to be out of line with the supposedly healthy national feeling was denounced. What's more, this attitude lasted long after 1945, when the voice of the people rang out, for example at the sight of certain non conformist groups: 'That wouldn't have happened with Adolf.' Of course that would not have happened, because they themselves would have informed 'Adolf' of it. On the whole utterances like this represent an echo of old denunciations.

The most famous denunciation of the 'Third Reich' is probably that of Jacob Schmid. On 18 February 1943 this Munich University caretaker, a qualified locksmith and electrician, observed Hans and Sophie Scholl throwing leaflets printed by the 'White Rose' resistance group into the atrium of the university entrance hall. He followed the students, apprehended them, and demanded that they accompany him to the custodian of the building. The custodian informed the university lawyer, who told the Gestapo. Even twenty years later Schmid justified his action by arguing that students could not be permitted to seed disorder in the university. Robert Musil comes inevitably to mind: 'Somehow order slips into the need for murder.'[35]

In the main, denunciations followed a simple pattern: an individual acted in a manner that was forbidden in the National Socialist state. They were observed doing so and denounced. It was generally police or party offices that were the first to be informed. There, the claim was checked and if necessary passed on to the Gestapo. Only then did the real organ of persecution spring into action. Cases like this, of denunciation followed by Gestapo action, happened everywhere. Members of communist underground organizations were betrayed, Jehovah's Witnesses were informed on from doorsteps, priests who had preached against the effects of the Nazi state were denounced, and Polish forced labourers who conducted intimate relations with German women were reported. Neighbours were denounced because they listened to 'enemy broadcasts' and locals were expelled from the village community after they had spread the latest 'Führer joke' in the pub. There seems to be no doubt that the extent of denunciations in Nazi society was on the whole significant.

Nonetheless, it is important to make certain distinctions: denunciations did indeed play a greater role in the prosecution of crimes on racial grounds, such as 'racial defilement' (*Rassenschande*) or 'friendship with Jews' (*Judenfreundschaft*)—57 per cent of all such cases in Würzburg can be attributed to denunciations from the public. But this was not the case for all other crimes. In Saarbrücken, denunciations to the Gestapo for treachery cases amounted to 87.5 per cent of the total, while for the persecution of homosexuals there were relatively few denunciations—only 9 to 15 per cent of the total amount. The proportion was barely higher when it came to the persecution of Jehovah's Witnesses: only around a quarter fell into the Gestapo's clutches and were then sentenced or punished as a result of active intervention by the local population.[36]

In other words, the denunciations followed a similar pattern, but the Gestapo's reactions did not. This was partly due to the fact that the Gestapo did not always rely on denunciations. In certain cases and with certain groups under investigation, denunciations played a minimal role, because the actual investigative work could be greatly enhanced by denunciations but not brought to any conclusion. This was the case for the persecution of communists and socialists. With these groups the most important sources of information for the Gestapo quite clearly arose from disclosures made under duress during interrogations. The arrests and raids that followed these statements, in particular the heedless imposition of punitive or protective detention and internment in concentration camps, happened whether there had been denunciations or not. For these purposes, the Gestapo possessed its own means of persecution. Denunciation did play a role in the persecution of the Jews, in particular in cases of 'racial defile-ment' or reports of minor everyday activities, such as a street trader selling roasted almonds to Jews. Nonetheless, the most successful campaigns were not initiated by reports from the local population: the arrests during the 'Night of Broken Glass' and the deportations of Jews were conducted at the highest political level and completely without the aid of denunciations.

For quite some time now, historiographical research has indicated that denunciations were significant as triggers and support for the persecution conducted by the Gestapo.[37] Faced with the 'unimagin-able extent' of proven denunciations you might even speak of a 'society under its own surveillance'. According to this view, it was not the Gestapo that was the principal investigator, but the 'normal' 'national comrade'.[38] Likewise, the precondition for these reports and denunciations was the atmosphere of the Nazi state, stirred up by propaganda and encouraging denunciation. The victims of denunci-ations were adequately determined by central political guidelines issued by the organs of persecution, the denouncers did not need to invent any new crimes. Calls for denunciations were publicly dissem-inated, as is shown in the following evidence from the south-west of the Reich: 'The Gestapa expects active participation; the most extreme vigilance is required to capture the internal and external enemies of the German people, who are once again particularly active in the border zone of Baden, before they inflict greater damage. Written or oral statements are to be directed promptly to the Secret State Police Office (Gestapa) or to the local police authorities.'[39]

It was no surprise, then, that many—in some cases too many—made such reports. The Gestapo leadership were not in the least concerned at the idea that there might in some places be a flood of denunciations that would be hard to deal with. Like every secret police force in a dictatorship, they worked on the basic principle that too much information was always better than too little. At the beginning of the war, Reinhard Heydrich even tried to introduce a legal duty to inform, according to which every German over 18 would be obliged to report to a 'National Report Service' (*Volksmeldedienst*) every crime and misdemeanour that would be considered punishable according to the 'healthy public feeling'—in the sense that it undermined the will to fight and destroyed the economic potential of the German people. Although he was not able to put through binding legislation, he still sent out a number of circulars demanding the 'total mobilization of the nation's political attention'.[40] He intended in this way to style the Gestapo as an all-seeing organ of surveillance, instilling fear and generating a willingness to adapt. Heydrich, head of the security police, intentionally allowed rumours of the omnipresence and omnipotence of the Gestapo to proliferate, in order to intimidate any internal political opponents. Any problems that arose from selfish or unfounded denunciations were acceptable as long as they strengthened the Gestapo's own position.

In addition, the Gestapo did not need to deal with all the denunciations alone, but could make use of the broad totalitarian infrastructure of the National Socialist regime. The system of organized informants included the involvement of various state and party institutions. All authorities and party structures were required to report anti-government activities to the Gestapo. Further, they were expected to receive 'statements' from the local population and forward them to the Gestapo if they were of political significance. 'Thus the complex network of authorities and party offices created a structural "range of denunciation options" to the local population. It shortened the denouncer's path to placing their report, and consequently lowered the inhibition threshold for denunciations.'[41] Very few reports landed directly on the Gestapo's desks, most taking a detour through block, cell, town, or district leaders, or being passed to chairmen of the German Labour Front (DAF) and its Information Office, which existed until 1937, or to individual police offices. These offices first checked which denunciations were well founded and which were simply based on personal enmities: by no means every report was passed on. State offices in particular tried to discourage people from making their report, bearing in mind the punishments that they might generate—a sign, by the way, that not every 'national comrade' had internalized the racist world view. Even if you assume a poly-cratic chaos typical of the Nazi state, and thereby presume that the co-operation between the Gestapo and their informants did not always run smoothly, it is safe to suppose that the support of the police, state, and party made it much easier, perhaps even made it possible, to deal with the large number of denunciations.

Help came above all from the clarification of 'treacherous offences' (*Heimtückedelikten*). According to the law against treacherous attacks on state and party of 20 December 1934, all 'malignant' and 'inflamma-tory' remarks directed against the Nazi regime became criminal offences and were to be threatened with drastic punishments. The spectrum ranged from telling a joke through passing on a rumour up to 'listening to enemy broadcasts'. The Treachery Act was designed to place private remarks and acts on an equal footing with public ones: the floodgates were thereby opened to denunciations from the private sphere. The Treachery Regulation of 21 March 1933 and the Treachery Act of 20 December 1934 were all-purpose weapons against critical utterances in an everyday setting, establishing a central criminal law norm that sought to suppress the exchange of information and opinions in normal life. A peak of 'treachery cases' was reached in 1936 with around 8,000 charges before the Special Court (*Sondergericht*) and then in 1937 with more than 17,000 Gestapo reports. Afterwards, the numbers dropped and the Gestapo leadership advised that first-time offenders should in future simply be released with a warning. The punishment was to be based less on the act or the content of the remark than on the perpetrator's personal attributes. Only 'genuine pests to the people' (Heydrich) should be punished.[42] The measures were then tightened again when the war began: after the outbreak of the Second World War in 1939/40, after the defeat at Stalingrad, and finally in the last months of the war in 1944/45, reports and denunci-ations because of 'treacherous offences', 'defeatist remarks', 'listening to enemy broadcasts' (the so-called 'radio crimes') or 'subversion of defence forces' had serious consequences, because the crimes were assessed in the context of wartime criminal justice conditions. Disseminating intercepted information was above all a punishable offence. The Special Courts, in Roland Freisler's words 'armoured corps of the judiciary', were required to dole out the death sentence to all those who were considered enemies in attitude or 'pests to the people'. Death sentences for trivial offences like theft of bread or listening to enemy broadcasts did indeed happen, but not as a rule. The Gestapo introduced 'state police measures' which concealed a whole set of sanctions: from 'cautioning', 'warning', and issuing a 'security fine' through imposing 'protective detention', to 'special treatment'. The latter was the National Socialist euphemism for execution. However, local studies show that very few treachery cases actually ended with the individual's life coming under threat in a concentration camp or with death.[43]

A typical treachery case took the following course: on 22 April 1941 a lorry driver delivering beer, presumably drunk, ranted about the war being raged by the Nazi regime: 'I tell you we're buggered, just like in 1914/18 when we were victorious but were still buggered. This whole war today, Germany's war, it's a swindle, just like the 1914/18 war. I was part of it, after all. We're going to lose this war just like we lost the last one.'[44] The driver's tirade was noted by an administrative inspector who happened to be there at the time, and who later reported it to an officer of the south German criminal police with whom he was acquainted. The officer reported the case to the local Gestapo office on 26 April 1941, which started an investigation into subversive remarks and 'undermining of military morale' (Wehrkraftzersetzung). The Gestapo officers then had to establish how well founded the accusations were. They began investigations, visited the 'scene of the crime' and interrogated witnesses, wrote reports, and attempted to get the accused to confess. How the denounced individual was treated depended on the quality of the original report and the 'credibility' of the witnesses. This was also how our delivery man was dealt with; he was taken into protective custody on the basis of statements by 'credible witnesses'. Amongst other things the Gestapo ascertained whether there was already any evidence against the man in a 'political,

political espionage or criminal context'. The local NSDAP cell chairman reported that the man was considered 'politically unreliable'. The Gestapo reported the case to their local headquarters and obtained an arrest warrant 'for crimes against the *Kriegssonderstrafrechtsverordnung* of 17 August 1939'[†] from the public prosecutor.[45]

In the end the decision as to whether the cases were 'particularly brutal' or harmless fell to the respective caseworkers, who had quite significant room for manoeuvre. The 'judgement' that they made depended on a number of factors:[46] in the first instance they looked at the accused and whether they were already known to the police or seemed particularly suspicious. In this case, as in our example, the 'political character reference' (*politische Leumundszeugnis*) was of great significance, and often decided how the case would progress. If, as here, the case appeared to be straightforward, it was passed on to the public prosecutor straight away in order to save time and effort. If not, then depending on the character reference the individual would get off with a warning or a fine. At the other extreme, they would be subjected to the Gestapo's own sanctions and placed in protective detention or in a concentration camp. If respectable citizens were accused of trivial offences then it was very possible that they would be released with no more than a warning. Even telling a political joke, which the National Socialists had made a punishable offence very early on, remained largely without consequence for Germans who were not of Jewish heritage and who had not engaged in any political activity. Most cases were not pursued at all, and with the odd exception the punishment was never greater than a few months' imprisonment.[47] For former communists, however, a denunciation for treachery could be fatal. Those on the margins of society or with poor character references were particularly at risk. Jews were the victims of denunciation precisely because they were dealt with especially harshly and brutally, although the apparent misdemeanours were utterly harmless

---

[†] The *Kriegssonderstrafrechtsverordnung* was the regulation that amended the German penal code for wartime, issued on 17 August 1938.

in themselves. The only difference was that the Gestapo knew no mercy in their cases. It comes as no surprise, then, that across the Reich the proportion of foreign forced labourers amongst those convicted of 'radio crimes' stood at around 20 per cent.

The most recent research has shown that the threat posed by the Treachery Act was not as significant as one might assume. The Gestapo did not press charges against most Germans who were politically and racially inconspicuous, but limited their terror to a few cases. Overall, it was far more common for the Gestapo to do no more than interrogate, caution and issue fines. Skilled in psychological matters, the Gestapo mostly had their victims sign a document with wording along the lines of: 'I acknowledge that I have been given a very strict warning by the Secret State Police [...] due to suspicions of listening to a foreign broadcast [...]. Furthermore I was informed that I should expect any repeat of this offence to result both in punishment by the court and in extremely severe measures by the state police and detention in a concentration camp.'[48] Only around 5,000 people were condemned for 'radio crimes' by the special courts.[49] If you set this figure against the number of German listeners that the BBC estimated were tuning into their broadcasts in August 1944—between 10 and 15 million every day—then it seems clear that the persecution was not on a grand scale. Or, to look at it from another angle, the interest was less in preventing people from listening than in preventing them from talking about what they had heard. However, exceptions were punished yet more harshly because the Gestapo obviously hoped that their actions would deter copycats. This is the only explanation for the fact that individuals were condemned and executed for very minor thefts.[50]

Was all this effort worthwhile? Was the burden not great—perhaps too great—for the Gestapo officers to pursue every report, only in the end to issue a warning or impose temporary detention if the evidence was too thin? If you consider the whole bureaucratic procedure necessary to check reports, it is easy to conclude that the number of cases overwhelmed the Gestapo and reduced their efficiency. Even the most paltry treachery offence had to be recorded in three copies, fully logged, and sent to the relevant local office for further processing. On the other hand, you must consider that even a harmless case could have a desirable result, in that the person reported to the Gestapo is suitably intimidated and subsequently conforms to the norms of the 'national community' (*Volksgemeinschaft*), so that they no longer make themselves conspicuous. Thus the Gestapo threatened to punish repeat offences more harshly, and—even with acquittals—carefully stored the personal records in their large index system. Seen in this light, an apparently inefficient police procedure could in practice have the desired results.

Although denunciation was widespread, the National Socialist society by no means policed itself. Unlike its treatment of political opponents, the Gestapo treated any non-conformist behaviour that was not part of a larger organization with exemplary measures. They made isolated use of terror, relying on a widespread deterrent effect. This was not generated directly by the Gestapo, but by their reactions to reports from the local population. They were reliant on denunciations for dealing with all forms of subversive daily protest, but were nonetheless not subordinate to those denunciations. The Gestapo leadership at least made the effort to retain control of the denunciations, using numerous decrees to inform their officers when they should respond leniently. Targeted information, disseminated by a controlled and censored press, the criminalization of political opponents, and the exemplary punishment and execution of certain marginal groups all made it possible for the Gestapo to exercise control with relatively few staff, to act as a deterrent, and to secure the regime's survival in times of internal political turmoil.[51] Despite denunciations, the 'Third Reich' remained a police state. There were more effective means of combating communists, Jews, and Eastern European foreign labourers than through the assistance of the local population. Most illegal remarks were not pursued. The actual number of offences was probably several hundred times higher than all the denunciations combined: 'Denunciations were the exception, not the rule, for the great majority of the German people.'[52]

Co-operation with the police, SS and Nazi Party organizations

Denouncers were by no means the only ones to help the Gestapo. Their most important helpers were usually uniformed members of the police, SS, and other Nazi Party organizations. The various organizations that collaborated from time to time with the Gestapo might well be seen as a kind of reserve Gestapo. In addition there were the various forms of support given by the state administration: the Gestapo was by no means the only investigating authority.[53] 'Administrative co-operation' (*Amtshilfe*) was always taken into account. In almost every Gestapo decree and in every law there are calls for the police, party, state, and population to support the work of the Gestapo. One of these decrees, for example, contains the following words: 'If the ultimate aim of the Secret State Police is to mobilize fully the whole population's attention against all activities that endanger the state, then it is all the more understandable that the Secret State Police expects in the first instance the most extensive co-operation and support from all state organs. In the case of the local and district police organs, this is not a voluntary duty but one decreed by the Reichsführer-SS.'[54] In other words, the networks of persecution in the 'Third Reich' by no means formed randomly. They were not improvisations, born of necessity, but very much intended, planned, and on the whole systematically organized.

From the point of view of the Gestapo leadership, the police and administration were not only their local arm, they were an integral part of the network of persecution. The Gestapo was the central core of a political administration that intended to shape every aspect of the population's communal life. After Werner Best's dictum, the Gestapo called itself 'doctor to the German national body'. The police, Nazi organizations, and bureaucracy were not equal partners of this doctor.

But they were important aides, their tools always at the ready and occasionally lending a hand themselves if the Gestapo were too busy. The fact that the Gestapo had a broad range of helpers on whom they could, and often did, fall back was thus not a sign of weakness. Without the practical support of various people and institutions, the Gestapo would probably not have managed to function and fully develop their potential as the agency responsible for persecution. The most recent research, which has investigated these questions by analysing networks, strengthens the thesis posed much earlier, that the Gestapo functioned solely as the spearhead of the terror apparatus.[55] Terror and persecution were based on the division of labour.

What is surprising is less that these various forms of co-operation existed, but that they worked so well. As opposed to the conflicts and rivalries evident so often within National Socialist structures, any persecution set in motion by the Gestapo was generally well organized, even if the division of responsibility between the leadership of the order police and security police was not always without controversy.[56] Despite failed investigations and problems with co-ordinating surveillance, despite delayed reports about events of relevance to the state police, as well as various difficulties in co-ordinating the imposition of sanctions, the co-operation between the Gestapo and other sections of the police was quite successful. The interplay between the decentralized persecution network and the centralized Gestapo apparatus does prove that the apparatus of persecution was far from monolithic, but divided into several branches. Nonetheless, it was kept well under control by the relevant SS and Gestapo offices. This success was due less to the Gestapo's preliminary investigations than to the fact that the police made an effort to fulfil the Gestapo's instructions dutifully. Owing to a mixture of obedience and sense of duty, perhaps also careerism and ideological indoctrination, 'normal' policemen were prepared to take part in the violent suppression and persecution staged by the Gestapo. To put it more pointedly: perhaps at the end of the day the persecution was so effective because it was not carried out solely by the Gestapo in the narrow sense. It was largely this support system, these 'assistant doctors to the German national body', that made the Gestapo's investigations successful.

Shortly after the National Socialists took power it became clear how important the normal police would be for supporting state police activities. The early seizures of communist and Social Democratic assets as well as the arrests that followed would not have been possible without the widespread support of conventional police units. It was officers from the Gendarmerie, not the Gestapo, who reported communist slogans plastered on walls or communist flyers. And when the Gendarmerie noticed a possible case of high treason, they did not hesitate but pursued the investigations through their own ranks and with the Gestapo's express approval.

The following case shows how essential this co-operation was for the achievement of state police aims. On 12 June 1934 a Nazi functionary made a report to the Gendarmerie of Walldorf near Heidelberg. He had been informed by a source that the former KPD member Georg Kaufmann had illegal documents in his possession. A gendarme subsequently performed a search of the suspect's flat, together with—as was laconically noted in the report—an 'SA man who had just arrived'. Together they discovered documents entitled 'Nazi leaders on the road to bankruptcy'. Kaufmann was arrested. Later it transpired that the so-called source who had triggered the investigations in the first place was Kaufmann's brother. 'I reported the matter because I didn't want to be suspected if it came out some other way,' he later explained. As the investigation progressed, several more KPD functionaries in the Walldorf district were arrested, following consultation with all the officers of the Walldorf Gendarmerie. Local police officers helped, too. Only one Gestapo member was present: a police secretary from the Heidelberg branch office, and he was only there because he happened to be in the area.[57] As none of those arrested was prepared to make a confession, and they all denied the accusations made by the source, the Gendarmerie searched the suspects' homes again. This time the suspects' wives were also interrogated and there were further arrests, all still without any Gestapo involvement. Then the Gendarmerie suddenly made a breakthrough: one of the suspects admitted knowing about the flyer: 'But Kaufmann ought to say where he got [the flyer] from, so that the others who have nothing to do with it can be freed.' Kaufmann, now worn down by endless interrogations, is presented with this statement. He then signs an interrogation report which, according to the version written by the gendarme conducting the interrogation, reads as follows: 'In the nights leading up to it, I underwent an inner struggle and reached the decision that I would under no circumstances pass these new flyers on to the courier. I saw for myself that what was written in the flyers represented a crime against the people. The workers would simply be deceived, lied to and stirred up by these documents. This is also the reason for my confession.' This document, very likely dictated by the police, was then presented to the other suspects. Impressed by the apparent 'betrayal' and discouraged after a personal confrontation with Kaufmann, the rest of the group made their confession, one after the other. Relieved, the gendarme wrote in his report: thus 'this case can be considered fully resolved.'[58] But he was to be proved wrong. In the following weeks the Walldorf Gendarmerie was entrusted with repeated investigations, arrests, and house searches—note: the Gendarmerie! The Heidelberg Gestapo did not consider itself responsible, and the head office in Karlsruhe only appeared to sign protective detention orders or to transfer prisoners to the nearest concentration camp of Kislau. All the preparations for the criminal proceedings against the Walldorf KPD group were left to the local Gendarmerie.

The Gestapo made certain of their helpers' services again and again. The Reich railway (*Reichsbahn*) was made responsible for border controls and passenger surveillance, the post offices for monitoring the post, the local passport offices for building up the Gestapo registry systems; various party offices and groupings of the NSDAP delivered political character references of suspicious persons and functioned as a contact point for denouncers. The National Socialists developed a surveillance network that extended far beyond the Gestapo. The two million block wardens (*Blockwarte*) in position in the German Reich before the war started, the Nazi welfare system, the German Workers' Front, and the National Socialist Women's League were also there to deal with the tasks of control and surveillance. They observed known opponents of the regime, Jews and all those in contact with Jews, or those who were simply 'politically unreliable'. Beyond these roles, minor party functionaries were also important as contact points for denouncers. The same applies to the various police offices. The order police reported politically suspect events and turned in forbidden pamphlets. They made their infrastructure available to the Gestapo, deployed their staff cars and provided their own staff to cordon off areas for executions. If trains needed to be checked, members of the criminal police were there. The Gestapo arranged the deportations to the concentration camps, but Schutzpolizei men accompanied the transports.

The criminal police in particular had become far more deeply enmeshed in the illegitimate National Socialist state than they managed to claim for years after 1945. They played a decisive role in the fight against apparent 'asocials', and in the persecution of 'homosexuals' and 'gypsies'. They took ruthless preventive measures against so-called 'career criminals', with often less than adequate evidence against their supposed criminal activities. It was precisely the preventive anti-crime measures practised by the Kripo that contributed to the tightening of penal justice, such as effectively suspending the basic rights of the accused, including the right to remain silent.

The number of those who, while not playing a full role, lent a hand in the complex of persecution and extermination extends far beyond Gestapo staff. This was also the case in the widespread surveillance of foreign workers that was set in motion after the outbreak of war. The Gestapo, nominally responsible for all offences by foreign workers, had no intention of handling such cases alone. To prevent a flood of such cases, which threatened to inundate the Gestapo simply because there were such huge numbers of foreign workers in the Reich, the authority nominally in charge of these matters engaged numerous helpers for the preliminary stages, tasked with making the first checks of incriminating cases. In all the milder cases of 'breaking of contract', the labour exchanges were in the first instance responsible for disciplining the workers: the basic idea being that 'if the labour exchanges' warnings prove fruitless, then further measures, e.g. short-term detention, can be carried out by the county administrative offices (*Landratsämter*). If the desired aim is still not achieved, the Gestapo will intervene.'[59] Preliminary investigations of 'GV crimes' were also often left to other sections of the police, as the following examples from the Black Forest prove. When a Polish forced labourer in Villingen was accused of having unlawful relations with a German woman, it was the Kripo that arrested and interrogated him. Subsequently, the Pole was brought to the nearest police prison—in a staff car of the local Schutzpolizei.[60] It was also often the case that the first questioning was carried out by the mayor and local police of the nearest village, which occasionally led to violence and maltreatment.[61] Faced with a German woman who had been involved with a Polish worker, an office clerk from Hinterzarten promptly cut off her hair with his office scissors; and is reported to have severely beaten the Pole. Furthermore, he threatened to hang the pair of them from the nearest tree if they refused to make immediate confessions.[62] Extorting confessions evidently took place in the offices of the provincial authorities, too. In each case, the Gestapo only became involved in the final stages.

Above all when it came to the deportation of Jews, whole networks were involved which were anything but improvised.[63] The SS was called on to cordon off the train station, the order police provided guards for the rail transport, the criminal police made female officers available to search female Jews, the Reichsbahn took care of the trains and timetable, the finance offices were involved in the withdrawal of assets, and the lists were compiled by the local registration office, which was also duty bound to de-register the deportees. After 9 November 1938 the deportations of Jews to the concentration camps were generally accompanied by police guards. Later, members of the Jewish community were obliged to provide assistants.

It was at the latest after the Second World War began that the measures taken by the 'normal' police very gradually diverged from those of the Gestapo. Just as the increasing range of employee types in the Gestapo led to a brutalization of their methods, so the deployment of various police and party units tended to radicalize the processes yet further.[64] The way that the Nazi state worked meant that the method of investigation with the greatest chance of success was always the most radical one.

However, it would be wrong to interpret the surveillance carried out by the persecution network as the direct reality of the 'totalitarian ambitions of National Socialism'.[65] The Gestapo was not omnipotent simply because it was supported by numerous helpers. This is disproved by the lapses and glitches cited at the beginning, which plagued the 'doctors to the German national body'. There were resistance groups which the Gestapo only learned about belatedly and rather by chance. Nor did the Gestapo ever get to grips with the stream of refugees that flooded over the green border into Switzerland, despite the considerable deployment of customs, rail, forestry, and hunting officials. The fact that they nonetheless had an omnipotent effect can be attributed to two main causes. First, and fundamentally, the great potential for violence by the persecuting authorities, which is not to be underestimated. The Gestapo was capable of acting beyond all legal and moral norms in order to strike brutal blows, to influence and destroy the fates of individuals at their own discretion. Secondly, the Gestapo benefited from the broad support of the National Socialist state in the form of the German population, a support which rubbed off on them, the enforcers. In other words, the Gestapo was working within a climate of willingness to consent and support, which extended far beyond their helpers in the police, party, and administration. We are thinking here not so much of denunciations as of the basic attitude of most 'national comrades', which lay at the root of denunciation. The fate of the others did not interest the majority. You put up with the Gestapo and tolerated their activities as long as their repressive measures were directed at the powerless and generally unloved sectors of the German population: Jews, communists, 'gypsies', the 'work-shy', and 'foreigners'.[66] And because the Gestapo were now not to be stopped, many citizens did something more than just accepting an unchangeable fate: they helped the Gestapo to carry out their bloody craft.

5

THE PRACTICE OF PERSECUTION IN THE REICH

Phases of persecution

The Gestapo was fully empowered to persecute unwelcome persons, first in Germany and later in Europe. Yet it was not all-powerful. For—just like the entire Nazi system—the Gestapo could only function because the co-operation, toleration, misinterpretation, and fidelity of numerous people made it possible. For most Germans, the National Socialist terror did not pose a real threat for a long time; it was primarily others that were affected.[1] The majority remained largely untouched and had a wholly different experience from those few declared enemies of the regime. Some were silent sympathizers while others, committed perpetrators, took part in one of the numerous networks of persecution. It was only towards the end of the regime that the terror was capable of affecting all those who opposed the futile orders for the 'final victory'.

The situation was fundamentally different for the declared opponents of the Nazi regime, those groups against whom the full force of the domination, oppression, and finally murder was directed. For the sake of clarity, we will differentiate here between various phases of persecution, which show that the Gestapo acted dynamically and was able to adapt to changing demands (as well as to the regional differences within the Reich).

In the early phase of persecution in 1933, unbridled terror reigned, for which above all the SA was responsible. Since the Gestapo as such did not yet exist, the 'auxiliary police' (*Hilfspolizei*), made up of party associations, was largely responsible for the persecution of opponents of the Nazi movement. In the early concentration camps and SA torture sites, communists, Social Democrats, and those of other political orientations were exposed to the whims of their guards. These included some actual private prisons, which regional rulers made temporary use of to satisfy their personal drives for power and revenge. We know of at least 160 such places of internment. The largest camp-like complexes were in Heuberg in Württemberg, Kemna near Wuppertal, and Osthofen in Hessen; in addition there were the Moor camps in Emsland. One of the most notorious camps was in the Vulcan shipyard in Stettin. At the climax of arrests in April 1933, around 50,000 people were interned in these improvised camps.[2]

The Gestapo had barely been founded in spring 1933 before it also got involved in murder. Albrecht Höhler, for example, who had shot dead Horst Wessel in the course of a private argument, was taken from gaol by Gestapo officers and murdered near Frankfurt an der Oder. The violence and terror of this early phase created fear and insecurity amongst those affected and their relatives, which made the Gestapo's later work easier.

In the following consolidation phase from 1933 to 1936, the Gestapo established its duties, systematized the repression, and brought together the forces that had been active until then under their leadership. They temporarily harnessed the random violence and introduced protective detention in a concentration camp as the harshest of the 'standard' punishments. From the beginning of 1934 the number of inmates began to lessen, only rising again as of 1936. The cases of 'intensified interrogation', in other words the use of physical violence during questioning, also increased after a brief reduction. The political left was still the prime target. When, after four years of persecution, the KPD and SPD underground organizations were as good as destroyed, the Gestapo could turn to other 'opponents'. This consolidation phase spans roughly the same period as when the Gestapo leadership focused on the aims and motives of the SS leadership under Heinrich Himmler and Reinhard Heydrich. But the Gestapo offices in the Reich could still function relatively independently during this time.

The Verreichlichung was followed by the phase of politico-racial persecution from 1937 to 1939, when actions against Jews and Sinti and Roma were expanded. The Gestapo now wanted to remove from the 'German national body' all forms of life and behaviour that they considered deviant. This meant that criminals, in other words so-called career criminals and the work-shy, as well as political or racial offences, were politicized and placed under the jurisdiction of the security police, which from then on included the Gestapo and the Kripo. The concept of internal security was now racially motivated. The deportation of Jewish citizens to Poland as well as the destruction of Jewish cultural assets—beautified as the 'Night of Broken Glass'*— were clear signs that the situation had intensified. After 1938 the persecution of the Jews became ever more intensive and ruthless. Preventive policing also became more widespread. Werner Best defined the tasks of the Gestapo and Kripo as follows: 'In order to secure the popular order against disruption and destruction it is necessary, in addition to the production and maintenance of external order, to repel and prevent every activity that aims to disrupt or destroy the popular order, even if it does not—or not yet—disrupt external order.'[3] The numbers interned in concentration camps increased greatly during this time. Yet an overwhelming majority of Germans, including numerous former communists and Social Democrats who remained under cover, were not particularly threatened by arrest and detention.[4]

At the same time, the Gestapo had been preparing for the impending war since 1937. The fact that this organ of persecution was adapting to war conditions was evident in the establishment of the Reich Security

---

* The German term for the pogrom of 9 November 1938, 'Reichskristallnacht', translates more directly as 'Reich Crystal Night', and as such 'beautifies' the event in a way that the English 'Night of Broken Glass' does not.

Main Office (RSHA). The intention was to be equipped to strike political enemies in the 'Inner-German Theatre of War', as Himmler put it. On Reinhard Heydrich's orders, arrests began on 1 September 1939. 2,000 to 4,000 political opponents, all recorded in the so-called A-index, were arrested and deported to concentration camps.

The beginning of the Second World War brought changes to the persecutors' perspective, too. In the first phase of war, from 1939 to 1941, maintaining German defence and economic forces was declared the highest priority. All forms of 'undermining military morale' were particularly harshly punished—including actions against the regulation of the war economy. Measures against 'politicizing clerics' became far harsher, reaching a new climax in 1941.The Gestapo also moved into the observation and oppression of foreign and forced labourers, who were arriving in the Reich in huge numbers. One part of the Gestapo apparatus was now dedicated to monitoring a range of sabotage cases, strikes, or refusals to work by this group. Dealing out death sentences for so-called 'GV Crimes' (sexual intercourse between German women and East European forced labourers) marked a new stage in the violence: for the first time, the Gestapo began to kill officially outside the concentration camps.

This opened the door to a progressive radicalization and brutalization that found its conclusion in the final phase, the second half of the war from 1943. Conditioned above all by their experience of extermination and murder in occupied Eastern Europe, where officers were sent on rotation, the Gestapo's propensity towards violence within the Reich increased. The bullying of 'foreign national' (*fremdvölkisch*) forced labourers reached new heights and peaked in gruesome mistreatment and torture.

Political persecution: communists and Social Democrats

The persecution of internal political opponents began in spring 1933, before the Gestapo was officially founded. Other police departments were therefore involved in the reprisals: in this early phase, National Socialist terror was directed almost exclusively against members of the recently banned political parties. Destroying the left, above all the communists, was the principal aim of the Nazi regime in its first eighteen months in power, because it was initially the only organized opposition to the regime. The basis for this persecution was the Reichstag Fire Decree, which Ernst Fraenkel has appropriately called the 'Third Reich's' 'constitutional charter'.[5] Arrests were made according to prepared lists, and at the end of June 1933 the concentration camps in Prussia alone held close to 25,000 people.[6] In total, 60,000 communist and Social Democrat activists were arrested in this early phase of persecution, of whom 2,000 lost their lives.[7] The new rulers used their first weeks in power to settle old scores, while transmitting a message to the public.[8] Large-scale raids and show deportations were laid on to convince the society that the National Socialists intended to do everything in their power to combat their opponents ruthlessly. Radio reports and newspaper articles reported that a process of 'cleaning up' (aufräumen) was taking place.[9]

During this first phase of political persecution, until autumn 1933, the political police had a solely supervisory role: they administered the lists of arrests and of confiscated items and they added to their index cards, but they rarely appeared themselves. It is highly likely that it was only the approved executive officers who were allowed to participate directly in the persecution. The actions were mostly carried out by the local police and by auxiliary police units composed of SS and SA men. So-called 'Raid commandos' (Rollkommandos) searched the premises of the workers' movement and their political parties, confiscated material, arrested the 'ringleaders' and sent them straight to concentration camps. It was characteristic for the persecutors to have a free hand on a political level even at this early stage. Hermann Göring, who as acting Minister of the Interior in Prussia was in control of the police, stated that anybody who used his gun in the course of his duties would be protected, regardless of the consequences: 'But anybody who fails due to false consideration can expect to feel the force of the law.'[10]

By the time the overthrow of power was declared complete, the Secret State Police had been founded, and its activities had developed into the more systematic and long-term combat of political opponents—who had quickly reorganized themselves after the initial suppression, setting up illegal groups and working underground. As a result, the persecution no longer resembled a revenge campaign. The Gestapo now began to benefit from the fact that the democratic political police had left behind considerable assistance: all the material about the KPD's organizational and membership structures, which fell into the hands of the National Socialists after 1933, was useful for the repeated raids and arrests that followed. Prior to the 'seizure of power', the NSDAP intelligence service had also compiled address lists for members of the KPD, SPD, Red Front Fighters' League, and other leftist groups.[11]

Some Gestapo officials became experts in the field of communist persecution. Collusion amongst the separate investigating authorities ran smoothly; local Gestapo offices even co-operated across regional boundaries in their arrests and interrogations, at times with the help of the Berlin headquarters. Whenever they heard about an illegal act by the political workers' movement, the Gestapo responded on a grand scale. When pamphlets had been distributed, every known member of the KPD or SPD was kept under close scrutiny, and large-scale raids were not unusual. The structure of the illegal groups often made it possible for the Gestapo to pick off the whole group one by one: each arrest brought others with it, snowballing until whole underground structures were shattered. The majority of communist functionaries had been arrested by autumn 1933, unless they had gone into hiding or fled the country. Further attempts by the remaining cadres to organize resistance through oral propaganda and disseminating pamphlets were then uncovered by the Gestapo at regular intervals in the following months. The Gestapo's response to resistance became yet more rigorous, often with random arrests on a grand scale, as outlined in a field report by the illegal KPD leadership: 'The deterrent tactics even go so far as simply condemning old people without any evidence against them.'[12]

The Berlin Gestapo achieved the most impressive intervention when, on 27 March 1935, they arrested the entire illegal leadership of the KPD in the Reich capital. Once the targets were in protective detention, they were mainly charged with 'Conspiracy and Preparations for High Treason' and condemned either to long-term imprisonment, internment in a concentration camp, or both. In the mid-1930s the Gestapo in Prussia, Bavaria, and Saxony began to take preventative measures against presumed communists. On 12 July 1935 Himmler had Heydrich issue the following order: 'The Reichsführer-SS has ordered that the number of prisoners from the ranks of the former K.P.D. functionaries in protective custody is to be increased by one thousand in the next month.'[13] Between October 1935 and May 1936 the Gestapo made more than 7,000 arrests, on largely vague charges: 'behaviour inimical to the state', 'political activity', or 'insults against leading figures'. In a further decree Heydrich continued: 'Those who have committed illegal acts since the change (Umbruch) are to be placed immediately in protective custody if their behaviour indicates that they continue to oppose the state and there is a suspicion that they are secretly agitating against the state. [...] Any communist who is placed in protective custody for a second time is not to be released for the foreseeable future.'[14] This intensification meant that, by April 1937, the concentration camps were overcrowded.[15]

This investigative work was made easier by certain forms of resistance, in particular on the part of the communists, which gave the Gestapo the opportunity for direct intervention. The production and dissemination of pamphlets, mail-outs (Briefkastenaktionen) or quasi-public oral propaganda put the members of illegal groups at direct risk of being discovered. In addition, the underground organizations were centralized and hierarchical. Once the Gestapo had arrested the head of an underground group, they simply needed to seek out those connected to him. Interrogations and the extortion of confessions played a pivotal role here, often conducted using extremely brutal means: threats, intimidations, psychological and sometimes also physical violence were common, even if the interrogation report makes no mention of them.[16] Suggesting to a prisoner that they had been betrayed by comrades, friends, or brothers also dissolved the bonds of solidarity within groups more rapidly, resulting in further 'confesssions'. Many felt that they had been 'sold' by their co-conspirators, and saw no reason to remain silent. Others gave in when they were told that their family members would be punished too. Some attempted suicide as an alternative to speaking out. There was, however, no shame in surrendering to the Gestapo, and it should not be viewed as 'betrayal' from today's viewpoint.[17] The cases of men and women who managed to remain silent and, with strategic aplomb, only to admit what the investigators knew anyway, are all the more exemplary.[18]

As of 1937 the Gestapo were able to state in their field reports that the political situation was largely calm; resistance from the workers' movement had clearly declined. The leftist groups were limited to small-scale resistance. There was only one further significant campaign during this time, against the Socialist Workers' Party (*Sozialistische Arbeiterpartei*, SAP) in 1938. Otherwise, the Gestapo made do with sporadic, though always rigorous, action in the isolated cases of 'oral propaganda' or other forms of illegal activity by the KPD, SPD, or SAP, in order to keep the political left in check.[19]

The persecution of religious communities

Amongst the long-forgotten victims of the Nazi regime are the members of the smaller religious communities, such as the Jehovah's Witnesses ('Earnest Bible Students').[20] Although this small group of around 25,000 to 30,000 people remained unpolitical and fully focused on the exercise of their belief, they were persecuted by the Gestapo. They conscientiously objected to the Nazi salute and military service and were consequently considered dangerous enemies to the state, since in the totalitarian state even the smallest deviation from the norm and normality of the national community was understood as a declaration of war.

The persecution of the Jehovah's Witnesses varied in its intensity. At first the Gestapo struggled to trace their illegal Bible-study activities. Only gradually did they gain deeper insights into the structure and composition of the communities—largely due to the fact that the members were often assertive in the public dissemination of their teachings. As with the banned workers' movement, the Jehovah's Witnesses were organized into small groups and structured hierarchically: at the head was a 'Reich leader', who was in charge of various 'district leaders'. These were then in contact with 'local servers' in the individual communities, who led the local cells. In this way, every member of the community remained connected to the headquarters and supplied with 'spiritual nourishment'—interpretations of the Bible and banned writings. This organizational structure gave the Gestapo the opportunity to unravel the whole structure from top to bottom, as is evident in the two waves of arrest in 1936/37 and 1937/38.

Since Christian commitment was fundamentally opposed to the National Socialists' neo-pagan, racist world-view, the Nazi regime viewed even the members of both of Germany's larger church communities as troublemakers and ideological competition.[21] But the 'political nature' of which the church was often accused was based less on real events than on the ideology of the persecutors, who saw in the pastoral ministry a political attack on National Socialism's claim to totality. Only a very few of the Catholic or Protestant clerics who were persecuted by the National Socialists had anything to do with open resistance or protest against the Nazi regime. They simply defended their religion and the values that it represented. But that was enough for thousands of them to be persecuted, above all from the mid-1930s onwards: they were subjected to house searches, surveillance, and interrogation by the Gestapo, which often—though not always—led to arrests, deportation to concentration camps, or death. Alongside the Gestapo, the SD also greatly influenced the campaign against the churches—not so much in daily acts of persecution as in providing a superordinate ideological authority. The SD ordained the direction in which the Gestapo then marched. However, the SD did not have the right to issue directives to the Gestapo. Reinhard Heydrich's functional decree in 1937 specified for the first time how the power was to be divided up. The SD was to deal with all general and fundamental questions related to 'churches, sects and other religious and ideological federations', while the Gestapo was exclusively responsible for the actual implementation of the persecution. Nonetheless an SD officer was to be present at all house searches, in order to receive the material and assets confiscated.[22] In church matters, then, the Gestapo was not in absolute control and there were no clear criteria for exactly when state police intervention was necessary. At times, their activities resembled more a small-scale improvised war, which until 1939 was defined and limited by tactical considerations. Thereafter the division of responsibility—a radical SD without executive authority on the one hand and a Gestapo without ideological penetration on the other— actually seemed to favour radical solutions.

The starting point was different for the two main denominations. There were two Protestant camps, the extremely Naziphile grouping of 'German Christians' on the one hand and the 'Confessing Church' that formed in direct opposition. The relationship to Catholicism was supposed to be regulated in the first instance by the Vatican concord that was signed on 20 July 1933. Accordingly, all forms of political Catholicism, including the German Centre Party, were officially disbanded. It soon became clear, however, that this regulation did not go far enough for the Nazi regime.

It is possible to identify different phases of persecution of varying intensity. Directly after the 'seizure of power' the focus rested on reducing the church to a purely 'sacristy Christianity' and largely to remove religion from public life. As of 1934, once the Centre Party had been disbanded and the Catholic associations and their press subjugated, the clergy shifted into the persecutors' sights. Pressure was also exerted on members of the erstwhile Christian unions. Religious associations, such as in 1935 the 'German Youth Force' (*Deutsche*

Jugendkraft), were banned. In addition, the Gestapo repeatedly ordered the surveillance of church services, above all when they feared that banned pastoral letters were being read out. SD officers were often sent to the services to help with this work. The Gestapo panicked when Pope Pius XI, in his encyclical 'With burning concern' of 14 March 1937, denounced the ills of National Socialism. Following this, all church services were to be watched to see if they read out the encyclical. Even the simple mention of it was a punishable offence. Interrogations, warnings, gagging orders, and short-term imprisonment were all regular instruments of state police action; yet penal proceedings remained the exception. There was a tendency to stop at threats: the 715 pastors of the 'Confessing Church' who had read out a banned declaration from their pulpits in March 1935, and were subsequently arrested, were released shortly afterwards.

The persecution of the churches reached a first peak in the defamation campaigns intended to drive wedges between clerics and congregations. In a veritable flood of court cases in 1936 and 1937, priests and members of the order were accused of supposed acts of indecency. This all happened under the overall control of the Gestapo, although it was conducted not by the department for churches that was normally responsible for such matters, but by a special commando of the departments in the Gestapo headquarters that dealt with homosexuality.[23] In a radio address on 28 May 1937, Goebbels described the Catholic church as a 'cancer in the healthy national body' and accused the church leaders of covering up homosexuality. The regime unleashed a witch hunt and hundreds of priests were imprisoned as a result.

The tone became ever harsher. Gestapo officers were increasingly called to leave the church themselves; 1937 saw the highest number of people leaving the church, and there was a renewed increase in 1941.[24] In a parallel movement, the persecution became more and more life-threatening for the victims. Here, the SD set the pace. At workshops in the Berlin RSHA the catalogue of measures for persecution was discussed: 'Repression of religious influence using all available means', banning of major declarations, the use of religious buildings for military purposes, 'the most intense surveillance of church dignitaries', imposition of gagging orders, 'the most intense persecution' of clerics and organizations 'which through speeches, writings or other activities undermine or attempt to undermine the people's will to resistance'.[25] Pressure was initially limited to protective custody, deportation, penalty or security payments, but as of 1940 deportations to concentration camps drastically increased in number. When a restructuring of the RSHA in 1941 transferred some of the SD's radical masterminds into the Gestapo, where they were given executive competencies, the persecution of the churches came to focus exclusively on ideological theories and political aims. After the attack on the Soviet Union, Himmler ordered that 'all rabble-rousing clerics [...] be detained long-term in concentration camps'.[26] For the first time, the idea of a 'Final Solution to the Church Question' made itself felt in the persecution headquarters, which could however not be accomplished because the hoped-for 'Final Victory' failed to materialize. Indeed, the Gestapo's persecution of the churches ebbed towards the end of the Nazi era, although harsher punishments such as deportation to a concentration camp remained in place. In total, 417 clerics were detained in concentration camps, of whom 108 died, while a further seventy-four lost their lives under other circumstances.[27]

The implementation of Jewish policy

National Socialist ideology branded the Jews as the Reich's 'main enemy'. Consequently, the 'Third Reich' terror was directed in particular against them. During the twelve years of Nazi rule they were discriminated against, then deprived of their rights, and finally murdered. It is possible to identify different stages of violence in this context, too, as well as the gradual radicalization of Gestapo involvement.[28]

The systematic and conceptual treatment of the 'Jewish Question' was the domain of the SD, while the practical implementation of the persecution was a matter for the Gestapo. They gathered information

about Jewish associations, emigrants—about every imaginable variation on Jewish life—and evaluated it. Later, the Gestapo organized
executive measures with the help of other police and administrative
departments. It is questionable whether they took a decisive role in the
conception of Jewish policy—aside, that is, from the leadership
around Himmler and Heydrich. But it is certainly true that the Gestapo
became the most important executive organ of this policy and developed it in their own way, by acting on their own authority or issuing
prohibitions. The SD and the Gestapo prompted the introduction of
new anti-Jewish legal norms at the ministerial level. On the whole,
working relations between the SD and the Gestapo functioned very
effectively.[29]

Compared to non-Jews, Jews were always more at risk of being
charged or persecuted by the Gestapo. Unlike national comrades
(*Volksgenossen*), they lived with the permanent threat of being arrested
for an arbitrary reason. It therefore became more and more difficult
for the Jews to escape the clutches of their persecutors. Yet during the
early years of the 'Third Reich' the Gestapo were largely uninterested
in the 'persecution of the Jews', because their main focus was the
persecution of political opponents and the regime was concerned to
avoid the foreign boycott that might follow if their witch hunt was too
obvious. If communists, Social Democrats, and unionists were Jewish,
however, they were pursued particularly invidiously and often even
publicly humiliated.

During the first years of Nazi rule the Gestapo limited itself to
isolated actions against Jewish individuals or traders. Similarly, Jewish
groups and associations were victimized and discriminated against.
Jewish emigrants who returned to the Reich were considered undesirable, and were automatically arrested on their return and then
detained in a concentration camp for at least three months. Individual
Gestapo chiefs such as Karl Berckmüller in Baden acted in yet more
perfidious ways against 'Jewish race-defilers', even before that became
an official criminal offence.

The Gestapo gathered incriminating material in a variety of ways. They made use of paid and unpaid spies, of postal monitoring, and of reports from local party offices and individual party members, but were also set on the trail of their victims by reports and denunciations.[30] The Gestapo profited in particular from the willingness of many Germans to make denunciations when it came to offences like 'race defilement' (*Rassenschande*). In the early years they relied more on reports from the local population than on their own surveillance or preventative measures. More than 50 per cent of all anti-Jewish reports came from the population, which usually arose from a combination of personal and political motives.[31]

The Gestapo received the reports and dealt with them at their own discretion. Many investigations brought to light untenable or poorly grounded accusations of Jews making negative comments about the regime or making the Nazi salute, which they were forbidden to do. Others were accused of attempting to move their assets abroad secretly. For the Gestapo, what mattered was not the motive of the denouncer but the apparent validity of the accusation. It was therefore even possible for slander to result in persecution. Individual officers could significantly influence the course of the persecution and decide whether to impose protective detention, detention in a concentration camp, or a simple fine, whether to end the investigation with or without warning, or to transfer the case to the justice system.

Beyond prosecution, the Gestapo was entrusted with purely administrative and organizational matters in the control and registration of Jewish organizations. Jews who wished to emigrate were kept under particularly close surveillance; and checks on the mail of the targeted individuals increased significantly. Jewish emigration was an important area of work for the Gestapo before the war, and they worked closely with the financial administration and customs authorities, particularly when it came to systematically robbing those Jews who had emigrated.[32]

When the 'Nuremberg Race Laws' were decreed on 15 September 1935, denying Jews German citizenship and prohibiting marriages with non-Jews, the Gestapo possessed the legal framework to continue their persecution. During 1935 and 1936 'Jewish matters' were increasingly bureaucratized in order—and this was the declared aim of Berlin's Gestapo leadership—to proceed more discreetly, precisely, and thus efficiently against Jews. 'Full agency in the Jewish Question', as official Nazi jargon called it, lay in the hands of the Gestapo and the SD. They were to suppress Jewish influence on all areas of public life and promote Jewish emigration. This began in local Gestapo offices with the creation of individual Jewish departments, run by 'case workers for Jewish matters'.[33] It was not necessary to have a particularly anti-Semitic attitude in order to work in this department; instead the case workers needed to be able to implement instructions assiduously, and to carry out their bureaucratic work and criminal investigations inconspicuously. Most of the new heads of these Jewish departments were not committed Nazis but long-serving, routine police officers.

This gradual bureaucratization was evident in particular in the compilation of 'Jewish card indexes', intended to record every single German of Jewish heritage. On 17 August 1935 Himmler ordered the Gestapo to apprehend all members of Jewish associations.[34] Jewish card indexes had already been developed in some regions. Data about the strength, leadership, real estate, and constitution as well as the membership lists of Jewish associations were to be compiled by normal police units and produced in triplicate. Initially, these activities were limited to the members of Israelite religious communities, but would later be extended to include all Jews and 'Jewish half-breeds' (jüdische Mischlinge).

The relatively relaxed persecution of the early years was brought to a close at the latest by the Verreichlichung, when the police was reconceived as a preventative force and the focus thereby moved onto racial persecution. The Gestapo leadership was no longer simply concerned with formally systematizing anti-Semitic actions in the Reich and bringing them under their own control, since they also soon demonstrated how decisively and brutally they intended to proceed. In October 1938 the chiefs of the security police radioed through the order that all Polish Jews over 18 currently in the Reich zone be arrested and deported to Poland.[35] The local stations were tasked with transporting these Jews to the selected 'loading stations' (*Verladebahnhöfe*). 'All security and order police forces are required to postpone other duties to assist in the transport of the prisoners to the loading stations', ordered the Berlin chiefs.[36] The victims of this first mass deportation included the relatives of 17-year-old Herschel Grynszpan, who had protested against the injustice by shooting dead an employee of the German Embassy in Paris, the Legation Secretary Ernst vom Rath. On 9 November 1938 the Nazi leadership, then assembled in Munich, took this act as a pretext to unleash an anti-Jewish pogrom across the whole Reich, with Hitler's agreement and following an inflammatory speech from Goebbels. Members of the Nazi Party and the SA set fire to synagogues throughout the Reich, destroyed around 7,000 Jewish shops, and laid waste to countless Jewish apartments. Around 100 people were murdered during the pogrom.

Gestapo offices were informed of the riots during the night itself. All Gestapo employees were called to their posts, in order to prevent looting and to stop fires spreading to other buildings. Their main activity, however, was to arrange the subsequent deportation of 26,000 men and youths to the concentration camps at Buchenwald, Dachau, and Sachsenhausen, where many Jews died as a result of physical and psychological abuse. Although the pogrom had not been started by the Gestapo chiefs, they took the opportunity to take control of the 'Jewish Question' and to define its future direction. In contrast to the principles of Jewish policy until this point, which along with raucous interventions and excesses on the streets were still shaped by economic interests and foreign policy concerns, the leadership of the security police began to systematize the removal of rights from Jews and quietly to speed up their enforced emigration. Any Jew who came to the attention of the authorities between 'The Night of Broken Glass' and the beginning of the war, for any offence, could no longer expect leniency. Most Jews were detained immediately in a concentration camp or sent there after being taken to court by the Gestapo. The Gestapo no longer reacted solely to the extensive evidence that came in from the local population. From this point on they were directly active: targeted state terror reigned.[37]

The victimization of the Jews took on a new dimension as soon as the Second World War started. A flood of new regulations, which were decreed by the Gestapo without even informing their nominal superiors at the Reich Interior Ministry, further limited their lives. This included limits to mobility, such as the nightly curfews that came into force at the start of the war, and restrictions to communication with the ban on owning a radio as of September 1939 and a telephone as of July 1940. A raid to confiscate all such devices was carried out on the orders of the Gestapo by Gendarmerie officers, who were repeatedly deployed for these purposes. Finally, on 24 October 1941, all friendly contact with Jews was prohibited. On 30 June 1942 all Jewish schools were closed on the orders of the Gestapo. The local Gestapo offices across the Reich were responsible for upholding these regulations: the wearing of the yellow Star of David, the prohibition of certain professions and possession of prohibited goods such as clothing coupons, soap, bicycles, skis, furs, or cakes.[38] The restrictions became ever more absurd: finally, Jews were forbidden from entering a forest or keeping pets.

Gestapo officers went out on patrol themselves and searched apartments belonging to Jews without either suspicion or legal permission. If they discovered woollen blankets, this could be enough for the resident to be deported to Auschwitz. Jews who had gone into hiding were hunted down. The Gestapo itself seized all their assets and interrogated the acquaintances and relatives of the missing person. If they surmised that others knew where he was hiding, they put pressure on those they interrogated using threats, detention, or the confiscation of food coupons.[39]

During the war the Gestapo was increasingly involved in the deportation of Jews, which began in February 1940 and was conducted systematically as of October 1941. They organized the collections of Jews from their homes; the local Gestapo offices drew up instructions, often minutely detailed; where necessary, such as in Berlin, they maintained the assembly camps; and they put together the transports. However, the actual arrests were usually only supervised at a distance by the officers. Further, the Gestapo was responsible for the checking and confiscation of assets that were left behind during deportations. A few days prior to a deportation the victims received an 'official disclosure', which they had to sign and which began with the words: 'Today the Secret State Police [...] informed me that I will be evacuated on 27.11.1941, that all of my assets retrospectively as of 15.10.1941 will be seized by the state police and that any disposal of assets since this date (gifts or sales) are rendered void.'[40] The Gestapo gathered in the asset statements and valuable items, searched the luggage for valuable documents, cash, and jewellery and submitted the victims to a strip search. Only a wedding ring or a 'standard wristwatch' was left with the victims, and even that was not always the case.[41]

The mass deportations required huge numbers of Gestapo officers and helpers from other police departments—even administrative civil servants were deployed. Herbert Titze, a member of the Gestapo's Jewish Department in Berlin, claimed only to recall the bureaucratic processes when he was called as a witness to an investigation in the early 1960s. He reported on how the deportation lists were compiled: 'The department head also announced that the leadership had ordered the evacuation of a particular number of Jews. Once the number of Jews to be evacuated had been given, the members of the Jewish Department, including me, although rarely, arbitrarily selected the relevant number of cards from my Jewish card index. Based on these cards, so-called "collection forms" and a preliminary transport list were completed. [...] Since there were more Jews to be deported than the members of the Jewish Department could manage, the members of other state police departments, including members of the criminal police and Schutzpolizei, had to help.'[42]

In the following years, Jews who had been in hiding or who had initially been allowed to stay in the Reich due to exceptional circumstances were deported to concentration and extermination camps in Eastern Europe, the last in February 1945. As of 1942, however, the Gestapo's involvement reduced significantly. The Jewish Departments became less important and their personnel was thinned out until they became entirely insignificant, since the majority of Jews had already been deported. In this phase, the Gestapo was one part of the murderous conglomerate of perpetrators in occupied Europe.

Dealing with homosexuals, the 'work-shy', and 'asocials'

Male homosexuality had always been punishable in Germany through Section 175 of the penal code. But the National Socialists saw in homosexuality less a transgression of dominant sexual morality and more an attack on the natural order enshrined in the national way of life. After the murder of Ernst Röhm, homosexuals were increasingly in the Gestapo's sights.[43] Homosexuals were to be 're-educated' as heterosexuals through threats, imprisonment, or detention in a concentration camp. The intensification of the penal code in June 1935 allowed persecution where there was suspicion of 'unnatural fornication'.

However, it was not exactly easy for the police to identify homosexuals—the Gestapo and the criminal police were often both active in this area. Unlike the persecution of the Jews, it was not enough simply to glance at the state administration's list of registered residents. In order to make the investigations easier, a secret decree of 1936 founded the 'Reich Headquarters for the Combat of Homosexuality and Abortion'. From this point on, all homosexuals in the Reich were to be registered with this agency. Nonetheless, the Gestapo was dependent on external support and benefited from the workings of chance. Denunciations were helpful in making the officers aware of offences in the first place, but often ended in failure, since it was hard to prove that illegal behaviour had taken place.[44] The Gestapo officers still tried to extort confessions from those under arrest. 'Relapsed' or 'chronic' homosexuals were brought before a judge, and after serving their sentence were usually taken into protective detention or sent to a concentration camp. For those with no prior convictions the Gestapo made do with a caution. There was no automatic process that ended in the concentration camps, no 'gay Holocaust'. But this is not to say that homosexuals were not severely persecuted: in concentration camps, the prisoners with the 'pink triangle' were right at the bottom of the camp hierarchy. Between 10,000 and 15,000 homosexuals were detained in concentration camps during Nazi rule, and 10,000 were imprisoned following a court case. In total only a small proportion of homosexual men were affected by state police measures, because many succeeded in keeping their secret.

Those considered 'work-shy' and 'asocial' were also persecuted by the National Socialists. Initially the criminal police was responsible for them as 'persistent offenders' or 'career criminals'. When they were arrested they were taken into protective custody.[45] As of 1937, with the emergence of the SS and police leadership's concepts of social hygiene and social biology, the Gestapo was entrusted with their persecution. In March 1937 Himmler ordered the arrest of 2,000 'persistent offenders', referring to those with a series of existing offences, even if they only amounted to trivial misdemeanours. The waves of arrests in 1937 and 1938 no longer affected only the Nazi regime's political opponents, but also the 'work-shy' and 'asocial'. Anyone who did not fulfil his duty to the national community could be taken into protective custody. The definition of those who fell into this category was not clear, which gave the Gestapo much room for manoeuvre. The unemployed were the most affected, as well as those accused of not achieving the levels of work demanded of them. 'Asocials' were beggars and tramps, pimps and prostitutes, those on benefits and alcoholics, hooligans and traffic offenders or sexually permissive women. Jews were disproportionately defined as 'asocial', too. Community welfare, work, health, and benefit offices voluntarily produced lists, gave suggestions, and set local priorities. For the National

Socialists, 'asocial behaviour' was the genetic precursor to criminality. The security police was expected to take preventative measures against it and commissioned either the criminal police or the Gestapo to pursue suspects. Big raids like the one in April 1938 resulted in almost 2,000 'work-shy' individuals being detained in concentration camps. In the course of the 'Work-Shy Reich' (*Arbeitsscheu Reich*) campaign of June 1938, which was run by the Kripo, between 9,000 and 10,000 people were deported to Buchenwald, Sachsenhausen, and Dachau; thus 'asocials' represented by far the largest contingent of concentration camp internees at the time. These arrests were increasingly motivated by economic demands: procuring free slave labour, which was urgently needed for the Reich's huge construction projects. After all, forced labour played an increasingly important role in military production sites for the SS, foreshadowing the mobilization and war to come.

Persecution of 'foreign nationals'

While the persecution of the Jews was intensifying, the Gestapo was faced with a new problem, which was to demand their particular attention once the war had begun: the fact that Germany was going to be infiltrated by millions of foreigners, which was considered dangerous from a Nazi perspective. This included prisoners of war as well as the foreign labour force within the German war economy.[46] The 'foreign nationals' were submitted to repressive laws and were intended to be largely isolated from the German population. The Gestapo considered that the employment of foreigners increased the security risk. Only very few workers came from countries with which Germany was allied in either peacetime or wartime. Moreover, the use of a foreign labour force in the Reich contradicted the *völkisch* principles of National Socialism, which the security police were supposed to implement. All the measures that had been introduced to 'purify the blood' of the German people, which included the repressive measures against the Jews, were as good as cancelled out by the deployment of the 'foreign nationals'.

The Gestapo found its own solution for this apparent dilemma: if they could not prevent the employment of 'racially inferior' ethnic groups for economic reasons, then the foreigners should at least be treated in a manner fitting to their 'rank'. The initial plans simply to record bureaucratically all the foreign workers were soon scrapped, owing to the single fact that civilian workers were increasingly joined by prisoners of war, amongst them many from the ethnic groups in Eastern Europe considered to be racially inferior. According to a note from the Gestapo field office in Heidelberg, the Gestapo intended to use 'all means necessary' to 'suppress' the 'racial-political and criminal' dangers represented by the Eastern European workers.[47] What these 'means' were soon became clear.

They included the planned murders of prisoners of war. The Gestapo was selected to carry out Heydrich's 'Einsatzbefehl No. 9' of 21 July 1941, which determined that all Soviet prisoners of war be investigated by the state police in order to establish which of them were dangerous according to National Socialist ideology: Jews, communists, or members of the Soviet secret service. Using the bureaucratically euphemistic terms 'selection' (Aussonderung) and 'special treatment' (Sonderbehandlung), those selected were to be taken to a concentration camp and executed. In fact, the criminal 'Commissar Order' (Kommissarbefehl) of 6 June 1941 ought to have prevented any of these groupings from surviving Germany's attack on the Soviet Union. However, since suspicious prisoners of war were discovered in German camps, the Berlin chiefs decided to take action within the Reich as well. The Gestapo became the executor of this retroactive Commissar Order on German soil. Einsatzkommandos, composed of three or four reliable police officers under the leadership of a criminal commissar from the regional Gestapo offices, co-operated with the relevant units of the army to complete the 'selections'. The process lasted until July 1942. Gestapo officers were permitted to concoct the criteria for the death sentence themselves. The Gestapo men believed

PLATE 1. Heinrich Himmler's march to the top: Hermann Göring officially appointed Heinrich Himmler as Inspector of the Prussian Gestapo on 20 April 1934.

PLATE 2.
Gestapo and SS working hand in hand: an SS-Kommando in front of the headquarters of the Gestapo in Berlin's Prinz-Albrecht-Straße, just days after the putsch against Röhm known as the 'Night of the Long Knives'.

PLATE 3.
Inside the Gestapo:
a photograph of the
interior of the Gestapo
headquarters in Berlin,
with busts of Adolf
Hitler and Prussian
Prime Minister
Hermann Göring in
the main reception
hall (1934).

PLATE 4. The 'perfect' National Socialist: Reinhard Heydrich, Chief of the Gestapo, head of the SD (Security Service) and the RSHA (Reich Main Security Office), and Deputy Reich Protector of the Protectorate of Bohemia and Moravia (1942).

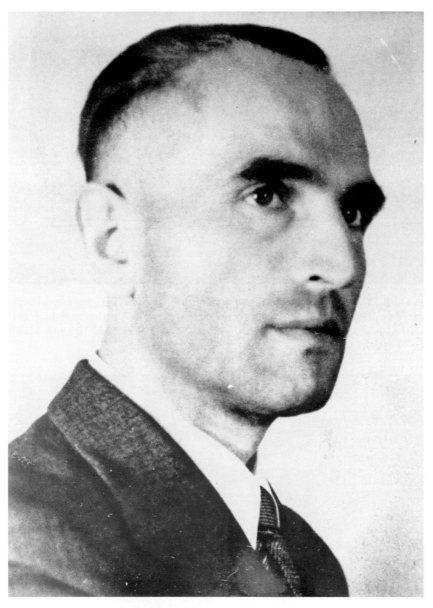

PLATE 5. The Gestapo's intellectual: Dr Werner Best, long-time head of the Gestapo's administrative department and Reinhard Heydrich's deputy (1942).

PLATE 6. A meeting to discuss the results of the investigation into Georg Elser's bombing of the Bürgerbräukeller in Munich on 8 November 1939. From left to right: Franz-Josef Huber, Arthur Nebe, Heinrich Himmler, Reinhard Heydrich, Heinrich Müller (27 November 1939).

PLATE 7. Two members of the Gestapo carry out a body search on a Jewish man in the Warsaw Ghetto (1942).

PLATE 8. Mass murder as a daily occurrence: mass execution of the Jewish population of Liepaja in Latvia by members of Einsatzgruppe A (15 December 1941).

PLATE 9. Brutal deterrence: the public hanging of eleven Soviet and Polish 'Frem-darbeiter' ('foreign workers') by the Gestapo in the Ehrenfeld district of Cologne (25 October 1944).

PLATE 10.
Public burial of seventy inmates of the town prison in Remscheid, in front of the town hall. The prisoners had been murdered by the Gestapo on 13 April 1945. The people of the town were ordered to be present at the burial by order of the Allied War Crime Commission (1 May 1945).

that they could recognize Jews through their circumcision alone—an error which Heydrich himself had to clear up with a reference to the Turkic peoples. The Gestapo commandos also worked with Russian collaborators, who tended to want to protect themselves by denouncing others. In addition, the Gestapo officers attempted to uncover further lines of enquiry through their interrogations. If the subject stated that he had been active in any way as a functionary, he sealed his fate without knowing it. At least 40,000 soldiers of the Red Army fell victim to the Gestapo's selection process.[48]

The Gestapo remained responsible for the prisoners of war who were not executed, too. They had to prevent soldiers coerced into labour in the Reich from coming into contact with the German population and they pursued any transgressions with particular severity. As of 1941 the Gestapo had finally assumed full control of the surveillance of foreign and forced labourers; criminal proceedings in normal courts were now to be the exception. The Gestapo used its own instruments of persecution: imposing protective detention or sending the subjects to a labour or concentration camp. Local Gestapo offices had significant freedoms in this particular area.

The surveillance and persecution of foreign workers required a great deal of the Gestapo's attention. In December 1941 alone, more than 5,000 foreigners were arrested in the Old Reich and Austria for downing-of-tools, compared to only 266 for 'communist or Marxist activities'. In 1943 around two-thirds of the Gestapo forces in the German Reich were occupied with combating the growing resistance amongst forced labourers. In autumn 1944 almost eight million civilian workers and prisoners of war were employed in the so-called 'Greater German Reich'. Faced with this large number of foreign workers, the Gestapo was dependent on support from numerous institutions and groupings: labour exchanges, local party offices and police stations, and above all the security offices within factories.[49]

The Gestapo possessed its own instrument of persecution and punishment, which lay outside the concentration camp system and beyond all judicial control: on their own authority they were able to send those who 'broke their employment contracts' (so-called *Arbeits-vertragbrüchige*) to a labour camp (AEL) for several weeks. These camps fell under the direct control of the regional Gestapo offices. This 'work education detention' (*Arbeitserziehungshaft*) was declared a preventative measure and set alongside protective detention. Almost every local Gestapo office had at least one such labour camp, where undesirable persons were detained.[50] Women's camps were set up in Fehrbellin, Salzgitter, and Stuttgart, while other AEL such as the one in Ober-lanzdorf had separate women's departments. Himmler decreed that these camps be constructed in places where the internees 'can be exploited for national and defence purposes, i.e. made available to a business for a low wage'.[51] The internees' wages were usually just a few pennies per working day. While at the beginning of the war it was mainly German 'work-shirkers', as they were called in Nazi jargon, that were treated in this way, this changed later. From 1942 it was primarily foreign civilian workers in the armaments industry who were sent to these labour camps, of whom around 60 per cent came from the Soviet Union and Poland. From this time onwards the number of prisoners and the number of camps grew. It can thereby be assumed that during the war one in twenty foreign civilian workers in the German Reich spent time in an AEL.

These workers were mainly sent to the camps because the company heads, armament commandos, or Reich Trustees of Labour (*Reichs-treuhänder der Arbeit*) had called on the Gestapo to intervene. Factory security offices and municipalities functioned as employers and detained the selected 'foreign workers'. In general, the Gestapo con-ducted few independent investigations, reacting instead to denunci-ations from the factories. The labour camps were constructed and maintained by a network of workers from the order police, the labour exchange, the NSDAP, private factory security offices, and security companies. 'Regional alliances' developed, which ensured the main-tenance of the camp and provided decisive support to the Gestapo.[52] As state police detention centres, the AEL were protected from exter-nal control, but were at the same time integrated into the local infrastructure. Further, the camps were used to discipline absconders. According to RSHA figures, around 45,000 foreign workers per month attempted to escape their contract by fleeing. In the wartime manhunts unleashed by the Gestapo, 35,000 of them were subsequently apprehended by various helpers from state and party, and sent to labour camps.

The treatment of the prisoners was by no means less brutal in the AEL than in the concentration camps. The death rate was high, especially in the camp at Watenstedt (Salzgitter) and in Rattwitz near Breslau, where almost 60 per cent of the prisoners died during their internment. And this happened despite the fact that, in contrast to those in a concentration camp, the internees of an AEL were supposed to be released (generally after six weeks) and returned to their employers. In practice, *Arbeitserziehung* ('education through work') meant nothing less than the physical abuse and psychological humiliation of the prisoners. The majority were given extremely arduous quarrying, earthwork, and mining jobs. The camp drill system was inhuman. The hygiene conditions and care were completely inadequate. The guards, who came in part from the ranks of the order police and in part from conscripted civilians, were permitted to shoot dead any prisoner who did not follow instructions or who moved more than three metres from their appointed workplace. The AEL were also used as execution sites for the implementation of 'Special Treatments'. During the war the Gestapo used labour camps in order to employ the widest possible arsenal of brutal persecution practices. They had the power to decide the life and death of foreigners subject to racial discrimination, and were able to act fully independently within the AEL. Towards the end of the war, they carried out targeted mass executions.

It has become clear that the treatment, care, and accommodation of the foreign labour force was not the same across the board, but reflected the 'racial principles' of National Socialism, which divided Europe up into a hierarchy of peoples. The 'Western workers' from France, Holland, or Belgium were at the top, superseded only by the neutral Swiss and to an extent the Italian allies until 1943. Poles and 'Eastern workers' from the Soviet Union, on the other hand, were considered to belong to inferior 'sub-peoples', and were publicly stigmatized and submitted to a wide-ranging system of repression. They were accommodated in barracks, were not permitted to attend German church services, and had to wear a label on their clothing: 'P' for Poles and 'OST' for Eastern workers. Poles were forbidden from using public facilities, ranging from express trains to bath-houses. In August 1941 the Gestapo expressly decreed that Polish civilian workers and prisoners of war were not permitted to enter public open-air swimming pools, 'since the national comrades cannot be expected to bathe with Poles. Furthermore, this fosters association with Poles.'[53] The Soviet men and women were in the worst position—their deaths due to inadequate nourishment or excessive work were taken as a given.

A number of misdemeanours by foreigners were punishable by death: rape, arson, but also leaving one's post without authorization or infringements against discipline at work. As soon as intimate relations between Polish workers and German women were discovered, which rarely involved the Gestapo's direct investigations, a bureaucratic mechanism was set in motion which ran like clockwork from arrest to execution. First, the responsible case worker in the field office had to write a report which was presented to the departmental head. He then had to check over the case again, sign the report, and forward it to the Foreign Workers' Department at the relevant head office. If the details of the case were not immediately clear, then further investigations were required, in order to move the accused towards a confession—using all available means. The investigators used brutal violence in many cases, even beating women in the face and threatening them with harsh sanctions. The regional head office then passed the case on to the RSHA in Berlin, where the final decision as to the fate of the foreign worker was made. The accused forced labourers were sometimes detained in concentration camps. If they were from Eastern European countries, the sentence was usually death by hanging.

In the main, Western workers got away with several years' detention.[54] As of 1942, Polish workers were examined for their 'ability to be Germanized' and if the judgement was positive, they were not executed. The German women were either taken to court and condemned to several years in prison or sent directly to the Ravensbruck concentration camp. Prior to this they had to put up with public vilification, as proven by a number of cases. They were driven through the town with a sign around their neck stating 'I am a Pole whore'.

Once the RSHA had condemned a Polish or Russian worker to death, the matter was passed back to the local Gestapo office so that they could begin preparations for the execution. The head of the field office where the offence had first been reported was now responsible for arranging the place of execution. Particularly favoured were places that permitted a large audience for the execution: after all, it was not only the whole staff of the Gestapo office and local party leadership that had to experience the spectacle, but also all foreign workers in the local area. The execution was intended to work as a deterrent.

The foreign workers from the local area were then taken to the place of execution by the local community administration and the Gendarmerie officers. Security police officers sealed the place from curious eyes. Two foreign workers were then selected to carry out the execution, in exchange for a little remuneration—either 5 Marks or some schnapps. The highest-ranking Gestapo officer present, usually head of a field office or the Gestapo chief himself, read out the death sentence, and an interpreter translated it into Polish. Next the executioners looped the rope around the victim's neck and pushed him down. The foreign workers were then required to file past the hanged man, while the translator told each of them that the same would happen to them if they were to get involved with German women. After the execution, the corpse was taken to the anatomical institute of the nearest university. The Gestapo instructed that the cause of death should not be recorded on the death certificate.

Until the last, the Gestapo used increasingly brutal methods to maintain their absolute control over forced and foreign labourers.

At the beginning of 1944 a group of forced labourers were hanged in public because they were accused of looting after a bombing raid. Foreign workers found guilty of sabotage were executed in their own workplaces. There, the executions took a similar form to the more public spectacles: the rest of the workforce had to watch, and normal policemen were brought in to ensure security.

As of summer 1944 the system of surveillance for Poles and Eastern workers was intensified. Disobeying the curfew was to be punished by protective detention, and for repeat offences by detention in a labour camp. The discovery of a resistance group composed of Russian forced labourers finally strengthened the Gestapo's will to act with extreme rigour. At this point, it also became evident that the Gestapo had long been part of a war of extermination within the Reich, a criminal system which they had implemented across almost the whole of Europe.

6

THE GESTAPO IN EUROPE

The nature of 'foreign deployment'

The National Socialist policy of expansion as of 1938 meant that the Gestapo's scope and the range of their duties had increased. The National Socialists referred to this in their bureaucratic jargon as 'foreign deployment' (*Auswärtiger Einsatz*). The Gestapo operated in Europe without the slightest legal foundations from the outset. The Gestapo Laws, which had been introduced in Germany just a few years previously, did not apply beyond the Reich borders. Here the sole authority came from the 'Führer's' mandate, or rather what Himmler and the security police leadership passed off as such: 'The Führer's mandate requires the Sipo (security police) to maintain the order of the German people in the state wished by the Führer, to protect them against all attacks, be they of a political or police nature, or purely criminal acts, and to take the required measures to achieve this.'[1] In a few words, the authorization was issued for a broad sweep of powers.

In Europe, the Gestapo was not only a civilian organ of persecution, but also played a role in implementing the plans for extermination. This programme was put into practice by the Einsatzgruppen—a wholly new instrument of state police activity. The Einsatzgruppen were to act alongside military campaigns, combating all apparent enemies of National Socialism as the army advanced. This unleashed a programme that can be described as 'manhunt and mass murder'.[2]

The so-called 'preventative combat of crime' in occupied Europe could begin immediately: apparent 'asocials', homosexuals, career criminals, and 'gypsies' were persecuted. Members of leftist organizations were tracked down and arrested, unless they were able to escape the National Socialist dominion. Buildings belonging to socialist organizations were occupied, union members were arrested, Jewish associations were dissolved, and religious establishments closed. Real estate belonging to Jews was seized. At the same time, racial 'cleansing' began: Jews and Slavs were mercilessly persecuted.

To a degree, the methods differed significantly from those used within the Reich. Although some boundaries were transgressed, for a long time the work of the Gestapo in Germany resembled regular police work. The attack on Poland, however, instituted a new mode: Gestapo officers could generally get by without tedious interrogations, and there was no need to extort confessions; suspects were often shot dead on the spot. Although, as will be seen, there were significant differences between the individual countries, methods essentially became increasingly brutal across the board. This process had begun in 1933, but now the final remnants of inhibition were cast off.

Their mobilization in occupied Europe also meant that the Gestapo lost its clear contours. Its personnel dispersed into new police structures, and the boundaries become blurred between the Gestapo's original duties and their new activities. For example, 2,000 men were supposed to be deployed for the Polish occupation in 1939, of which two-thirds were to be provided by the Gestapo and the criminal police, with the rest coming from the SD. When the Soviet Union was invaded two years later, the proportion of Gestapo men in the Einsatzgruppen was significantly smaller, in particular in the lower ranks. The truck drivers were almost exclusively conscripted workers, sent by the labour exchanges. Of the 990 men in Einsatzgruppe A in the Soviet Union less than 10 per cent came from the Gestapo, while 35 per cent were members of the Waffen-SS. The Gestapo increasingly merged with other sections of police, SS, and SD offices, building a complex network of security police and security services that could barely be distinguished from one another. The same was true of their outward appearance: regardless of which organization they belonged to, all Einsatzgruppen men wore the SD symbol on their uniform. But it was by no means only German men who served in the Einsatzgruppen. Rather, the murder commandos developed increasingly into multi-ethnic security consortia under the leadership of the Gestapo.[3] The importance of collaboration becomes clear at this point, and it took different forms in every country under German occupation, but in particular in Eastern Europe.[4] The security police Einsatzgruppen were not only supported by SS and police units. The German army was involved in the war of extermination, too.

Einsatzgruppen were deployed across almost the entire war zone: Einsatzkommando Austria during the 'Annexation' in March 1938, Einsatzgruppen Dresden and Vienna when the Sudetenland was occupied in September 1938, and Einsatzgruppen Prague and Brno at the invasion of Czechoslovakia in March 1939. Einsatzgruppen I–VI and Einsatzgruppe z.b.V. (for special assignment) then followed during the Polish campaign, with Einsatzgruppe Serbia formed in April 1941. For the attack on the Soviet Union Einsatzgruppen A–D were formed in June 1941, followed by Einsatzgruppen E in Croatia, F in Hungary, G first in Romania and later in Hungary, H in Slovakia, and K and L during the Ardennes campaign in December 1944.[5] This list is by no means complete, since further commandos were formed ad hoc for various tasks, especially in the last months of the war.

Those who were sent by the Gestapo to wage ideological warfare usually came from a disbanded local Gestapo office, or one that had been downgraded to a field office.[6] Those involved were then willing and able to make up for their demotion, their loss of power and status, by operating in the field. There was also often negative selection of personnel: delegates were those who had made themselves known in their local offices for either ineptitude or corruption.[7] Across the broad ranks of Gestapo officers there seems to have been no consistent enthusiasm or willingness to volunteer for 'foreign deployment'. Service in the East was particularly unpopular, since there was an increased risk to one's own life there.[8] Reinhard Heydrich consequently made frequent references to the importance of the Eastern deployment in memoranda, and warned of 'homeland warriors' and 'shirkers'.[9] It is impossible to say whether Heydrich's admonitions bore fruit in individual cases. But it is clear that a significant proportion of Gestapo officers took part at least temporarily in the 'foreign deployment', and were thus directly or indirectly part of the National Socialist war of extermination. As we have seen, these individuals were by no means all committed National Socialists. Nonetheless, they were almost without exception prepared to fulfil murderous orders—many developed a significant number of their own initiatives, some showed sadistic characteristics and enjoyed their 'work'. Some, on the other hand, took part only reluctantly in the murders—but they took part nonetheless.

Research into Nazi perpetrators has taken on a new momentum over the past few years, but it is still far from reaching a conclusive answer or from synthesizing the various approaches into a comprehensive whole.[10] You might foreground the perpetrator's anti-Semitic motivation, their generational characteristics such as objectivity and emotional coolness, or the significance of fundamental socio-psychological mechanisms within the acts themselves—the multi-layered nature of the perpetrators has already been described by Raul Hilberg: 'The personality characteristics of the perpetrators did not fall into a single mold. The men who performed the destructive work varied not only in their backgrounds but also in their pyschological attributes.'[11] This general feature of the perpetrators is also true of the Gestapo officers: they did not follow any simple model that could be described in a few words. Thus there can be no comprehensive characterization of the Gestapo officers as *perpetrators*. Instead, the *acts* themselves shift into the foreground, acts which were carried out in their millions across Europe during the deployment.[12]

The beginnings of expansion: Austria, Sudetenland, and Czechoslovakia

The Gestapo was officially deployed outside the borders of the German Reich a year and a half before the Second World War broke out:

the 'annexation' of Austria in March 1938 was the first field for the Gestapo's experimentation in 'foreign deployment'. Special commandos, made up of Gestapo and Kripo officers, were deployed for the first time to arrest opponents of the regime. As early as 1935 lists were being compiled for this purpose in the Austria Department of the Berlin Gestapo headquarters. On 12 March 1938 the German army marched into Austria, to the jubilant cries of the majority of the local population. Austria became National Socialist and under its new rulers it resembled Germany in the weeks following the 'seizure of power'. Indeed it was worse: the Austrian National Socialists seized the opportunity to terrorize their opponents in the most brutal way. Over 70,000 arrests were made in a very short time. Many officials, including Austrian NSDAP and SS members, sensed their chance in the chaotic conditions to set themselves up as the new overlords. It took a good week for the German police leadership to get a grip on the situation, and it was Berlin's wish that riotous behaviour and instances of unruly persecution should not be repeated. The construction of a new police force in Austria was obviously significant, since Himmler, Heydrich, and Daluege stayed in Vienna during the annexation, along with a number of other high-ranking police leaders, in order to keep a close eye on the reconstructions of the police.[13]

By the end of 1938 seven Gestapo offices had been established in Austria, each responsible for the political police in their own region. Tirol and Vorarlberg were both dealt with by the Innsbruck Gestapo office.[14] From the outset, the Gestapo apparatus in 'annexed' Austria was set up in the same way as that in the German Reich, which was unlike the set-up in other occupied countries later on. Germans took the top positions, Austrian career policemen became their deputies. A special unit of the security police was set up to oversee the re-structuring and Heinrich Müller was brought in as Inspector of the Security Police for the whole of Austria. His close friend and colleague Franz Josef Huber was made head of the Gestapo office in Vienna.[15] Thus two central positions were occupied by experienced German officers. When Müller returned to Berlin in September 1938,

Ernst Kaltenbrunner—later Reinhard Heydrich's successor as head of the RSHA—exercised significant influence over the Gestapo: first as 'State Secretary for the Security Services in Austria', later as Higher SS and Police Leader for military district XVII.[16]

The SD, too, took part with its own Einsatzkommando: under Adolf Eichmann's leadership its activities were directed primarily against Austrian Jews. The newly established 'Central Office for Jewish Emigration' gave rise to the so-called 'Viennese Model', which expedited the expulsion of the Jews in a perfidious mixture of brutality and bureaucratization.[17] Those who did not emigrate despite all this were later deported. Eichmann and his men laid the tracks for the 'Final Solution to the Jewish Question', to be passed on in its entirety to the security police and SD. Later additional Central Offices were set up in Prague and the Netherlands, all under Eichmann's control. On 21 December 1939 his post was moved to the Gestapo and from then on he functioned as head of Section IV B 4 in the RSHA.

If the first deployment in Austria was at least somewhat improvised at first, the occupation of the Sudetenland in September 1938 was far more methodical. Commandos were set up in advance, which caused conflict between the SD and the Gestapo as to who should take control. The Gestapo gained the upper hand at least nominally, since the campaign was referred to as a special deployment of the state police, but for the first time the SD also took an executive role.[18] Two Einsatzgruppen were formed, one in Dresden and the other in Vienna, comprising a total of 863 men. They are thought to have arrested more than 10,000 people, though the exact figures are unknown. The arrests became so random that in December 1938 Heydrich wrote to the relevant Gestapo head offices: 'There have been a number of arrests on the basis of charges that have later proved to be unfounded or grossly exaggerated...'.[19] It was very difficult to direct from above the individual dynamics of state police activities on the ground. The deployment abroad seemed to lower yet further the inhibition threshold for violence, which was already very low in any case. Along with the arrest of potential or supposed enemies, the Gestapo took on an important role in the 'Germanization' of the Sudetenland. The plan was gradually to incorporate the Sudetenland into the German Reich, by either expelling the Czech population or pressurizing them to take German citizenship. The Gestapo administration followed this principle too, and Gestapo head offices were set up in Reichenberg, Karlsbad, and Troppau in October 1938.[20] Further branches followed. The mobile Einsatzgruppen formed the basic staff of the Gestapo structures there.

While the Sudetenland was gradually being incorporated, the army leadership forged plans to destroy Czechoslovakia completely. On 15 March 1939 the army met no resistance as it marched into Bohemia and Moravia. Two security police Einsatzgruppen operated in their wake: the EG I Dresden and the EG II Vienna with seven Einsatzkommandos. Just as in October 1938, the units comprised Gestapo officers and SD men. The units were now headed by leading Gestapo officers, who thereby demonstrated their executive competency. These Einsatzgruppen and commandos remained in operation until 5 May 1939: more than 6,000 people were arrested, around 15,000 of whom were sent to concentration camps by the Gestapo.[21] Once the operation was complete, the staff for the newly founded Gestapo offices were recruited from these mobile units. This model was repeated later in a different form in other European countries.

Poland 1939: the beginning of the war of extermination

The invasion of Poland offered Himmler and Heydrich the opportunity to extend greatly the limited powers of the police and SS beyond the borders of the German Reich: they were to implement Hitler's plan of *völkische Flurbereinigung* (ethnic cleansing). The Gestapo and the SD played a central role in these endeavours. The first general discussion about the institution of Einsatzgruppen composed of security police and SD members had taken place on 5 July 1939, under Heydrich's leadership and in the presence of Werner Best. Best was also responsible for building up and equipping the Einsatzgruppen.[22] Initially, five Einsatzgruppen were set up, each attached to army units that they would follow, in order to carry out the security police work in their wake: 'The duty of the security police Einsatzkommandos is to combat all enemy elements in enemy territory behind the battle lines.'[23] This definition of the enemy was not only vague but gave those in power on the ground the capacity to determine who should and should not be considered an enemy element. The army particularly feared voluntary fighters, and security police units did indeed encounter many armed Poles behind army lines. Thus Himmler telegraphed the following instruction to the Einsatzgruppen on 3 September 1939: 'Polish resistance fighters who are caught in the act or with a weapon are to be shot dead immediately.'[24] In fact, the voluntary fighters were an illusion. It was only after the military operation had come to an end that the partisan movement formed out of the destroyed units of the Polish army.[25] Those arrested during the September campaign were mainly soldiers who had been surprised and overrun by the German army's swift advance—a problem, then, that to some degree was caused by the Germans themselves.

The war took a dynamic course, and additional personnel were soon required: on 3 September 1939 the Einsatzgruppe z.b.V (for special assignment) was formed of four police battalions and a special commando of the security police, numbering 350 men, while on 9 September Einsatzgruppe VI was set up in Frankfurt an der Oder and on 12 September the independent Commando 16 was established in Danzig.[26] The security police and the SD deployed around 2,000 men at this stage, of whom three-quarters came from the Gestapo and Kripo. The Einsatzgruppen and commandos mainly recruited from local Gestapo offices. The leadership was largely composed of academics, many with doctoral degrees—mostly in law.

Although the army leadership had demanded additional police support behind the lines, the activities of the Einsatzgruppen led to conflicts between the army on the one hand and Himmler and Heydrich on the other. For one, many army officers were outraged at the mass executions carried out by the security and order police units just days after war broke out. For another, it was questioned whether the army had executive powers in Poland and could make use of the Einsatzgruppen, or whether the Einsatzgruppen could operate independently. Heydrich got his way with the commander-in-chief of the army, Walther von Brauchitsch, in this debate, and with Himmler's promotion to 'Reich Commissar for the Consolidation of the Ethnic German Nation' on 7 October 1939 and the detachment of the Einsatzgruppen from army jurisdiction, the path was smoothed to full independence for the security police. From this time on, there is a clear increase in the number of executions. Further, the main aim of the Einsatzgruppen, the liquidation of the Polish elite, was clearly articulated by Heydrich.

The last Polish units had surrendered on 6 October 1939, the military campaign was over, but the Einsatzgruppen's murderous campaign continued. There is no exact figure for the victims, but by the end of 1939 tens of thousands had been shot dead in Poland, around 7,000 Jews along with the Polish elite. This high number, combined with the manner of the killings, only permits one conclusion: it was not a case of collateral damage or spontaneous over-reaction, but the war of extermination began in Poland in 1939 and not in the Soviet Union in 1941. Although the decision as to the 'Final Solution to the Jewish Question' had not yet been made, the Holocaust was already in the air. For the Gestapo and the SD the deployment in Poland meant a clear increase in power and it is no coincidence that the Reich Security Main Office was officially created on 27 September 1939, during the Polish campaign: the shared schooling in mass murder can be understood as the foundational act of the RSHA.[27]

The area of Poland under German occupation was divided into two parts and incorporated into the Reich: the northern part became Reich District Danzig-West Prussia, and the western part Reich District Wartheland. The southern and eastern part was brought together as the 'General Government for the occupied Polish lands' and not integrated into German administrative structures. Once their activities were complete, the Einsatzgruppen men were distributed across the newly created posts: on 7 November 1939, for example, a state police head office in Poznań and regional Gestapo offices in Inowrocław (Hohensalza) and Łódź (Litzmannstadt) were established.[28] By the end of 1939 additional field offices were set up according to the structures in the Old Reich. Starting with Danzig, offices of the security police and SD were also set up in the Danzig-West Prussia district.[29]

In the Warthe district (Warthegau), the Gestapo was responsible for the surveillance of the Jewish population, sanctions, internment in concentration camps, and executions. More comprehensive measures such as 'resettlement', mass executions, and combating partisan activity fell within the remit of the newly created Higher SS and Police Leader (HSSPF), since they required all available police and SS forces. To a degree, the persecution of the Jews in the Warthe district was therefore no different from that in the rest of occupied Poland. Nonetheless, the exclusion and extermination of the Jews saw some particularities and innovations: ghettos were set up for the first time, for example. The ghetto in Łódź was the longest-standing; more than 200,000 Jews lived there for periods of up to four years.[30] Furthermore, poisonous gas was used for the first time in the Warthe district for the 'euthanasia' campaign, when disabled Poles were murdered in December 1939.[31] This created a direct link to the Holocaust: it was Herbert Lange's Special Commando that carried out the gassings. The same Lange was in charge when the first extermination camp was set up in Chełmo in the Warthe district in November 1941.[32] It was built because attempts to deport the local Jews into the General Government had failed. Consequently, Jews were exterminated in the Warthe region itself as of September 1941, initially with mobile gas vans and then with the static variation.

The Gestapo was directly involved in this process: security police men controlled all the administrative posts in Chełmo, and local Gestapo offices played an important role in the concentration and extermination of the Jews. However, it is important to note at this point that the mass murder was not planned and executed by the SS and Gestapo alone: the concentration camps were guarded by the Schutzpolizei, for example, and the civil administration of the Warthe district was also involved in the Holocaust—headed by the Gauleiter and Reich Governor in Poznań Arthur Greiser. By 1944 the German authorities had made good progress in their common aim to render the Warthe district 'free of Jews'. This aim was part of the 'General Plan East', which sought amongst other things to Germanize the region. Yet in the summer of 1944 there was nowhere in Europe that housed so many Jews in one place as the ghetto in Łódź. The clearing of the ghetto began in June 1944 with deportations to the extermination camp in Chełmno, which had been temporarily deactivated. The last deportations from Łódź, however, went to Auschwitz, when on 30 August 1944 the ghetto was finally liquidated. In 1939 around 435,000 Jews had been living in the Warthe district, only 3.5 per cent of whom survived the German occupation and Gestapo rule in this area.[33]

The General Government was initially organized differently from the other Reich districts, and the intention was that it might serve as a model for all future German colonies.[34] This had consequences for the security police and its structure. In the General Government the security police was subordinate to Section IV D 2 of the RSHA.[35] Based in Cracow, the Commanding Officer of the Security Police and SD (BdS) functioned as the local RSHA representative. His subordinates were the Commanders of the Security Police (KdS) in each of the four districts, who had control over several field offices; below the district level, however, there were no offices.[36] This system meant that the Gestapo, Kripo, and SD were brought yet closer together, and integrated offices were set up for the first time. This was the closest it ever came to Himmler's and Heydrich's ideal of a National Socialist state protection corps, made up of a conglomerate of these different forces and agencies, although, for example, under the KdS in Radom the SD was accommodated in a different building from the security police and the criminal police. More than 350 civil servants were employed in that district— well over half in the service of the Gestapo.[37] In total, around 5,000 civil servants worked for the security police and SD. Despite these differences compared to the situation within the Reich and the newly incorporated regions, the security police did not develop an autonomous policy.[38] As a result, state police practice was completely arbitrary, far more than within the Reich. This was accompanied by a negative personnel policy: those deployed in the General Government did not represent the elite of the security police. Alcoholism, corruption, internal conflict, and brawling were not unusual.

In addition, SS and Police Leaders (SSPF) were instituted in the four districts of the General Government, all subordinate to the HSSPF East, Friedrich-Wilhelm Krüger.[39] The division of duties and chains of command of the BdS and KdS on the one hand and the HSSPF and SSPF on the other were not always clear and occasionally led to friction, but on the whole this did not prevent the security police from functioning effectively. Furthermore, by spring 1940 a civil administration under the leadership of Hans Frank had been established in the General Government.[40] In August 1941, following the invasion of the Soviet Union, a fifth district was added: Eastern Galicia. Frank tried in vain numerous times to incorporate the police apparatus into his own operations; nevertheless, for a long time the civil administration was in charge of general issues relating to 'Jewish policy', while the Gestapo only had to carry out 'police' measures such as executions and internment in camps.[41] This was not only the case for the Jewish population: in May 1940 the security police conducted a large-scale 'Extraordinary Operation of Pacification' (*Außerordentliche Befriedungsaktion*), whereby 4,000 mainly non-Jewish Poles were murdered and thousands deported to concentration camps—including to the camp at Auschwitz that was specially built for the purpose.[42]

The persecution of the Polish intelligentsia and political opposition and the combat of the resistance movement were the main tasks of the Gestapo in the General Government. Here, alongside informants, they made use of their two main weapons: torture and form-filling. The Gestapo's principal problem was not getting hold of information—for this the officers' brutal interrogation methods, informants' reports, and denunciations proved to be more than adequate. The difficulty

arose when it came to evaluating and filtering the mass of information. The Gestapo in Radom sorted the material into a card index with
fourteen categories: '1. The person and main card index (light green
cards); 2. The organization index (pink cards); 3. The profiling or
special index (blue cards); 4. The index of pseudonyms (red cards); 5.
The "gang" index; 6. The insurgency index; 7. The index of confidential
informers; 8. The pamphlet index (yellow cards); 9. The local index
(orange cards); 10. The street index; 11. The industry index; 12. The photo
index; 13. The officers' index; 14. The prisoners' index (orange for Poles
and light blue for Germans).'[43] However, even this highly nuanced
system could not cope with the flood of information. The weakness of
the executive was an even greater problem: despite the problems outlined above, the Gestapo had penetrated deep into the organization
and structures of the Polish resistance movement, and were aware of
individual campaigns. The exact time of the Warsaw uprising was
therefore known in advance, but there was no way of delaying it, let
alone preventing it altogether. It was unthinkable that the resistance
movement might be wholly defeated.[44]

However, the Gestapo had more success when it came to the
persecution and extermination of the Jews. During the first weeks of
the Polish campaign in the autumn of 1939, around 7,000 Polish Jews
were murdered by the Einsatzgruppen. In the following months up to
the end of 1940 Jews were increasingly divested of their rights, driven
from their homes, and in some cases ghettoized. The persecution
intensified during the spring and summer of 1941, not least because
the army was advancing towards the Soviet Union.[45] In the General
Government, what is generally known as the Holocaust developed in
four phases.[46]

First came the decision in favour of mass murder, after other plans,
including the bizarre notion of deporting Jews to Madagascar, had
failed.[47] The treatment of the 'Jewish Question' was lent dynamism by
the activities of the Einsatzgruppen in the Soviet Union in the summer
of 1941, as will be explored in more detail. At the same time, the mass
murders of Jewish men were committed by SS and police units in

Eastern Galicia, which had become the General Government's fifth district.[48] By the end of the year 60,000 people had been murdered there. The local offices were well informed as to the new systems. In addition, from September 1941 the police began to execute Soviet prisoners of war and Jews who had escaped from camps or ghettos without first trying them in court. From the point of view of the German occupiers, there was no longer any space for Jews in the General Government, and so they had to be eliminated altogether. In the euphemistic language of the National Socialists, it was termed 'the Final Solution to the Jewish Question'.[49] Initially, then, there were a number of independent regional initiatives that led to the Holocaust. These were accompanied by plans and discussions in the control centre of Berlin, in which Heydrich and Müller were involved and which climaxed in the so-called Wannsee Conference.[50] The second phase began in spring 1942: on 16 and 17 March police units transferred the Jews they considered unable to work from the ghettos in Lublin and Lvov (Lemberg) into the new extermination camp at Belzec— 'Operation Reinhard' had begun.[51] By May 1942 it was already clear that this was not just a local event. The next step was taken with the establishment of another concentration camp at Sobibor in the Lublin district.[52]

From May or June 1942 large-scale ghetto clearances in all five districts marked the beginning of the third phase. During this time the civil administration of the General Government lost its responsibility for Jewish matters, which was transferred to the SS and police apparatus. Since the Gestapo, who were actually responsible for it, did not have enough personnel for the huge task at hand, the SS and police chiefs took over some of the duties.[53] Odilio Globocnik, the SSPF in Lublin, played a central part in rolling out 'Operation Reinhard'.[54] Only with his support and that of the order police could enough men be deployed for the ghetto clearances and deportations. The deportations to extermination camps were now carried out on a massive scale: along with Chełmo in the Warthe district, and Belzec and Sobibor mentioned above, Treblinka was used from July

1942 and Lublin-Majdanek from October 1942. Auschwitz, already in use, was extended to include an extermination camp at Birkenau. In total between 2.5 and 3 million people were murdered in these camps. The camps were under the control of the SS, but the Gestapo was part of the concentration camp system in the form of the camps' political departments.

However, not all Jews went like lambs to the slaughter: in April 1943 there was an armed uprising in the Warsaw ghetto, which was mercilessly suppressed.[55] The last ghetto in Eastern Galicia was cleared and destroyed on 18 June 1943. Since Belzec had already been closed by this point, they reverted to the trusty option of mass shootings. From the summer of 1943 any Jews still living in the General Government were either in forced labour camps or in hiding: the fourth and final phase had begun. When uprisings broke out in the extermination camps at Sobibor and Treblinka in October 1943, Himmler ordered 'Operation Harvest Festival' (*Aktion Erntefest*): the murder of all Jews still living in the Eastern part of the General Government. On 2 and 3 June more than 40,000 people were shot dead by soldiers from the SS, the Waffen-SS, the order police, and the security police. Following this, any Jews in hiding were generally captured by police patrols and shot dead.

If you look at the police apparatus in the General Government in terms of administrative science, you see not a perfectly functioning machine but rather a 'colonial administration as corrupt and criminal as it is amateurish'.[56] Nonetheless, this amateurism was evidently adequate to carry out a crime of unimaginable proportions. The Gestapo forces were relatively small in number, but they formed the core of the terror and extermination network: they cleared out the ghettos and deported the Jews to extermination camps or straight to the place of execution. The men of the security police who were involved in such acts also became direct perpetrators, almost without exception: individuals even boasted of having killed a thousand people with their own hands.[57] The acts themselves took on apocalyptic characteristics: children were thrown into the air like clay pigeons and shot in flight, mothers killed as their children watched, children's heads smashed against walls until they cracked open, while their mothers looked on.

To reiterate: it was not only the security police elite who were deployed in Eastern Europe. They were positioned at pivotal points, as commanders of the security police or heads of a local office, and in this way they directed the Holocaust. On the ground, the murders were carried out by average men, who were more than prepared to do so for different reasons: they could gain personal riches, act out their hatred for Jews without restraint, or satisfy a general sadism—in a sexual respect, too—without fear of punishment. But it was also the case that many of the men felt that they were doing the right thing and fulfilling a great duty.

The General Government took on a prime importance for a variety of reasons: it was the main location for the acts of brutality and in some respects it was at the core of the Holocaust. Only in the occupied areas of the Soviet Union did the extermination reach a similar level. In addition, the General Government was the worst affected area of Poland—proportionally, Poland had the highest numbers of victims. And ultimately, Jews from the whole of Europe were deported to the General Government and murdered in the extermination camps.

The Gestapo in Northern and Western Europe

In the two countries that fell under Nazi control after Poland, the Gestapo were faced with a whole new set of conditions: according to Nazi racial doctrine, Norwegians and Danes were Nordic peoples and consequently viewed as 'race-relations', in contrast to the Poles. In addition, there was only a small Jewish population in both countries. This impacted on the conception and practice of the state police operation, as did a series of conspicuous differences between the two countries.

In Denmark, free elections continued during the war, the country was spared open combat, and it remained remarkably stable through-out the National Socialist occupation. Some, of course, fell victim to

German police rule, but their numbers remained relatively low: estimates range from 200 to 500 deaths in total.[58] For a long time the Gestapo played a rather minor role in Denmark. It was only with Werner Best's promotion to Reich Plenipotentiary (*Reichbevollmächtigter*) in November 1942 and the growth in sabotage activities by the Danish resistance movement that the security police took on increased significance. The German police's first open operation in Denmark took place in late summer 1943. The Gestapo's activities there were dedicated almost exclusively to the resistance movement, since a spectacular initiative allowed almost all of Denmark's 7,000 Jews to flee to Sweden in October 1943. The 'counter terrorism', as Gestapo measures against the Danish resistance movement were known in Nazi jargon, meant nothing other than brutality and arbitrary despotism. The period of leniency in Denmark was now over. Werner Best made a strategic decision to act in moderation, but gradually lost control over the Gestapo. The so-called 'People's Strike' in summer 1944, when the majority of Danish workers refused the German occupiers' demands, showed the powerlessness of the occupying forces and led to conflict between Best and Hitler as to the best way forward. Following this and until the end of the war, the security police chiefs under BdS Otto Bovensiepen became ever more autocratic and intensified the 'counter terrorism' to which 102 Danes fell victim between summer 1944 and the end of the war.[59]

Although Norway also ranked as a Germanic country, the conditions differed from those in Denmark. There was initially a hope that the collaborative government under Vidkun Quisling would provide additional forces for co-operation, and that the German occupying force could be kept to a minimum. When in autumn 1940 it became clear that this would not work, security police chiefs began to build up a police organization. At the end of the war the security police and SD in Norway numbered 887 men and 178 clerical staff.[60] The HSSPF Friedrich Wilhelm Rediess was the highest-ranking police officer in Norway, but in practice played only a marginal role. Reich Commissioner Josef Terboven was so hard-line that it was impossible for the

HSSPF to develop any standing of his own. The line taken by the security police was also largely determined by Terboven, since the long-term BdS for Norway, Heinrich Fehlis, was closely allied to the Reich Commissioner, which was viewed with suspicion in the RSHA.

Terboven also called for the security police in Norway to be harsher—a demand that was obviously met: from autumn 1941 'intensified interrogations' found their place here, too. The Gestapo met the growing active and passive resistance with unrelenting severity. But the Norwegian resistance movement was not to be intimidated. On the contrary, attacks on German institutions and assassinations of members of the security police increased from spring 1944 and led to 'Operation Flower-Picking' (*Aktion Blümchenpflücken*), when the Gestapo formed a special commando that murdered around two dozen individuals thought to be involved in the resistance movement. Norwegian Jews were also persecuted by the Gestapo. In April 1940 over 1,800 Jews were living in Norway, of whom several hundred managed to escape to Sweden in the first days of the German occupation. Of the 1,100 to 1,400 that remained, more than 750 were then deported. The majority of the deportations happened between November 1942 and February 1943, and almost all those deported were subsequently murdered.[61]

In the Netherlands, which was invaded on 10 May 1940, the situation was similar to that in Norway and Denmark: the National Socialists considered the Dutch to be a Germanic people, too. Thus—as in Norway—a Reich Commissariat was established there.[62] Einsatzgruppen were formed, mainly recruiting from field offices near the border, and were gradually transformed into static units, as had been the case in other countries. The first BdS in the Netherlands was Dr Wilhelm Harster, who had held several executive positions in the security police and SD in Stuttgart, Innsbruck, Cracow, and Kassel.[63] He was particularly close to Reinhard Heydrich, who valued him greatly. Harster built up an organization based on the RSHA and expected extensive co-operation with the Dutch authorities. During the first six months, however, there were frequent changes of personnel, and the new officers had first to orientate themselves on the ground. The Security and SD had their national headquarters in The Hague, with around 200 employees, and there were five field offices in Amsterdam, Arnheim, Groningen, Maastricht, and Rotterdam, with a further 500 employees in total. Additional Dutch investigative services made up for these low numbers.

Gestapo and SD operations in the Netherlands did not pass without incident, either: the so-called February Strike of 1941 caught the security police apparatus completely unawares. On 25 and 26 February the population reacted spontaneously to anti-Semitic measures laid down by the German-led city administration in Amsterdam and by the order police. Nonetheless, until spring 1943 the Gestapo's operations ran relatively smoothly—from the National Socialists' point of view, at least. Almost all Dutch Jews were arrested and deported and resistance activities were kept to a minimum. The Gestapo co-operated with numerous government agencies and administrative authorities in the occupied Netherlands.[64] Various German and Dutch institutions were involved in the deportation of the Dutch Jews in particular. Alongside the security police and the SD these were police battalions, the local Dutch police, and the voluntary auxiliary police, a militia of local National Socialists. In total 105,000 Jews were deported from the Netherlands, most to Auschwitz and Sobibor.[65]

In spring 1943 the basic attitude of the Dutch people changed, triggered by the German army's decision of 29 April 1943 to make all officers of the Dutch army prisoners of war. The whole country was outraged and many took to the streets in protest. In response, the security police and the SD arrested several hundred so-called 'ringleaders', condemning 116 of them to death. Once again the German security police apparatus had been caught unawares, and from then on it came under increasing pressure. The German agents consequently adopted more brutal methods, abusing those under arrest and reacting with excessive violence. Hundreds of political prisoners and resistance fighters were executed in July and August 1944 alone. A silent ceasefire between the security police and the Dutch resistance movement only began in September 1944: as the war neared its end, attempts were made to avoid violent confrontations.[66]

In Belgium and France, which were also conquered unexpectedly quickly in a 'Blitzkrieg' ('lightning war') in spring 1940, the situation was different: both countries were put under military administration. Initially the Gestapo did not have such a free hand here as in the other occupied countries. The army chiefs did not want to be marginalized by Himmler and Heydrich again, as had been the case in Poland. Thus the RSHA field office in Belgium was set up solely as a 'Field Office of the Security Police and SD under the Military Governor', and was re-named 'Representative of the Head of the Security Police and SD under the Military Governor' in Feburary 1941.[67] The security police were able to extend their area of influence gradually and to demonstrate their competence with the deportation of over 25,000 Belgian Jews, but the military administration remained intact and in control until the summer of 1944.[68] Himmler only succeeded in installing a Higher SS and Police Leader for Belgium and Northern France on 18 July 1944, with the appointment of Richard Jungclauss to the post in Brussels.[69]

In France executive police powers remained with the military administration until June 1942. The security police was not wholly inactive, however: although the army leadership had gained the upper hand as to whether they or the RSHA would rule, in June 1940 Heydrich had managed to install Helmut Knochen as a Commissioner of the Chief of the Security Police and SD. Knochen, just 30 years old, brought along most of his men from the SD. He gradually increased his personnel from twenty in 1940 to more than 200 in 1942.[70] The co-operation with the military administration on the one hand and the Gestapo on the other was reasonably good. There were only real conflicts when young security police commanders were transferred to France from the East and found it difficult to cope with the 'more moderate' conditions there.

With the institution of a Higher SS and Police Leader the relationship between the security police and the army in France was restructured:

on 1 June 1941 the SS-Brigadeführer Carl Albrecht Oberg took over the office of HSSPF France and held this position until the end of the war.[71] Knochen was promoted to BdS. In the course of the restructuring the security police took over the relevant personnel from the military administration and from the Secret Field Police (*Geheime Feldpolizei*) and set up new offices throughout France.[72] In total seventeen Security Police Commanders (KdS) were instituted.[73] The new apparatus allowed Oberg and Knochen to devote themselves more effectively to the 'Jewish Question'.[74] An initial deportation of 1,100 Jews had already taken place in March 1942, with the second on 5 June of the same year. But from then on the pace picked up: by August 1944 over 75,000 Jews had been deported from France, most to Auschwitz. Only around 2,500 survived. A further 2,000 to 3,000 Jews died in the internment camps. Around 1,100 were murdered in France.[75] It is important to note, however, that the deportations were not carried out by the Gestapo, security police, and SD alone—numerous French collaborators gave energetic assistance. The persecution of the Jews in France was almost completely in the hands of the French administration and police. The Gestapo's role was to instigate and inspect.[76]

The Gestapo's second focus was combating the French resistance movement—*La Résistance*. The various French resistance groups are still today known under this collective label. On Himmler's orders the security police acted with full severity. Since Gestapo numbers were relatively low, the measures for the 'Combat of Terrorists and Resistance Groups' were usually carried out in conjunction with the security police and SD, the army, military police, and order police. 1,200 individuals fell victim to these troops' operations between 1 October 1943 and 1 May 1944 alone.[77] These numbers are small compared to the war of extermination waged by the security police in Eastern Europe and the Balkans. One thing became clear: there was no such thing as chivalrous combat in Western Europe, either.[78] The small French village of Oradour, in which 643 men, women, and children were murdered by the 2nd SS Panzer Division 'Das Reich' on 10 June 1944, is only the most visible expression of this war of terror being conducted in the West. Although they did not take part in the massacre in Oradour, the Gestapo in France was one of the ensemble of persecutors responsible for tens of thousands of victims.

The provinces of Lorraine and Alsace were in an unusual situation, since they were ethnically French but annexed by the German Reich. A chief of the civil administration was installed in both regions: Robert Wagner for Alsace and Josef Bürckel for Lorraine. Hitler's instructions were that the regions should become 'German, and that means purely German', and that he would not ask about the 'methods used to Germanize the region'.[79] Robert Wagner tackled the challenge with great enthusiasm: 'We have begun to liberate Alsace from all those elements that for centuries have brought calamity on the Alsatian people. We have removed the Jews, the French and their obstinate hangers-on.'[80] Wagner expelled or prevented from returning from southern France around 105,000 people in the second half of 1940. Security policemen under the BdS Strasbourg and the BdS Metz also took part in these measures, functioning as Wagner's direct deputies. As in other countries, Gestapo structures developed out of Einsatzkommandos, which went on the hunt for enemies of the Nazi state immediately after occupation. As for the Germanization of Alsace, the Gestapo also took responsibility for investigating 'Alsatian-French mixed marriages in racial, political, economic and linguistic terms'.[81] Robert Wagner had his own concentration camp built in Vorbruck near Schirmeck as early as mid-July 1940. The RSHA also maintained a large concentration camp on land at Struthof near Natzwiller (Natzweiler). Here several thousand people died between 1941 and 1944, including allied prisoners of war, who were deported from the German Reich to Natzwiller by the Gestapo in so-called 'Night and Fog' missions, to be quietly shot and cremated.[82]

The escalation of the extermination: the Gestapo in South-Eastern and Eastern Europe

Before the summer of 1941, when the German war machinery was directed at full tilt at the Soviet Union, there was an interlude. Hitler had ordered the attack on Greece, 'Operation Marita', in December 1940 since, without discussing it with the Reich, Italy had invaded the country on 28 October 1940 but was clearly not in a position to conquer it alone. Since the German-friendly government of Prince Paul in Yugoslavia had been overthrown in March 1941, this country was also brought ad hoc into the military planning. The attack on both countries began on 6 April 1941 and the Balkan campaign was over within a few weeks. Yugoslavia was defeated: Slovenia was divided up between the German Reich and Italy, and the allies Bulgaria and Hungary also helped themselves to Yugoslavia's assets. The state of Croatia became a new fascist ally of the German Reich. The rest of Serbia was placed under German military administration.

At first glance, the occupation structure in Serbia was similar to that in France, with SS-Gruppenführer Harald Turner at its head as chief of the military administration. Turner attempted to take control of the newly formed security police and SD Einsatzgruppe and the Reserve Police Battalion 64 from Cologne, but this attempt was vetoed by Heydrich.[83] This made no difference in practice: while in Poland the army leadership had complained about the activities of the Einsatzgruppen, the co-operation between the army, SS, security and order police was now smooth.[84] The initial aim was to divide duties along typical lines: the army would fight the military enemy, while the security police would deal with the communists, Jews, and partisans. But this changed within only a few weeks. Because of weaknesses in the police organs, the army was charged with fighting partisans from summer 1941, and between October and December 1941 soldiers murdered over 25,000 people as part of 'retribution operations', including more than 6,000 male Jews and gypsies.

The army therefore took a direct part in the murderous measures against Serbian Jews, which temporarily qualified the role of the security police. By contrast, Gestapo activities followed standard patterns. The Gestapo used the Jewish Council that it had established to ensure that the bureaucratic processes of deportation functioned smoothly. The council was required to pass on the directives of the German organs. However, the 'reprisal measures' (*Sühnemaßnahmen*) that were carried out by infantry units meant that the initiative in the 'Final Solution to the Jewish Question' was largely transferred to the army: nowhere else was the army so deeply involved in the Holocaust. Not until the winter of 1941/42 was responsibility for the extermination of the Serbian Jews passed back to RSHA organs. The principal problem was now the murder of the approximately 15,000 women and children who had been spared by the army's 'reprisal operations' and deported to the Sajmište concentration camp near Belgrade.[85] At the end of January 1942 SS-Untersturmführer Herbert Andorfer took over the commando. He came from Department III of the BdS Belgrade and was therefore not officially responsible for 'Jewish matters'. The concentration camp was guarded by 25 men from Reserve Police Battalion 64. In early March 1942 a lorry arrived from Berlin: it was a gas truck.[86] Every day in the weeks that followed, under the pretence of resettlement, groups of 50 to 80 women and children were loaded into the truck and gassed during the journey; the corpses were then hastily buried on a military drill ground. The murderous operation ended on 10 May 1942: Serbia was 'free of Jews'. The example of Serbia showed that any unit had the potential to become perpetrators. It was barely possible to differentiate between army, SS, and police apparatus in this murderous business. In Serbia, the co-operation between security police and SD, order police and army worked more smoothly than in any other country under German occupation.

Greece, which in spring 1941 had been overrun just as quickly as Yugoslavia, was divided into three zones: north-eastern Thrace was allocated to Bulgaria, and the rest was divided into an Italian and a German zone.[87] In the smaller German zone, security police and SD offices were established in Athens and Thessaloniki; however, their activities remained limited for a long time, largely restricted to the surveillance of communists.[88] By the end of 1942 there had still been no anti-Jewish measures, since the plan was to proceed against the Greek Jews in a joint effort with the Italians. The Italians were dragging their feet, however, so the RSHA finally agreed to take the initiative: in February 1943 two 'Judenberater' (Nazi 'advisers' on Jewish affairs), Dieter Wisliceny and Alois Brunner, were sent to Thessaloniki with a commando.[89] Together they set up a Jewish security service, which was to supervise the ghettoization of the 56,000 Jews resident in Thessaloniki. Transports to Auschwitz began on 15 March 1943, with up to six trains departing per week. By August 1943 almost all Jews in the German zone had been deported to Auschwitz. The Gestapo's 'Judenberater' had completed their task and were able to leave.

A few days later, following Italy's capitulation in September 1943, German troops occupied the Italian zone of Greece. The Jews living there now fell under the control of the Gestapo. Wisliceny returned from Slovakia.[90] He began preparations for deportation straight away, although they were complicated by the fact that there were no address lists of Jews. By March 1944 only 1,500 Jews had registered. Consequently Wisliceny's successor, Anton Burger, conducted mass raids throughout the whole of Greece on 24 and 25 March 1944: units from the security police and SD, German order police, army, and Greek police combed the country for Jews. All those arrested were immediately deported. Once again, successful co-operation between the different organs of persecution under the Gestapo's leadership, as well as a readiness for collaboration, was in evidence. By April 1944 almost all Jews on the Greek mainland were in custody or had been deported.[91]

After the Balkan intermezzo, Hitler could attend to the real objective of his war: the destruction of the Soviet Union. On 22 June 1941 the German army and their allies set out on 'Operation Barbarossa'. This campaign was a war of extermination from the outset.[92] Compared to the previous campaign in Poland, the co-operation between the army and the security police Einsatzgruppen was now better organized. The army high command had given a secret order to the troops on 28 April 1941: 'Regulation of the Deployment of Security Police and SD in association with the Army'.[93] Directly behind the front line, the Einsatzgruppen were to operate in close consultation with the army, while in the rear lines they had more independence. Initially the RSHA established four Einsatzgruppen with a high-ranking leadership: Einsatzgruppe A under the experienced Franz Walter Stahlecker; Einsatzgruppe B under Arthur Nebe, Head of Office V (Criminal Police) of the RSHA; Einsatzgruppe C under Dr Dr Otto Rasch, also an experienced commander, and Einsatzgruppe D under Otto Ohlendorf, Head of Office III (SD-Domestic) in the RSHA. At the beginning of July 1941 an Einsatzgruppe for special assignments was put together from BdS forces in Cracow, and it advanced into the Eastern Polish regions.[94]

The Einsatzgruppen formed the core of the war of extermination against the Soviet Union, although they never numbered more than 3,500 men. This clearly suggests that the Einsatzgruppen depended on close co-operation not only with the army but also with Waffen-SS troops and police battalions.[95] The mass murders were conducted through division of labour: the murder of Soviet prisoners of war was at its core a genuine army crime, as was the implementation of the Commissar Order at the Front.[96] The large-scale combat of partisans, so-called 'Operations for Combating Gangs' (Bandenbekämpfungsaktionen), was mainly carried out by the army and Waffen-SS together. More minor operations, on the other hand, were dealt with by the Einsatzgruppen. The extermination of the Jews in the occupied Soviet regions was also a matter for the Einsatzgruppen, although Waffen-SS and army units, as well as police battalions, were also involved.

Einsatzgruppe A, the largest in terms of personnel, was responsible for the Baltic region and northern Russia. It consisted of four Einsatzkommandos and followed the Army Group North. Although it was nominally an Einsatzgruppe of the security police and SD, the Gestapo provided only eighty-nine and the SD merely thirty-five of the total 990 members. The Waffen-SS provided the largest contingent with 340 men, particularly in the lower ranks. The situation was similar with the other Einsatzgruppen: as the German sphere of influence expanded, there were no longer enough security police officers available. Furthermore, the delegated men were often from posts that had been dissolved or downgraded, and were not being used to their full capacity in the Reich—in the 'wild East' they now hoped for career progression and promotion, since they had the chance to prove themselves at the security police frontline.[97] The dynamics of the war meant that Einsatzgruppe A was the first to be stationed in a fixed location: as of the end of September 1941 Walter Stahlecker functioned both as head of the Einsatzgruppe and as BdS Ostland, based in Riga. The offices of the Commanders of the Security Police and SD in the General Districts Estonia, Latvia, Lithuania, and Belarus were all formed out of the Einsatzkommandos. At the same time mobile units continued to function, labelled Einsatz- or Sonderkommandos.[98]

The Baltic states were particularly open to co-operation with the German occupying forces, and Lithuanian and Latvian police units were extensively involved in the extermination campaigns.[99] In Estonia significant security police functions were carried out by locals. This could even be reconciled with the SS's racist principles—Himmler himself considered the Estonians to be a 'valuable' people.[100] Just a few days after the outbreak of war, the men of Einsatzgruppe A, supported by order police units and local forces, carried out the first mass shootings, initially of communist functionaries and male Jews. From mid-August 1941 the country's entire Jewish population was affected. At the same time, ghettos began to be established in the larger cities such as Riga.[101] Stahlecker gave 1 February 1942 as the deadline for his Einsatzgruppe to have murdered 218,050 Jews in the Baltic states.

Einsatzgruppe B under Arthur Nebe was somewhat smaller. It consisted of 655 men, and remained roughly this size until 1944.[102] This Einsatzgruppe followed the armies of the Army Group Centre (Heeresgruppe Mitte) through the Byelorussian lands and remained rather more mobile than Einsatzgruppe A. It was supported in its activities by Police Battalions 316 and 322 and Reserve Police Battalion 131.[103] The Einsatzgruppe was also allocated the 'Vorkommando

Moskau' under the Head of Office VII (Ideological Enemy Research), Professor Dr Franz Alfred Six, since the early success of the war initially led them to expect the Russian capital to be taken early.[104] In order to close the gaps in the network of security police, the KdS in Warsaw and Lublin sent out support forces into newly occupied Eastern Poland, so that Einsatzgruppe B could advance further east. In December 1941 the forces were at least partially stationed in fixed positions, and a duty station was set up in Minsk. From here the murders of Jews in Byelorussia were planned and the combat of partisans organized. The Einsatzgruppe was supported in these murderous activities not only by police battalions but also by the army, Waffen-SS, secret military police, and local auxiliary police—as so often the case, institutional boundaries became blurred in the war of extermination. According to its own records, Einsatzgruppe B murdered over 140,000 people by 31 March 1943, the overwhelming majority of them Jews.[105]

Einsatzgruppe C was deployed in Ukraine and followed the 6th and 17th German Army. It comprised a command staff, two special commandos, and two Einsatzkommandos, with a total of between 700 and 800 members. In the first weeks of the military campaign the men mainly murdered Soviet functionaries and the so-called 'Jewish intelligentsia'. At the same time there were a number of pogroms throughout Ukraine, particularly in small towns, which were conducted by Ukrainians. The Einsatzgruppen individually fomented these riots or—and this was more often the case—turned them into mass executions. At the latest from August 1941, the murderous force of the Einsatzgruppe was directed against all Jews living in its zone of operation, which comprised around one million of the 1.5 million Jews in Ukraine. According to its own records, the Einsatzgruppe murdered 118,000 people, while the total number of Jewish victims in Ukraine was around 1.4 million. This makes it clear that Einsatzgruppe C was only one component in the ensemble of extermination there.[106] It also involved Ukrainian protection squads (*Schutzmannschaften*) and auxiliary police, who were often more than willing to make common cause with the German occupying forces.[107]

Sonderkommando 4a of Einsatzgruppe C took part in one of the largest massacres in the Second World War: under Paul Blobel's leadership and with help from officers of police battalions 43, 303, and 314, more than 33,000 Jews from Kiev were shot dead in the Babi Yar ravine on 29 and 30 September 1941. The following assertion will no longer come as a surprise: this mass murder was by no means a singular occurrence, it was just its extent that surpassed the average murderous activity of the various commandos. Towards the end of 1941 Einsatzgruppe C was provided with several gas trucks and mobile murder tools. However, the trucks did not always work well, and so mass shootings continued.

Between January and July 1942 the commandos of Einsatzgruppe C were reconfigured as stationary duty posts: in this way a BdS Ukraine was established, held by the second head of the Einsatzgruppe, Dr Max Thomas. Einsatzkommando 5 became KdS Kiev, and Sonderkommando 4b evolved into KdS Stalino, near Donezk. As the German army retreated, the stationary duty posts were either dissolved or moved, and the commandos were allocated to various combat groups. In June 1944 Einsatzgruppe C was finally officially disbanded.

In the southernmost section of the front, Einsatzgruppe D was active—the smallest with only 500 men. This is the best researched of all the Einsatzgruppen.[108] It advanced behind the 11th German Army and the 3rd and 4th Romanian Armies, from the Romanian lands through the Bukovina and Bessarabia, through the Crimea and into the Caucasus. As with the other Einsatzgruppen, it was made up of only a few security police and SD personnel, with the majority coming from the reserve police, Waffen-SS, and conscripts. Nonetheless, the leadership was made up of experienced specialists from Gestapo offices and SD districts within the Reich or from the occupied lands. The Einsatzgruppe began executions as soon as it crossed the border. As early as September 1941 the commandos had begun to murder entire Jewish communities.

At the beginning of October 1941 Himmler visited some of his units on the Eastern Front. On the 4th of that month he met Otto Ohlendorf, head of Einsatzgruppe D, in Nikolajew and gave a speech to his men. He is said to have suggested that the war was about gaining land for settlement and that the extermination of Jews and political opponents was therefore essential. This was a difficult task that nonetheless had to be fulfilled.[109] Himmler's argument at this stage was at its core the same as that two years later in the so-called Poznań Speech. With a few exceptions, the men of Einsatzgruppe D did indeed fulfil their murderous duty, even if it was a burden for some of them: the head of Sonderkommando 11, for example, complained vociferously about the lunch provided during a shooting, because it included tinned blood sausage. He screamed at the administrator: '...saying what a disgrace it was, and accusing him of trying to raise hell. In this situation, he said, we would do without provisions like that.'[110] The head of the commando was not being cynical here. He spoke frankly and demanded that the provisions be appropriate to the task: blood sausage, in his view, was not a fitting snack, since it reminded him of the activity that had just been committed.

Einsatzgruppe D murdered 90,000 people by the end of March 1941. Alongside the murder of Jews and Soviet functionaries, the commandos also took part in the 'euthanasia' programme: they searched sanatoria and asylums, checking whether the inmates and patients were 'worthy to live'. Anyone who failed the selection was murdered in the gas trucks parked outside. At the beginning of January 1943 Einsatzgruppe D neared its end, since the German army was retreating from the Caucasus. A large part of it was deployed in partisan combat as 'Kampfgruppe Bierkamp'; in May 1943 this unit, and thereby the whole of Einsatzgruppe D, was administratively disbanded. The personnel were distributed to various duty stations.

The exact number of people who fell victim to the Einsatzgruppen in the Soviet Union is not known. It is certain, however, that they murdered around a million people, of whom the overwhelming majority were Jewish. As elsewhere, the Einsatzgruppen were only part of the network of persecution and extermination. Yet to a certain extent the Soviet Union represented the murderous climax in their parade of destruction through Europe: never before in history had so many been murdered by so few in such a short space of time.

Zones of deployment in the second half of the war: Africa, Italy, Hungary, Croatia, Slovakia

The Gestapo was active in several other countries in addition to those already discussed. At first glance, perhaps the most exotic zone of deployment was Africa. A mobile unit was set up there in July 1942, and allocated to Rommel's army. The group was officially an SS Einsatzkommando, although some Gestapo officers were also involved. The operation guidelines were in part taken verbatim from those for the Soviet Union, since these had proved particularly useful in practice. The commando leadership was drawn from various young security police or SS chiefs in their late twenties and early thirties. In total this mobile unit numbered 100 men and was charged with organizing the extermination of the Jews in the Middle East, with the assistance of Arab collaborators. However, the course that the military campaign took meant that this never came to pass. The commando was disbanded in spring 1943.[111]

Italy was another case altogether. As a former ally, it only came under German control in September 1943—at a time when National Socialist expansion had already reached its apex. Dr Wilhelm Harster was sent from the Netherlands to take up the position of Security Police Commanding Officer (BdS) in Italy, with the task of building up the security police and SD apparatus. In this he was effectively independent from the HSSPF for Italy, SS-Obergruppenführer Karl Wolff. Harster structured his agency along similar lines to the RSHA, and his staff included smaller Einsatzkommandos and partisan-hunting commandos. The BdS personnel in Italy were constituted from several different groups: along with members of the Einsatzkommandos and officers from the German police apparatus there were German specialists and experts on Italy. In time up to forty security police and SD duty stations were set up in Italy. When the war ended in 1945 approximately 1,000 men were deployed there. It is no longer possible to say for sure whether this number had previously been higher, although it might be assumed that this was the case.[112]

As previously in other countries, the persecution of the Jews in Italy was one of the Gestapo's core duties, and the 'Jewish Question' came into focus only a month after German occupation. Since the BdS, Wilhelm Harster, and his apparatus were not yet available, Eichmann dispatched an Einsatzkommando to Rome under the leadership of the experienced 'Judenberater' Theodor Dannecker, in order to begin preparations for the deportation of the Italian Jews.[113] Dannecker and his men set to work with systematic and single-minded purpose: they examined files that detailed the social structure of Rome's Jews and conducted a large raid on 16 October 1943, during which 1,259 people, mainly women and children, were arrested. The majority were deported to Auschwitz two days later. In total over 6,400 people had been deported from Italy by 14 December 1944, of whom only around 800 survived.[114] In addition 1,100 Jews were deported from Trieste, which had been annexed by Germany and belonged to the 'Operational Zone of the Adriatic Littoral'.

The security police were also charged with the surveillance of the urban areas, in particular in the largely industrial north of Italy. In spring 1944 the security police temporarily lost control here, and there were general strikes in Turin and Milan. The so-called 'ringleaders'— around 1,200 workers—were deported to the concentration camps at Mauthausen and Dachau. German rule was not only tested by the strike, however. The Italian resistance movement often posed a serious challenge to the occupying forces, such as in a March 1944 attack on a German police battalion training company in which thirty-four men were killed. 335 prisoners were murdered by the security police in a 'reprisal measure'.[115] Since Italy was viewed as a collaborating state, such mass killings were relatively rare and deportations more common, although these were often also journeys to death.

Hungary was another long-term ally of the German Reich. For various reasons, however, the German army marched into Hungary on 19 March 1944. On the one hand, Hitler rightly feared that Hungary might pull out of the war, and the invasion was an attempt to prevent this. On the other hand, a number of economic, political, and military aims came into play.[116] Einsatzgruppe E was activated alongside the German army units. Established in March 1944 in Mauthausen, it was composed of forces from the security police and Waffen-SS, as well as customs officials: 800 men in all. The group was made up of seven Einsatzkommandos, which became stationary units once the military operation had concluded. There was an additional eighth commando with sixty-five men from Section IV B 4 of the RSHA, under the leadership of Adolf Eichmann himself. Experienced 'Judenberater' such as Dieter Wisliceny and Theodor Dannecker were also members of this special commando.[117] Their task was the 'Final Solution to the Jewish Question' in Hungary.

Hungarian authorities helped them in their activities, while mass denunciations dealt with the rest. In addition, army and Waffen-SS units committed numerous crimes, raiding and ransacking Jewish homes. Within a very short space of time Jews were deprived of their rights and excluded from Hungarian society: by April 1944 close to 200,000 Jews had been interned in hurriedly established, makeshift ghettos. The RSHA experts then began to prepare the deportations, most going straight to Auschwitz, which received the biggest influx of inmates in its history. On 15 May 1944 the first train set off, and at the beginning of July the deportations were suspended. In this short time well over 400,000 men, women, and children were deported, the majority from rural areas. The Hungarian Gendarmerie gave extremely brutal assistance to the Gestapo men, and abuse and torture were a daily occurrence.[118]

The Hungarian Regent Horthy stopped the deportations in July 1944 following protests from several foreign governments and the Pope.[119] In October 1944 the Germans finally forced Horthy to step down and installed a fascist government under Ferenc Szálasie, the head of the Arrow Cross movement.[120] On 20 October 1944 Arrow Cross Party members and Hungarian police began to arrest Jewish men in Budapest, to help with the construction of defences in the south and east of the city against the advancing Soviet forces. Three days previously Eichmann had returned to Budapest in order to re-start the deportations: this time the Jews were to be sent to Germany as slave labour. A lack of trains meant that tens of thousands were sent on so-called death marches, and anyone too weak to continue marching was liquidated on the spot. Hungarian Gendarmes and Arrow Cross supporters were also involved in these marches. International protests ensued once again. In November 1944 the deportations were finally stopped, though there were also logistical and economic reasons at play. Eichmann left Budapest a few days before Christmas, shortly before the Red Army surrounded the city. By then over 500,000 Hungarian Jews had been deported. What had taken over a decade in the German Reich had been implemented here by the Gestapo within a few months, with the assistance of numerous helpers and collaborators.

Security police and SD Einsatzgruppen were also deployed in the satellite states allied to the 'Third Reich', such as Croatia and Slovakia. Their main duties in both countries were the combat of resistance movements and the murder or deportation of the Jewish population. Einsatzgruppe E in Croatia was founded in spring 1943 and lasted until the end of the war in May 1945, but was unable to do much against the strong Yugoslav partisan movement. After Italy capitulated in September 1943 it did manage to deport the Jews from the coastal region of Dalmatia. Einsatzgruppe H was established in Slovakia in August 1944, following the armed uprising there. It largely consisted of Slovakian collaborators, ethnic Germans, Waffen-SS men, and a whole year group from the Security Police College in Fürstenberg, numbering 2,500 in total. As well as dealing with the uprising, the commandos deported 12,000 Jews to concentration camps and murdered 4,000 *in situ*. Two Einsatzgruppen were also founded for the German army's last major offensive, the Battle of the Ardennes:

Einsatzgruppe K under Dr Emanuel Schäfer in Euskirchen and L under Dr Ludwig Hahn in Cochem. Schäfer had previously been BdS in Belgrade, while Hahn, as KdS in Warsaw, had concluded the liquidation of the Warsaw ghetto. When the battle was finally lost in January 1945, both Einsatzgruppen were disbanded: the end of the war was nigh.[121]

Radicalization in ruins: the repercussions of 'foreign deployment'

The unrestrained violence of state police operations in occupied Europe had an impact on the Gestapo's activities within the German Reich. The final phase of the war, which began at the latest when allied forces crossed the Reich borders in autumn 1944, was characterized by a number of features. The British and American bombing campaign, which had been going on for years, now reached its apex and resulted in apocalyptic scenes in a number of German cities.[122] Social norms dissolved, looting was a daily occurrence, and state activities moved ever closer to purely prerogative activities. The state was transformed into 'more or less organized anarchy', as émigré political scientist Franz Neumann stated fittingly in August 1944.[123] In other words: German society was in a state of catastrophe.[124]

In this apocalyptic mood, Gestapo officers turned to the methods that they had already made use of in occupied Europe. But now they were not carrying out these deeds hundreds or thousands of miles from home. And now these deeds did not take place behind the walls of concentration camps and prisons.[125] At the latest in this final phase of the war, the murderous practices of the Secret State Police were anything but secret, and were carried out before the eyes of the population. Although for a long time the average 'national comrade' was generally not at risk of becoming a victim, from autumn 1944 onwards almost anyone could enter the persecutors' sights. The Gestapo alone were not responsible for this crime, however, since SS, Volkssturm, party agencies, and the army were also involved.[126] The Gestapo officers were not even the dominant perpetrators. They were mainly responsible for the mass executions of forced labourers.[127]

Gestapo employees had been in crisis mode since the attempted assassination of Hitler on 20 July 1944. Although after the event almost all the conspirators were captured, the attack itself caught the Gestapo completely unawares. In addition there were constant rumours prophesying an uprising of forced labourers; and the allied landings in Normandy and the advance of the Red Army seemed to signal that the end of Nazi rule was just around the corner. On 21 October 1944 Aachen was the first German city to be taken by allied forces: the end of the 'Third Reich' seemed to be just weeks away. But the military situation stabilized and the war was to go on for over six months. The Gestapo took advantage of this time to commit further crimes: 'The more helplessly the regime was exposed to its external enemies, the more bloodthirsty its attacks on all those inside its borders whom it identified as enemies.'[128]

Although this ongoing murder in the face of imminent defeat might seem utterly incomprehensible, there were numerous reasons for the Gestapo officers' behaviour. On the one hand their acts were a kind of compensation: the 'Russian' could not be defeated with military means, but it was possible to take revenge on all Russian forced labourers in the Reich. And indeed the Gestapo's violence was mainly directed at Eastern workers. Furthermore, in the final months of the war the chain of command up to the RSHA dissolved, giving the middle- and lower-ranking officers an ever greater sphere of influence. Since most Gestapo officers suspected that there would be no prospects for them after the war, an apocalyptic mood took hold: they would take as many as possible with them into their imminent ruin. In addition, a perverted understanding of order was at play. The forced labourers were mostly in a very sorry state: starving, often ill and dressed in rags, they presented a disturbing picture. By murdering them, it was seemingly possible to create order in the chaos. The forced labourers also served as a scapegoat for the ever growing criminality and looting, which was nonetheless also the work of 'national comrades'.[129]

The following figures give a sense of the extent of gang activity: from March to September 1944, 2,700 Soviet prisoners of war were arrested, having joined together in resistance groups.[130] But this was not the climax of such activity. The Nazi leadership had long feared that the foreign workforce would develop resistance organizations, yet little is in fact known about resistance by foreign civilian workers. It was above all Soviet prisoners of war who formed resistance cells.[131]

To reiterate: in the final phase of the war, Gestapo operations in the German Reich bore an increasing resemblance to security police operations in Eastern Europe. Almost all the officers who were involved in these crimes had already been active abroad. Towards the end of the 'Third Reich', these shared experiences levelled out the differences between the various groups of Gestapo officials. The fact that Germany itself had become a theatre of war, coupled with the fear of uprisings by forced labourers, led the Gestapo to seek refuge in new models of organization and activity. Following the patterns established in the previously occupied zones, new security police stations were set up. In the West German border zones in particular, security police and SD combat groups and Einsatz companies were founded.[132]

This was also the initial focus of the crimes.[133] It is thought that in the final months more than 10,000 people, above all 'foreign labourers' and prisoners of war, deserters who were subsequently arrested, politically dubious Germans, Jews, and inmates of the AEL, fell victim to the war that the Gestapo waged on German soil together with Werwolf and Volkssturm units and Nazi functionaries. The final reckoning of the foundering 'Third Reich' could affect almost anyone. The circle had closed: the Gestapo had gone far in its twelve-year history, undergoing numerous metamorphoses, but its murderous practice ended where it had all begun—in Germany.

In the final days of the Second World War the security police apparatus collapsed and, like so many others, Gestapo and SD employees attempted to erase the traces of their actions. They destroyed files on a grand scale, so that only a fraction remain available to researchers today. Many leading officials attempted to go into hiding with false papers, others committed suicide or died in the final moments of combat. The Gestapo headquarters, the Reich Security Main Office, which had already been destroyed in a bombing raid on 3 February, finally wrapped up its activities on 22 April 1945.[134] At the same time the SS and police apparatus began their retreat in two directions: in the region around Flensburg, known in military terms as 'Fortress North' (*Festung Nord*), Himmler was joined by a large proportion of the central SS institutions, the main office of the order police, and Offices III, V, and VI of the RSHA as well as a few Higher SS and Police Leaders. The Gestapo headquarters, Office IV of the RSHA, was evacuated to the region around Berchtesgarden—into the so-called 'Alpine Fortress' (*Alpenfestung*).[135] But the supposed defences were brittle and within a few days this final episode was also over.

7

THE GESTAPO AFTER 1945

Suicide, flight, persecution: from the end of the war to the Nuremberg Trials

The end of the Second World War meant the end of the Gestapo, too. With the demise of the 'Third Reich', the main National Socialist organ of persecution ceased to exist. Considering that the Gestapo's final function had been as an 'internal army' and executor of the war of extermination, there was a certain logic to the fact that both military and secret police power collapsed simultaneously: the Gestapo had also made an unconditional surrender. What is more, and unlike most other 'Third Reich' agencies, it achieved immediate notoriety for having taken a significant role in all the atrocities and crimes of the Nazi regime. It was now known that the Gestapo was guilty, if not of everything, then of a great deal, and many who had once supported it wanted nothing more to do with this institution. The extended Gestapo—its network of persecutors, supporters, helpers, and facilitators—disappeared under cover of the war's end and acted as if there had been only *one* Gestapo. The ideal type of the Nazi criminal was from now on an SS man in the service of the Gestapo, who had murdered Jews, opposition or resistance members in occupied Europe or in the German Reich. Crimes committed by the other police departments, which had provided significant support to the Gestapo, were barely mentioned. The criminal police, for example, largely managed to hide their mass crimes.[1] In the main, the activities of the uniformed police between 1933 and 1945 was also hushed up, played down, or kept quiet. It sometimes seems as if the police in the Nazi state had merely pursued petty criminals and gone on traffic duty.

This meant that the Gestapo lost all structural backing almost overnight. This is perhaps also why plans made by the security police leadership, which had aimed to deploy Gestapo officers as guerrilla 'Werewolves' against the allied occupiers within the Reich, had foundered. Without assistance, the Gestapo could no longer function effectively. Detached from its network, it could no longer make any headway against the massed enemies in the Reich. The only killings committed by the Gestapo after the Nazi surrender were suicides, and even these did not take place in large numbers. Any that did occur were mainly committed by leading figures such as Dr Max Thomas, once head of Einsatzgruppe C in the Soviet Union, who committed suicide on 6 December 1945 in order to avoid his imminent prosecution.[2] Reichsführer-SS Heinrich Himmler, who had also been Reich Interior Minister since August 1943, also chose this path and killed himself with a poison capsule on 23 May 1945, while in British custody.

Nonetheless, the allied troops feared surprise attacks from secret police paramilitaries, and consequently took all the Gestapo officers they could lay their hands on into custody. The allied occupation worked on the principle that all those they considered criminals due to their rank within the NSDAP or one of its organizations would be automatically arrested. After the war ended, many former Gestapo officers disappeared behind the barbed wire of internment camps, where they were sent for a given period to bring them to justice for their crimes. The dual character of penance and prevention had also defined the Gestapo's own conception of political cleansing in the early war years.

Despite these measures, and although few specifics are known about them, the number of high-ranking Gestapo men who did manage to go into hiding or flee abroad was not insignificant.[3] The so-called 'rat line' took criminals like Klaus Barbie or Adolf Eichmann via Italy to South America. Many a Gestapo henchman made use of his contacts and in the confusion of the regime's collapse managed to elude arrest, to take a false name and thereby cover up his own past. Klaus Barbie even became an important military-political power broker and CIA agent in Bolivia. But flight and repression were far from being the rule.

The security officers of the allied tracing agencies were well informed: as early as October 1942 the formation of a 'United Nations Commission for the Investigation of War Crimes' (later United Nations War Crimes Commission) had been announced in London and Washington, and it began work a year later. The allies collected evidence of atrocities, massacres, and mass executions. The results of the investigations and later the successful allied manhunts were impressive. While the American agencies followed up all clues in order to promote denazification, the English and French concentrated almost exclusively on the crimes that had been committed against allied citizens, above all prisoners of war and forced labourers.[4] In principle the Soviets also attempted to seek out and punish every single member of the Gestapo, whenever they received relevant evidence from the population. However, there was no systematic search for Gestapo employees there, either.

If Gestapo members did appear in court, then it was initially only in allied military trials, where they had to answer for crimes committed against foreigners. The allies had agreed during the war that the Nazi perpetrators should be punished in the places where the deeds had been committed. The basis for this decision was the 'Declaration on Atrocities' made at the Moscow conference of 30 October 1943. As a result some Gestapo officers were sentenced and executed in Eastern Europe. But Gestapo officers also faced British military courts in Germany, where they were tried for the murder of prisoners of war, sentenced to death, and executed.[5] The principal war criminals, whose crimes could not be assigned to one geographical location, were to be tried in one single grand trial: the Nuremberg Trial of the Major War Criminals, which lasted from 14 November 1945 to 1 October 1946. The aim of the trial was to condemn the principal offenders as individuals, but also to condemn whole organizations or groups, as was laid out in Article 10 of the Statute of the International Military Tribunal of 8 August 1945.[6] Like the SD, the Gestapo was accused of the persecution and extermination of Jews, atrocities and murders in concentration camps, excesses in the administration of occupied zones as well as the abuse and murder of forced labourers and prisoners of war.[7] And they were convicted of these crimes, since the trials gave the first insight into the full extent of NSG crime.* During the trial itself, most Germans took the view that the crimes had to be brought to light and the culprits brought to justice.[8]

The Nuremberg Judgment categorized as Gestapo members all those who had taken part in the criminal deeds in an official capacity: from the members of the administrative departments to the executive officers and the border police officers.[9] However, it excepted border guards (Grenzschutz) and the Secret Field Police, as long as there were no charges against them, as well as those employed solely for 'pure office work'.[10] On the basis of this judgment, any Gestapo member could be put on trial. The criminal character of the Gestapo was considered proven once and for all, and did not need to be newly proved in each individual case. Gestapo members were able to insist that they had had to follow orders, a line of defence that was soon elevated to the status of 'the necessity of following orders' (Befehlsnotstand),[11] which could be taken as a mitigating factor. Active participation in the criminal organization beyond following orders was only assumed if the criminal acts had been carried out either in full awareness or with the express involvement of members, which was not always easy to prove.

The Nuremberg Trials had thus laid down important principles, but had left much open. The political accountability of the Gestapo leadership as well as the competencies, inner structures, and connections

* The abbreviation 'NSG' stands for 'Nationalsozialistische Gewaltverbrechen', or 'National Socialist Violent Crimes', and refers to the crimes committed by National Socialist elements during the 'Third Reich'.

between headquarters and field offices remained unexplained. The focus on the major offenders and criminal organizations meant that the reality of state police operations, which functioned by way of a network of helpers, could retreat into the background. One of the major offenders was Reinhard Heydrich's successor and the last head of the Reich Security Main Office, Ernst Kaltenbrunner, who was condemned to death. Shortly before his execution in October 1946 he wrote that it was a 'glorious feeling to have lived a life that demanded and found peril and readiness for duty'.[12] He was obviously convinced to the end that he had done the right thing, and showed no remorse.

One of the twelve so-called Subsequent Nuremberg Trials also dealt with crimes committed by Gestapo members.[13] In trial 9, for example, twenty-four high-ranking Einsatzgruppen heads were charged. The case lasted around six months and ended on 10 April 1948 with the highest number of death sentences in any of the subsequent trials. In the course of several amnesty initiatives in the early 1950s, however, only a few of these sentences were carried out.[14] Along with three others, only Otto Ohlendorf, head of Einsatzgruppe D, was executed in January 1951. The West German justice system did not address this issue again until ten years later, with the Ulm Einsatzgruppen Trial.

Spruchkammer trials and denazification

Part of the process of denazification was the broad-brush punishment of Gestapo employees as members of a 'criminal organization'. However, this was detached from attempts to evaluate political and personal criminal acts individually and to pass judgment on them, which took place in specially created lay courts, so-called Spruchkammer.[15] The 'Law for Liberation from National Socialism and Militarism' of 5 March 1946 allowed that formally incriminated persons such as Gestapo officers could be exonerated by relevant witnesses. Individual cases then provided the opportunity to establish to what extent they could be made personally responsible for the crimes of the Gestapo.[16]

Contemporary criticism and historiographical research concur that the decisions made by the Spruchkammer were hugely diverse.[17] Individuals with much to incriminate them were given relatively minor judgments, while arguably minor cases were punished with harsh retribution measures. The concession that allowed witnesses and evidence to be brought for self-exoneration resulted in a market in 'certificates of blamelessness', from which individuals and groups profited in different ways. Gestapo officers also tried to whitewash each other. Affected collectively by the retributive measures of political cleansing, they sought solidarity in an attempt to elude criminal persecution. This kind of comradely assistance was widespread, and evident in the many cases in which former officers took action together against the investigations. The heads of the personnel office of the former Reich Security Main Office, Werner Best and Georg Schraepel, were often even cited as guarantors.

It was above all Best who took pains to co-ordinate the Gestapo officers' attempts to justify their actions. In his wake and clearly strongly influenced by him, the lawyers in the Nuremberg War Criminals Tribunal, Rudolf Merkel and Joseph Weisgerber, published a defence paper that was intended to steer the Gestapo members' defence into Spruchgericht and Spruchkammer trials.[18] Paying particular attention to Werner Best's representations, they sketched a harmless image of the Gestapo, with only rudimentary reflection on their participation in the persecution. In Best's view the Gestapo should be prosecuted only for the major crimes named in the Nuremberg Judgment: the persecution and extermination of Jews, atrocities and murders in concentration camps, excesses in the administrations of occupied zones, operating the forced labourer programme, and the murder of prisoners of war. All other crimes, large and small, such as the extortion of confessions and torture, should if possible disappear behind these larger crimes. Many Gestapo officers also argued that state police surveillance had already been in operation long before the 'Third Reich' and was also known to happen in other countries. Members of the border police or counter-espionage units argued that these branches had not been part of the Gestapo proper. It helped the apologists that the new police structures in the 'Third Reich', with their fusion of state and party functions, were far from transparent for the investigators. It also proved difficult to find witnesses for the prosecution who were able to counter the defendants' window-dressing. This was easiest when dealing with the persecution of the political left, since there were numerous survivors. Jews or foreign labourers, however, could rarely appear as prosecution witnesses in the denazification trials.[19] A widespread view has it that against this background the Spruchkammer increasingly developed into a 'Fellow Traveller Factory' (Mitläuferfabrik), whereby there was no longer any connection between the efforts made in a case and its final result.[20]

Due simply to the sheer numbers of cases and the extremely complex bureaucratic processes involved, the attempts made by the authorities of denazification to investigate all incriminated Nazis and where necessary to punish them were only partially successful. The fact that apparently minor cases were dealt with first, in order to avoid long delays to social and professional reintegration, was particularly problematic. This well-intended measure became a shortcoming, as over the years the denazification process lost intensity and the Spruch-kammer consequently became less engaged.[21] This situation worked in favour of the majority of Gestapo employees: as time went on they were able to benefit more and more from the laws of termination (Abschlussgesetzen) and amnesties.[22] The desire to bring all the crimes to light, which had initially dominated the public sphere, made way for a 'politics of the past' in all political camps, which prioritized 'repealing punishments and accomplishing integration in favour of a million-strong army of former party comrades'.[23] For many Gestapo members the retribution measures were consequently softened.

All in all, however, it does seem that—despite all breaches, errors, and lapses—the allies' political cleansing was rather effective.[24] The majority of Gestapo members were directly affected by the measures and as a rule the main body of officers spent three years in internment camps: a normal internment lasted from mid-1945 to the middle or end of 1948. Camp internment was the harshest of all the political cleansing sanctions available for denazification.[25] This sufficed to trigger a 'profound life-historical crisis' in most Gestapo members,[26] which led the majority into bitterness and despair.

Nonetheless it was still difficult in the mid-1950s to collate incriminating documents on individual Gestapo officers, such as in the case of the former Hamburg Gestapo chief, Bruno Streckenbach.[27] It was only at the end of the fifties, when the crimes of a larger circle of perpetrators came to the attention of the public and judiciary investigations and a large number of criminal trials were instigated, that the state of information about the activities and functional mechanisms of the Gestapo improved. A number of cover-ups from the early phase of denazification were checked again, and knowledge about the extent of the 'SS state' expanded rapidly.[28]

Criminal prosecution in German courts

As of the end of 1945 the allied occupying forces had empowered German courts to pursue any crimes committed against German citizens that could be classified as 'crimes against humanity'. However, German investigative procedures could initially concentrate only on particular sets of offences; the focus rested on the so-called final-phase crimes in the last year of the war. From 1949 onwards more severe crimes could be investigated. On 2 June 1949 the Hamburg Gestapo trial convicted twelve men for their activities in the Hamburg police and Gestapo.[29] A few months later, on 9 November 1949, the biggest trial to date was opened at the High Court in Cologne, against five former members of the local Gestapo office. Here crimes that had been committed *before* the war were investigated for the first time. 160 witnesses and a broad resonance in the media suggested a palpable interest in the judicial and moral treatment of Gestapo activities.[30]

On 1 January 1950 the German courts were finally granted unrestricted jurisdiction, so that they could now in theory conduct more than just individual cases. But investigative activities did not increase immediately, not least because public interest in the legal process noticeably declined during the 1950s—the lowest point was reached in 1954, with 183 cases.[31] Following the foundation of the Federal Republic, all dealings with the Nazi past were clearly influenced by a 'politics of the past', and demands for amnesties for the condemned perpetrators and even for a general amnesty grew louder.[32] In early July 1954 there was another trial against former Gestapo members in Cologne. The public prosecution in the High Court had originally investigated over a hundred former officers of the Cologne Gestapo regarding their involvement in the deportation of Cologne's Jews, but in the end only three individuals were brought before the court and the sentences were mild. The press, too, paid little attention to the trial.[33]

The majority of Gestapo members were not summoned to court, and numerous crimes remained unpunished. The daily human rights violations in the AEL were above all hardly ever brought to court. Criminal prosecution processes in the GDR showed similar tendencies. Although the GDR leadership constantly accused the Federal Republic of integrating Nazi elites into society, and the East German Stasi regularly delivered evidence for show trials, at the same time it blocked investigations against Nazi perpetrators at home if they ran counter to the GDR's propaganda image.[34] After the 'Waldheim Trials', the official view was that all Nazi criminals, and therefore all Gestapo employees, had been brought to justice. Gestapo members still living in the GDR therefore no longer had to fear criminal proceedings, provided they came to terms with the new order.[35] Cases against Nazi criminals were rare, and when they did occur they were treated as show trials. From the mid-1960s onwards one department of the Stasi was occupied with seeking out former National Socialist criminals—although this had more of a political than judicial grounding. However, this landed the Stasi itself in the soup. For their investigations regularly unearthed extensive lists of Einsatzkommando and police battalion members who had lived unchecked in the GDR for over twenty-five years. Nonetheless, the

GDR intended to prosecute only those for whom a life sentence was very likely because of the gravity of their crimes, the burden of proof, and the likelihood of a successful trial. For this was the only way to uphold the GDR's anti-fascist founding myth that there were just a few deplorable individual offenders who had cleverly managed to disguise themselves in the socialist society. It is therefore impossible to say how many Nazi criminals were spared criminal proceedings.[36] The Dresden Gestapo officer Henry Schmidt lived undercover until the end of the 1980s, and until then the Stasi continued to work on bringing him to justice—in an attempt to present the supposedly morally superior Germany to an international audience as the determined persecutor of Nazi crimes.[37] Thus the role played by the division of Germany in the fate of the National Socialist perpetrators was not insignificant, though it is impossible to say with certainty whether it encouraged or hindered the punishment of Nazi crimes. Such conclusions will vary depending on your viewpoint.[38] Regardless of these issues, it is fair to say that both East and West Germany made only sporadic attempts at pursuing Gestapo crimes.

For the former Gestapo officers in the Federal Republic, the early fifties were the least troublesome years: parliament and government were committed to amnesty and integration for former National Socialists. The old functional elites were needed in the re-emerging social order and experts, regardless of their particular focus, could hope for a rapid return to professional life. One of the first laws passed in the Federal Republic was the Immunity Law of 31 December 1949. This amnestied all crimes committed before 15 September 1949 for which the punishment was less than six months, which included bodily harm resulting in death, as long as the perpetrator had not acted out of 'cruelty, dishonour or profit-seeking'. Numerous Gestapo officers now saw the opportunity to emerge from the underground, to profit unashamedly from the new legal situation. 'Now that [...] the law on immunity has been passed, I would not like to miss the opportunity to catch up on my denazification', one Gestapo officer was recorded as saying.[39] And he was by no means an exception: around 700,000 people must have benefited from this law.[40]

The legal scope for prosecuting members of the Gestapo was now hugely restricted. All homicide offences were subject to a period of limitation of fifteen years, after which they could not be brought to court.[41] For murder the limit was originally twenty years. Since most trials investigating NSG crimes only began after 8 May 1960, numerous offenders were no longer legally liable, as many Gestapo officers claimed that they had been dragged along in the chain of command, which generally ruled out a murder charge. A 'procedural trick' could even turn a charge of accessory to murder into manslaughter.[42] From then on only murder could be prosecuted, which required evidence of 'base motives'—a motive that it was ultimately impossible to prove with any former Gestapo officer. In 1979 the limitation period for murder was finally abolished.[43] And yet it transpired that the murder clause in the German penal code was not well suited to deal with state-legitimized persecution on political or racial grounds. The principles of German law did not allow for the ideological foundation of the crimes to be taken into account. For good reason, some see in this a problem inherent in the system: 'because the internal conception and structure of the democratic criminal code is not up to processing a dictatorship'.[44]

This apparently gave the Gestapo officers a sense of security, too. However, the more self-assured the former officers became, and the more they insisted on their supposed right to be reinstated into public service, the more attention the public began to pay. The outspoken performance of the former police chief of Memel, Bernhard Fischer-Schweder, who did not shy away from describing his murderous deeds with the Tilsit Einsatzkommando of Einsatzgruppe A, led in the end to the Ulm Einsatzgruppen trial, which set the stage for a new, large wave of trials against Nazi perpetrators and which can therefore be seen as a turning-point in the history of the NSG trials. After the years of 'conscious silence' between 1949 and 1958, the public had clearly been sensitized once again and considered it necessary for Nazi crimes to be dealt with strictly by the state justice system.[45] A series of major scandals that sent shockwaves through the whole republic during the sixties increased the sense that there was a serious problem. Ever more critical questions were being asked: whether the democratic Federal Republic had really shed its National Socialist heritage or whether it was in fact still contaminated by old Nazis, as SED propaganda never tired of emphasizing. As we now know, the GDR had also integrated numerous tainted figures, whose existence was kept quiet for political reasons. In the West things were different: there it was now clear 'that investigations had to precede the punishment of Nazi crimes against which criminal proceedings had not yet been brought, and that these investigations had to surpass significantly all the state prosecution's prior attempts to shed light on the crimes'.[46] For this reason the Central Office of the State Justice Administrations was founded in Ludwigsburg in December 1958, which in the following years systematized the known facts about Nazi crimes and soon began to co-ordinate thousands of NSG trials.[47] The murders committed by the Einsatzgruppen in occupied Eastern Europe formed one focus of the investigations. The continuing investigations by public prosecutors and—linked to these—the shift in public opinion, which pushed for former Nazi perpetrators to be punished, may have resulted in only a few Gestapo officers ending up in prison, but it did rob several others of a quiet retirement. Many were called to the witness stand for the first time. Michael Wildt's description of the RSHA leadership can also be applied to most Gestapo officers: the self-assuredness, the ignorance, and the reluctance to engage in self-reflection started to falter in the 1960s, when a new social climate, supported by the assiduous work of a group of committed public prosecutors, confronted the former Gestapo members with their earlier deeds.[48]

Even if most Gestapo members got off scot-free, the efforts to prosecute have proved to be important and valuable to this day. Countless witnesses and former participants were interrogated, the backgrounds to individual deeds were reconstructed, and Gestapo mechanisms were re-created. The quality of historical research on the Nazi era, which we now take for granted and which has made this era perhaps the most intensively investigated and most widely discussed in history, has its foundation in these investigations: the court documents are an important and irreplaceable historical source which hugely extend our understanding of the crimes—which indeed, in some cases, have made that understanding possible in the first place.[49]

The Frankfurt Auschwitz Trial, which began on 20 December 1963 at the High Court in Frankfurt am Main and was known officially as 'Criminal Case against Mulka et al., Reference 4 KS 2/63', is also to be viewed in this light. The trial lasted 20 months and took in 183 court days, on which a total of 359 witnesses were heard, including 248 former inmates of Auschwitz. The trial was the most significant attempt to prosecute the genocide in a systematic fashion, and to devote its investigations fully to this aim: it intended to shed light on the horrific events. The general public prosecutor in Hessen, Fritz Bauer, took great pains to initiate and maintain the investigations. Around 1,500 witnesses were questioned in the pre-trial hearings alone, which concluded in October 1962—more than in any prior case. The Auschwitz Trial became the longest and most comprehensive High Court trial in German legal history. It revealed to the public the full extent of the Nazi crimes.[50] These included the acts committed by Wilhelm Boger as the Gestapo representative in the camp's political department.

Fenced in by the huge number of trials, most Gestapo members attempted to play down their part in the crimes and to trivialize their own level of responsibility. This is displayed most clearly in the case of Adolf Eichmann, whose defence during the whole trial against him in Jerusalem was repeatedly based on the notion that he had only acted on orders and according to the Führer principle, and was therefore not culpable in a legal sense. He also claimed never to have directly participated in the murder or deportation of people, but as a 'cog in the system' had merely passed on orders—an attitude that was later summarized by Hannah Arendt as the 'banality of evil'. Eichmann was condemned to death on 15 December 1961 and executed on 1 June

1962. But it was not only Eichmann; most Gestapo officers also claimed not to have known about the extent of the persecution or they argued that only those 'principally responsible' in the Nazi state were guilty, on whom justice had already been passed in Nuremberg or in the other allied military trials. As individual Gestapo members, they styled themselves as characters who only did what was demanded of them, without ever getting an insight into the bigger picture. As we have seen, this was not the case.

The Frankfurt Auschwitz Trial was the biggest Nazi case in the history of the Federal Republic. But there might have been an even bigger trial a few years later. In 1963 the public prosecutors in Berlin began comprehensive investigations against employees of the Reich Security Main Office and members of the Berlin Gestapo. If the RSHA Trial had actually taken place, it would probably have been the biggest and most significant trial not only concerning the murder of European Jews but also the crimes committed against Poles, Soviet prisoners of war, forced labourers, 'asocials', and other victims.[51] But things took a different course: the investigations were concluded in March 1967, and in nineteen cases the matter was brought to court. Most Gestapo members had died in the meantime or couldn't be tried due to insufficient evidence. Others could not be located. On 22 February 1969 the general public prosecution in Berlin's Supreme Court finally raised charges and applied for trials against eight defendants. The final main trial was only against three of them, lasting 16 months and ending without sentence for all three defendants. The trial against the main accused, Otto Bovensiepen, was closed after he suffered a heart attack. The remaining defendants were acquitted because, according to the existing legal principles, their liability for the deport-ation of Jews from Berlin could not be proven. From today's view-point the result is unsatisfying and inadequate: 'Although the Berlin deportations were researched in minute detail, although a majority of those responsible were named and arrested, although these figures admitted some involvement in the deportations, the extermination of Berlin's Jewish population has remained unpunished and unatoned.'[52]

A second, no less spectacular case arose from the failed RSHA trial: on 11 March 1969 Werner Best was arrested in his flat in Mülheim an der Ruhr and brought to Berlin. As head of Department I of the Gestapa he had been responsible for the deployment of the Einsatz-gruppen in Poland. For this reason the public prosecutors considered him to be a major perpetrator, responsible for the tens of thousands of murders committed in autumn 1939. The fact that Best had not even been interrogated as witness or accused during the years of investiga-tions in the RSHA case is only superficially surprising: he held a doctorate in law, was the theoretical and organizational mind of the RSHA, and had excellent contacts in post-war Germany. When deal-ing with Best the public prosecutors could allow themselves no weakness or error—if a case against such an exposed figure should fail it would have fatal consequences for future Nazi trials. The con-tinuing investigations were extensive but successful, and the docu-ments gathered would likely have led to Best's conviction. However, the trial was never opened because Best changed his strategy: realizing that the burden of proof was overwhelming, he chose the 'medical' path. Several references cast doubt on whether he would be fit to face a long trial—and thus in August 1972 the court decided to adjourn the case. The most ambitious NSG case alongside the RSHA case had failed. For the last seventeen years of his life, Werner Best remained free.[53]

However, not all attempts at large and even spectacular trials failed. This was evident in the case against Kurt Lischka, formerly head of the Berlin Gestapo headquarters as well as temporary chief of the Paris Gestapo, whose conviction was brought about above all by Serge and Beate Klarsfeld through their public protests and attempted kidnap-ping.[54] On 23 October 1979 the trial against Lischka and two of his colleagues was opened at the Regional Court in Cologne, which ended with Lischka being sentenced to 10 years in prison, of which he served two-thirds. Herbert Hagen, head of the security police and SD field office in Bordeaux, was sentenced to 12 years for accessory to murder. However, this was only possible because charges had been brought as early as 1960 and the results of preliminary investigations were held by the Central Office in Ludwigsburg. This meant that the period of limitation was interrupted and the accused did not fall under the 'cold amnesty'.[55] But these convictions do not suggest that the treatment of NSG crimes had changed across the board: they must instead be seen 'as an exception rather than a consistent development in the Federal Republic'.[56] The former Gestapo chief of Auschwitz, Johannes Hermann Thümmler, a fanatical agent of National Socialist racial politics, was never brought before a court despite several attempts.[57] The majority of Gestapo employees could make a cosy life for themselves in post-war Germany, some leading respectable careers.

Careers in post-war Germany

In their defence statements the former Gestapo employees revealed their inability and unwillingness to reflect on the past from a moral viewpoint. They also refused to admit their own transgressions for fear of criminal proceedings. The Gestapo men often remained indifferent to their own past. Barely any of them could manage a word of pity, let alone remorse. And yet the political cleansing set in motion a collective process of detachment from the National Socialist past, which took root in the politically secure and economically prosperous Federal Republic. By blanking out their own responsibility within the National Socialist police apparatus, the Gestapo members created their own new reality, in which there was no longer any room for memories of earlier activities. If we consider this attitude to be based on a superficial rejection of the National Socialist past, albeit only a rhetorical denial, then the denazification and cleansing measures at the end of the war must have been more successful than they at first seemed.[58] After the unpleasant experiences of the post-war years, no Gestapo officer wanted to stick his head above the parapet as a result of his former duties. The once so feared persecutors now wanted above all never to leave the normal world of the average German in West and East. And in both the Federal Republic and the GDR they found a politics of the past that made it possible to live unobtrusively. As it became increasingly clear that the Bonn Republic was a highly successful undertaking, because it was politically stable and economically prosperous, so it became easier for the former Gestapo employees to adapt to the new status quo.

In the East some even managed to make their way into SED structures, which then also promised a certain stability.[59] But most withdrew into a quiet, inconspicuous, and largely unpolitical private life. An association of former Gestapo officers was never established—not least because leading defence strategists such as Werner Best did not consider it politically opportune. Numerous Gestapo officers adapted to the new norms of the democratic state and accepted that it was necessary to distance themselves—at least in a rhetorical sense—from National Socialism, particularly as this presented them with the prospect of professional continuity and precluded criminal proceedings. The same applied in the GDR insofar as former National Socialists were particularly quick to agree to co-operate with the Stasi if that spared them criminal proceedings and exclusion from society. This form of state-legitimized opportunism, fostered by many former Gestapo members, may be reprehensible from a moral viewpoint. But it did contribute to the fact that the feared members of the National Socialist police apparatus were transformed into a relatively harmless troop of adapted individuals, who subordinated themselves either to the new democratic and market-oriented structures of the West or to the real socialist conditions of the East.[60]

While this integration tended to pass off quietly in the GDR, so that the claims of the anti-fascist state were not undermined, in West Germany things operated to a degree in the open. In the Federal Republic, an important step on the path towards professional reintegration for the former Gestapo members was therefore undertaken by the legislature: in article 131 of the Basic Law the young Federal Republic obliged itself 'to regulate through federal legislation [...] the legal position of persons including refugees and displaced persons (*Vertriebene*), who were in public service on 8 May 1945, were discharged for reasons other than civil service law or collective bargaining law, and have not or not yet been employed in their previous position'.[61] This article was actually intended to rehabilitate those in the service of the state who had lost their livelihoods at the end of the war, such as former career soldiers and civil servants for the military, or refugees and expellees from the former Eastern lands. Soon, however, the obligation to re-employ was also applied to those who had lost their jobs in the West after the war because of their culpability as Nazis. A short time later there was political consensus that the 'victims' of the allied cleansing should be granted a return to public service.[62]

The first implementation law of 11 May 1951 contained a regulation along these lines.[63] Public employers were obliged to make 20 per cent of their planned positions available for those from the '131' category. Until such a position was allocated, the person entitled to maintenance had to be paid a transitional benefit, which greatly increased the pressure to appoint incriminated individuals. In Schleswig-Holstein employers even boasted of having re-employed 50 per cent of those affected—far more than the law had originally intended.[64]

Those who had lost their posts during denazification now got their entitlement to maintenance and work prospects back. Certain regional regulations even made it possible for those who were politically incriminated to find their way back into public life.[65] The Gestapo officers were originally supposed to be expressly exempt from this regulation, as noted in paragraph 3 of the law. However, paragraph 67 provided an exception, which allowed Gestapo officers to be included as long as they had been transferred to the persecuting authority 'ex officio'. This apparently unspectacular passage permitted a majority of the Gestapo personnel to count themselves in the '131' category from the outset; for all those who had started their police careers before the Gestapo was founded, or who as criminal or order police were drafted into the Gestapo later, were considered to have been transferred 'ex officio'. An 'ex officio' transfer was therefore by no means the same thing as a transfer 'against one's will'. This, however, is precisely what countless former policemen in the service of the Gestapo asserted, in order to cover up their actual motives—careerism or professional ambition. Although exact figures are not available, it is safe to assume that almost half of all Gestapo members benefited from the 131 regulation.[66] The numerous amendments, exemption clauses, and special provisions that followed even made it possible to transfer one's former Gestapo rank to the new position or to have it taken into account in pension calculations. It also soon became possible for promotions to be taken into account, in particular if a higher position would have been reached in any case, such as if the particular officer had not been transferred 'ex officio' to the Gestapo.[67] There was a certain automatism in all amendments: as soon as it could be ascertained that an 'ex officio' Gestapo officer could not be accused of any personal transgressions or crimes, he was able to enjoy *all* the perks that had been generated over time.[68] As denazification continued to lose intensity from 1948 onwards, once seriously incriminated Gestapo members were transformed into simple police officers, who were soon handed deeds of honour declaring 'gratitude and recognition for 40 years of faithful service'. Around a third of the Gestapo chiefs of 1938 managed to reach a position appropriate to their qualifications in the Federal Republic.[69] As a rule the employment structures followed the pre-1933 model. Only those who had already been found guilty of a serious charge in a Spruchkammer case were fully excluded from professional rehabilitation.[70]

Along with this legally regulated re-employment in public service, other career paths were open to former members of the Gestapo. Those who had joined the service from other sectors and therefore had no police training were dependent on alternatives outside of public service, and the prospects were far from rosy. Many sought a simple and inconspicuous career or attempted to live off sporadic state benefits or their own family. In these cases most were granted a state benefit that covered subsistence, in the main in the context of a partial pardon. Leading Gestapo officers with a legal background, on the other hand, either worked as independent lawyers, in the semi-public arena of union management, or found work in the private sector. In April 1950 Johannes Hermann Thümmler, former Gestapo chief of Chemnitz and Auschwitz, found a position as an unskilled worker for the Zeiss Optics factory in Oberkochen, advancing quickly to a position in the accounts department, and finally becoming head of the company's economic department and managing director of the independent Zeiss construction company.[71] Werner Best worked as legal adviser for the Stinnes firm in Mülheim an der Ruhr, where a number of his former colleagues had also found positions in industry. In the early 1950s Best even attempted to infiltrate the FDP association of North-Rhine-Westfalia along with other former National Socialists, although he was unsuccessful.

Those Gestapo officers who were able to present themselves as experts in enemy surveillance and counter-espionage could hope for a particular appointment. The secret service in both East and West Germany recruited former high-ranking Nazi functionaries as agents: in this way, heavily incriminated war criminals found jobs. These people were desired because of their informal knowledge as well as their connections to former SS comrades. The higher their status and function within the Nazi regime, the more the secret services seemed to want them on board. It has been widely researched that the Stasi also systematically and intentionally recruited Nazi perpetrators as informants and agents in the West and East.[72] Erich Weinmann, head of the 'Occupied Zones' group in Office IV of the RSHA and from 1942 Commanding Officer of the Security Police and SD in Prague, is thought to have been involved in constructing an Egyptian secret service from the mid-1950s onwards. Three other leading RSHA figures worked for the intelligence service of the Federal Republic after the war.[73] One of the most spectacular appointments is that of Heinz Felfe, a former SD leader, in the Gehlen organization. Felfe brought a whole coterie of SD comrades with him, who all worked as double agents for the KGB.[74] There were also rumours that the former head of Office IV in the Reich Security Main Office, the notorious 'Gestapo-Müller', worked for a foreign secret service—in Washington or Moscow, depending on the political position of the observer.

Others claimed to have seen him in South America. However, none of the clues was well-founded, and nothing was proved. The only sure thing is that Heinrich Müller's mystifying disappearance nourished once again the myth of the mysterious power of the Gestapo—a myth that to a degree continues to this day.

CONCLUSION: WHAT REMAINS OF THE GESTAPO?

Despite all the myth-making, in its bureaucratic set-up the Gestapo was a police authority like many others: it created files, recorded investigations, and interrogated suspects. In terms of criminal investigation techniques it was unsurpassed in its time. Apart from the top functionaries of the Reich Security Main Office, who came from the SD, most of those who served in the Gestapo were ordinary police officers. In one sense this is not surprising, as persecution was a craft that became normal practice for a policeman. But all this did not exclude participation in 'special operations'. On the contrary, Gestapo employees were expressly encouraged to take part in the extra-legal abuse and murder of disenfranchised groups. In the event, most officers were involved in these crimes. Bureaucracy and terror were by no means mutually exclusive, they were two sides of the same coin: the terrorist side of the Gestapo spread fear, while the bureaucratic side ensured efficiency.

The Gestapo was supported by a large number of helpers, from amongst the police, the state administration, Nazi Party members, and the general population. It therefore amounted to more than the sum of its official officers and employees. Terror and rule had a broad foundation. Mobilization, repression, social conformity (*Gleichschaltung*), and the persecution of dissidents: all this was accepted by the majority of the population. This proved fundamental to the Gestapo's functioning: in some respects it legitimized an authority which could then set itself up as a self-proclaimed elite of enemy persecution, as a 'doctor for the German national body', and surround itself with a myth of omniscience. It was assumed that Gestapo spies were at large in every inn, in every association, that their informants were lurking in every bus and tram. The supposed danger of being denounced and punished for a thoughtless remark intensified the climate of fear. This could only please the Gestapo: people were to believe that paid and unpaid spies lurked at every corner, and that the police were in the know about everything.

Influenced by this intentional self-image, but above all directly affected by state police measures, the persecuted painted a picture of a strong, powerful Gestapo.[1] Contemporaries considered the secret police apparatus of persecution to be a highly effective organization, which achieved everything that it set out to do. The myth of an omnipotent Gestapo was further established in the final weeks of the Nazi regime and indiscriminately projected back onto the whole Nazi era by the press—which also helped individuals to legitimize their own participation in the 'Third Reich'.[2] The idea that the Gestapo had been an omnipresent organization was then further promoted by the theory of totalitarianism propagated in the 1950s. It was only in the 1990s that historiography began to scrutinize the myth and to assess the historical Gestapo according to its actual deeds.[3] The fact that this myth could be sustained for such a long time must also have to do with the numerous comparisons that have been made across the world between any secret police work and the Gestapo. How many Hitlers or Himmlers, how many Gestapos were identified after 1945? Did this not, beyond all rhetoric, give rise to modes of evaluation that have also influenced the implicit memory of the historical Gestapo? Today 'Gestapo' is still a metaphor, a shibboleth, used to devalue unpleasant institutions and to vilify.

So the question returns: what remains of the Gestapo? The awareness that it was neither an accident of German history nor of the German police. The Gestapo was not an artificial product grafted onto German society—however artificial the police structures of the Nazi system might have been. In terms of personnel and its institutional structure, it was more an individual growth which, after producing its ugly buds, was able to disappear once again into the undergrowth of bureaucracy, civil service, and state loyalty. In a moral respect this post-war regression was bought at too high a price for many observers. However, if you consider that an association of Gestapo veterans has never been founded, and that thanks to numerous investigations such as the Auschwitz Trial or the cases investigated by the Central Office of the State Justice Administrations in Ludwigsburg a remarkable level of knowledge has been reached about terror and rule in the Third Reich, the balance sheet of dealing with the past is not only negative: the end of the Gestapo was and is definitive. New versions and continuations should not, may not, and will not develop.

In order to uphold the 'Never Again' maxim, at the bidding of the allies the founding fathers of the Federal Republic developed a principle that resulted from the negative experience of the Gestapo: the imperative to separate police and intelligent services. Intelligence duties, which were traditionally carried out by the political police, are still today the responsibility of the regional authorities and of the Federal Office for the Protection of the Constitution (*Bundesamt für Verfassungsschutz*), which nonetheless do not have executive functions.[4] The police, on the other hand, are dependent on the investigations and enquiries of the intelligence service. On the whole, this division of duties works very well in practice.

Nevertheless, in a time of global war against terrorism some of these lines of separation are once again the subject of discussion: it is said that the large amount of information that has to pass between police and intelligence services lessens the effectiveness of the security services. Some go even further: the military should be deployed for the good of internal security as well. What is conceived as a sign of strength turns into its opposite: military deployment at home is the sign of a weak state.[5]

At the same time, notions of preventive policing are also once again finding a voice: it is surely for the best if the criminal or terrorist is investigated and neutralized before they commit their crime. The notion of pre-emptive control and increased surveillance, coupled with the call for harsher and marginalizing punishments, is becoming increasingly accepted in the Western world.[6] The prohibition of torture is no longer a taboo in this context, either. It is sobering to note that, in the wake of a debate about security policy, the central achievements brought about through the defeat of a dictatorship can be challenged again so quickly. To prevent misunderstandings: we are not seeking to instrumentalize the history of the Gestapo, its ideological objectives and criminal acts, in the service of current debates about internal security. The gravity and sheer extent of the crimes committed alone makes this inappropriate. However, the Gestapo was more than just a purely historical phenomenon. It makes it very clear what people are capable of when state power gives them a mandate. If this power is corrupt or perverted, and based on the wrong values, then this leads to criminal acts. The individual agents are often not aware of any moral guilt, but are rather convinced that they are doing the right thing. The question of how such developments might be prevented in the future is relevant today.

GLOSSARY OF TERMS

Official Titles, Organizations, Abbreviations

Abschnitt An SS district

AEL Arbeitserziehungslager (Work Education Camps), Gestapo-run detention centres active from 1939/40 until the end of the war

BdS Befehlshaber der Sicherheitspolizei und des SD (Commanding Officer of the Security Police and SD), heads of RSHA field offices during the war. Some took over the roles of IdS

Block leader (Blockleiter) Nazi Party representative responsible for the political supervision of a particular neighbourhood. Subordinate to a Cell leader (Zellenleiter)

Block warden (Blockwart) Nazi Party representative responsible for the political supervision of a particular neighbourhood

Bürgermeister Mayor of a town and, depending on its size, responsible either to the Landrat or to the Regierungspräsident but with certain autonomous powers under the principle of 'self-administration' (*Selbstverwaltung*)

County administrator (Landrat) civil-service official in charge of a district roughly the size of an English rural district council and subordinate to the Regierungspräsident

DAF (Deutsche Arbeitsfront) German Labour Front, National Socialist trade union organization

District governor (Regierungspräsident) civil-service official in charge of a district roughly the size of an average English county

EG Einsatzgruppe der Sicherheitspolizei und des SD, security police and SD groups operating behind army lines as the German army advanced eastwards during the Second World War. Particularly responsible for the murders of Jews and partisans. Sub-groups known as Einsatzkommandos

Free Corps (Freikorps) armed groups of volunteers made up of anti-revolutionary and anti-democratic soldiers returning from the battlefields of the First World War

Gauleiter Head of a Nazi Party Gau, a district the size of a large city or province

Gestapa Geheimes Staatspolizeiamt (Secret State Police Office), the

headquarters in Berlin of the secret
state police (Gestapo)
Gestapo Geheime Staatspolizei (the
secret state [political] police)
HSSPF Höhere SS- und Polizeiführer
(Higher SS and Police Leader);
senior SS official in charge of the
SS and police in a large region
IdS Inspekteur der Sicherheitspolizei
und des SD (Inspector of the
Security Police and SD), new office
established in 1936 to secure the
centralization of the security police
and SD at a regional level and to
prepare for the mobilization of the
Gestapo and Kripo. During the war
its main function became the
complete fusion of the security
police and SD into a National
Socialist state security force. To
this end, it gradually took over the
functions of regional Gestapo
offices, and some inspectorates
were turned into commanding
officer stations (BdS)
IKL Inspektion der
Konzentrationslager
(Concentration Camp Inspector
[ate])
KdS Kommandeur der
Sicherheitspolizei und des SD
(Commander of the Security Police
and SD), subordinate to BdS in
RSHA field offices during the war.
KL/KZ Konzentrationslager
(concentration camp)
KPD Kommunistische Partei
Deutschlands (German
Communist Party)
Kripo Kriminalpolizei (Criminal
Police Department)
NSDAP Nationalsozialistische
Deutsche Arbeiterpartei (National

Socialist German Workers Party =
the Nazi Party)
Oberabschnitt An SS district larger
than an Abschnitt
OKH Oberkommando des Heeres
(Army High Command)
Old Reich (Altreich) Germany in its
pre-1938 borders
Ostland The Baltic States and
Byelorussia (White Russia)
Reich Governor (Reichsstatthalter)
the most senior official in a federal
state (Land), a new post introduced
in 1933 and normally held by a
Gauleiter
RFSS Reichsführer-SS
RKF Reichskommissar(iat) fur die
Festigung deutschen Volkstums
(Reich Commissar[iat] for the
Consolidation of the Ethnic
German Nation), Himmler's
official post and office
co-ordinating all resettlement
programmes, initially confined to
Poland, but eventually extended to
the whole of German-occupied
Europe
RSHA Reichssicherheitshauptamt
(the Reich Security Main Office),
established in 1939 to bring the
Security Police (Gestapo and
Kripo) and SD under one roof
SA Sturmabteilung (lit. Storm
Department = stormtroopers)
SAP Sozialistische Arbeiterpartei
Deutschlands (German Socialist
Workers' Party)
SD Sicherheitsdienst (Security
Service), Nazi party organization
established by the SS in 1931 as an
intelligence operation. Originally
partly a kind of ideological think-
tank for gathering information on

and developing policy towards
Nazism's ideological opponents,
it began to acquire executive
functions in the late 1930s

Sipo Sicherheitspolizei (Security
police), an amalgamation in 1936
of the Gestapo and Criminal
police, though the two retained
distinct organizations

SPD Sozialdemokratische Partei
Deutschlands (German Social
Democratic Party)

SS Schutzstaffel (Protection squad)

SSPF SS- und Polizeiführer (SS and
Police Leader)

Stapo Gestapo

State Secretary (Staatssekretär)
the most senior permanent
civil-service official in a ministry

völkisch Term dating from c.1900
denoting an ideology and
movement that stressed the
importance of ethnicity in
determining national identity and
considered that human mentalities
and behaviour and national
cultures were largely shaped by
race/ethnicity ('blood') and that
there was a qualitative hierarchy of
ethnicities. These beliefs were
usually accompanied by
anti-Semitism

Volkssturm A home guard
established 25 September 1944

Waffen-SS Armed SS, the military
organization of the SS

Werwolf A commando force
operating behind enemy lines as
the allied armies advanced into
Germany

z.b.V. (*zur besonderen Verwendung*) 'for
special assignment'

Table of SS Officers' Ranks

	British Army	US Army
SS-Obergruppenführer	Lieutenant-General	Lieutenant-General
SS-Gruppenführer	Major-General	Major-General
SS-Brigadeführer	Brigadier	Brigadier-General
SS-Oberführer	Senior Colonel	Senior Colonel
SS-Obersturmbannführer	Lieutenant-Colonel	Lieutenant-Colonel
SS-Untersturmführer	Second Lieutenant	Second Lieutenant

NOTES

Abbreviations

BA	Bundesarchiv Berlin
GLA	Generallandesarchiv Karlsruhe
GStA PK	Geheimes Staatsarchiv Preußischer Kulturbesitz Berlin
HStAD	Hauptstaatsarchiv Düsseldorf
IMT	*International Military Tribunal*
MBliV	Ministerialblatt für die innere Verwaltung
RGBl	Reichsgesetzblatt
SAPMO-DDR	Stiftung Archiv der Parteien und Massenorganisationen der DDR im Bundesarchiv Berlin
StALB	Staatsarchiv Ludwigsburg
StAMS	Staatsarchiv Münster

Preface

1. Reinhard Heydrich, 'Politisches Soldatentum in der Polizei', in *Völkischer Beobachter*, 17 February 1941.

2. Alfred Schweder, *Politische Polizei. Wesen und Begründung der politischen Polizei im Metternichschen System, in der Weimarer Republik und im nationalsozialistischen Staate*, Phil. Diss. (Berlin, 1937), 164.

3. Franz Neumann, *Behemoth: The Structure and Practice of National Socialism* (New York, 2009), 546. First published in 1942, without the appendix from which this quotation is taken.

4. Ernst Fraenkel, *The Dual State: A Contribution to the Theory of Dictatorship* (Clark, NJ, 2006), 28. First published in 1941.

5. Carsten Dams, *Staatsschutz in der Weimarer Republik. Die Überwachung und Bekämpfung der NSDAP durch die preußische politische Polizei von 1928 bis 1932* (Marburg, 2002); Michael Stolle, *Die Geheime Staatspolizei in Baden. Personal, Organisation, Wirkung und Nachwirken einer regionalen Verfolgungsbehörde im Dritten Reich* (Constance, 2001). See in particular the following essay collections: Gerhard Paul and Klaus-Michael Mallmann (eds), *Die Gestapo. Mythos und Realität* (Darmstadt, 1995); Gerhard Paul and Klaus-Michael Mallmann (eds), *Die Gestapo im Zweiten Weltkrieg. 'Heimatfront' und besetztes Europa* (Darmstadt, 2000).

6. For example: Edward Crankshaw, *Gestapo: Instrument of Tyranny* (London, 1956); Jacques Delarue, *The Gestapo: A History of Horror* (London, 2008); Jochen von Lang, *Die Gestapo. Instrument des Terrors* (Hamburg, 1990); Frank Gutermuth and Arno Netzbandt, *Die Gestapo* (Berlin, 2005).

1. Foundation and Early Years

1. Joseph Goebbels, *Die Tagebücher von Joseph Goebbels. Sämtliche Fragmente*, ed. Elke Fröhlich, Teil I. *Aufzeichnungen 1924–1941*, vol. 2 (Munich, 1987), 40.
2. Dams, *Staatsschutz*, 67–119.
3. Memorandum 'Die Nationalsozialistische Deutsche Arbeiterpartei', in *Staat und NSDAP. 1930–1932. Quellen zur Ära Brüning*, introd. Gerhard Schulz, ed. Ilse Maurer and Udo Wengst (Düsseldorf, 1977), 75 f. There is a complete copy in the GStA PK, I. HA, Rep. 84 a, Nr. 3157, Bl. 23–122.
4. Stolle, *Geheime Staatspolizei*, 46.
5. Christoph Gusy, *Weimar—die wehrlose Republik? Verfassungsschutzrecht und Verfassungsschutz in der Weimarer Republik* (Tübingen, 1991).
6. Dams, *Staatsschutz*, 53–66.
7. Martin Faatz, *Vom Staatsschutz zum Gestapo-Terror. Politische Polizei in Bayern in der Endphase der Weimarer Republik und der Anfangsphase der nationalsozialistischen Diktatur* (Würzburg, 1995), 144; James H. MacGee, *The Political Police in Bavaria*, Phil. Diss. (University of Florida, 1980), 278.
8. *Gestapo Oldenburg meldet... Berichte der Geheimen Staatspolizei und des Innenministers aus dem Freistaat und Land Oldenburg 1933–1936*, ed. and introd. Albrecht Eckhardt and Katharina Hoffmann (Hanover, 2002), 17.
9. Christoph Graf, *Politische Polizei zwischen Demokratie und Diktatur. Die Entwicklung der preußischen Politischen Polizei vom Staatsschutzorgan der Weimarer Republik zum Geheimen Staatspolizeiamt des Dritten Reiches* (Berlin, 1983), 90.
10. Carsten Dams, 'Kontinuitäten und Brüche. Die höheren preußischen Kriminalbeamten im Übergang von der Weimarer Republik zum Nationalsozialismus', in *Kriminalistik* 58 (2004), 478–83 (p. 480).
11. Dams, *Staatsschutz*, 177.
12. Karl Schäfer, *20 Jahre im Polizeidienst (1925–1945)* (Heusenstamm, 1977), 21.
13. 'Polizei-Anzeiger des Polizei-Präsidium Bochum', Nr. 25, of 24 December 1932, in StAMS, Polizeipräsidien, Nr. 206, Bl. 112 ff.; 'Namentliches Verzeichnis der Beamten der politischen Polizei in Bochum und Dortmund', of 1 April 1933, in StAMS, Reg. Arnsberg, Nr. 14 601, Bl. 14; 'Durchsicht aller Nachweisungen der Staatspolizeistellen über die beschäftigten männlichen Kräfte des Innen- und Außendienstes nach dem Stande vom 25. Juni 1935', in GStA PK, I. HA, Rep. 90 P, Nr. 14, Heft 2.
14. 'Der Polizeipräsident Aachen an den Regierungspräsidenten Aachen', 6 October 1934, in HStAD, BR 1031/185, Bl. 210 ff.; 'Amtliche Bekanntmachung des Polizeipräsidenten Köln', 24 September 1931, in NS-Dokumentationszentrum

der Stadt Köln, 24 September 1931; 'Nachweisung aller männlichen Kräfte des Innen- und Außendienstes der Staatspolizeistelle Köln', 25 June 1935, in GStA PK, I. HA, Rep. 90 P, Nr. 14, Heft 2; Volker Eichler, 'Organisation, Struktur und Schriftgutüberlieferung der Gestapo in Frankfurt am Main', in *Frankfurt am Main. Lindenstraße, Gestapozentrale und Widerstand,* ed. Institut für Stadtgeschichte (Frankfurt am Main and New York, 1996), 71–85 (p. 72).

15. Evaluation of the personnel database at the *Institut für Zeit- und Regionalgeschichte* in Schleswig in 1998, checked against the male personnel in domestic and field service at Kiel state police station as of 26 June 1935, in GStA PK, I. HA Rep. 90 P, Nr. 14, Heft 2.

16. Robert Gellately, *The Gestapo and German Society: Enforcing Racial Policy 1933–1945* (Oxford, 1990), 50–4.

17. Law concerning the Institution of a Secret State Police Office of 26 April 1933, in *Preußische Gesetzsammlung 1933,* 122.

18. Reinhard Rürup (ed.), *Topographie des Terrors. Gestapo, SS und Reichssicherheitshauptamt auf dem 'Prinz-Albrecht-Gelände'. Eine Dokumentation* (Berlin, 2005), 11.

19. Law concerning the Institution of a Secret State Police Office of 26 April 1933, in *Preußische Gesetzsammlung 1933,* 122.

20. Decree by the Minister of the Interior regarding the new organization of the political police of 26 April 1933, in MBliV 1933, Sp. 503–07 (Sp. 503).

21. Andreas Schwegel, *Der Polizeibegriff im NS-Staat. Polizeirecht, juristische Publizistik und Judikative 1931–1944* (Tübingen, 2005), 46.

22. Graf, *Politische Polizei,* 420 ff.

23. Holger Berschel, *Bürokratie und Terror. Das Judenreferat der Gestapo Düsseldorf 1935–1945* (Essen, 2001), 76 f.

2. Organizational Development

1. Gellately, *The Gestapo,* 38.

2. George C. Browder, *Foundations of the Nazi Police State: The Formation of Sipo and SD* (Lexington, 1990), 96–116; cf. Peter Longerich, *Heinrich Himmler: A Life* (Oxford, 2012), 155–61.

3. Ludwig Eiber, *Unter Führung des NSDAP-Gauleiters. Die Hamburger Staatspolizei (1933–1937),* in Paul and Mallmann, *Die Gestapo,* 101–17 (pp. 103 ff.); Stolle, *Die Geheime Staatspolizei,* 80 ff.

4. Josef Ackermann, 'Heinrich Himmler—"Reichsführer-SS"', in Ronald Smelser, Enrico Syring, and Rainer Zitelmann (eds), *Die Braune Elite 1: 22 Biographische Skizzen* (Darmstadt, 1999), 115–333; Johannes Tuchel, 'Heinrich Himmler: Der Reichsführer-SS', in Ronald Smelser and Enrico Syring (eds), *Die SS. Elite unter dem Totenkopf* (Paderborn, 2003), 234–53; Longerich, *Heinrich Himmler.*

5. *Der Dienstkalender Heinrich Himmlers 1941/42,* ed. and with commentary and introduction by Peter Witte et al. (Hamburg 1999), 22.

6. Robert L. Koehl. *The Black Corps: The Structure and Power Struggle of the Nazi SS* (Madison, Wisconsin, 1983), 32, 53, 79.
7. Peter Longerich, *Geschichte der SA* (Munich, 2003), 206–19. Hans-Ulrich Thamer, *Der Nationalsozialismus* (Stuttgart, 2002), 168–77.
8. Ian Kershaw, *Hitler 1889–1936: Hubris* (London, 1998), 500–17.
9. Günter Neliba, *Wilhelm Frick. Der Legalist des Unrechtsstaates. Eine politische Biographie* (Paderborn, 1992), 248–51.
10. Friedrich Wilhelm, *Die Polizei im NS-Staat. Die Geschichte ihrer Organisation im Überblick* (Paderborn, 1997), 73.
11. Michael Wildt, *An Uncompromising Generation: The Nazi Leadership of the Reich Security Main Office* (Madison, 2009), 133–5.
12. Werner Best, 'Der Reichsführer-SS und Chef der Deutschen Polizei', in *Deutsches Recht* 6 (1936), 257 f.
13. Browder, *Foundations*, 163–200; Longerich, *Himmler*, 180–201.
14. Patrick Wagner, *Hitlers Kriminalisten. Die deutsche Kriminalpolizei und der Nationalsozialismus zwischen 1920 und 1960* (Munich, 2002); Wagner, *Volksgemeinschaft ohne Verbrecher. Konzeptionen und Praxis der Kriminalpolizei in der Zeit der Weimarer Republik und des Nationalsozialismus* (Hamburg, 1996).
15. Decree by the Reichsführer-SS and Chief of the German Police regarding the consistent naming of Secret State Police offices in the Reich, 28 August 1936, in RMBliV 1936, Sp. 1344–1346.
16. Gellately, *The Gestapo*, 42.
17. Ulrich Herbert, *Best. Biographische Studien über Radikalismus, Weltanschauung und Vernunft 1903–1989* (Bonn, 2001), 150–61.
18. Law concerning the Secret State Police, 10 February 1936, in *Preußische Gesetzsammlung 1936*, 21 f. (p. 21).
19. George C. Browder: 'The Numerical Strength of the Sicherheitsdienst des RFSS', *Historical Social Research* 28 (1983), 30–41.
20. Wildt, *An Uncompromising Generation*, 145.
21. George C. Browder, 'Die frühe Entwicklung des SD. Das Entstehen multipler institutioneller Identitäten', in Michael Wildt (ed.), *Nachrichtendienst, politische Elite, Mordeinheit. Der Sicherheitsdienst des Reichsführers-SS* (Hamburg, 2003), 38–56 (p. 41).
22. *Organisation der Geheimen Staatspolizei* (no date), in BA R 58/781, Bl. 20.
23. Decree of the Reichsführer-SS and Chief of the German Police concerning the appointment and training of the candidates for the Security Police and Security Service of the RFSS, 18 February 1938, RMBliV, 1938, Sp. 289–294; Jens Banach, *Heydrichs Elite. Das Führerkorps der Sicherheitspolizei und des SD 1936–1945* (Paderborn, 2002), 268–71.
24. Decree of the Reichsführer-SS and Chief of the German Police concerning the deployment of members of the Security Police in the Schutzstaffel [SS] of the NSDAP, in RMBliV 1938, Sp. 1089–1091.

25. Michael Wildt, 'Radikalisierung und Selbstradikalisierung 1939. Die Geburt des Reichssicherheitshauptamtes aus dem Geist des völkischen Massenmords', in Paul and Mallmann, *Gestapo im Zweiten Weltkrieg*, 11–41 (pp. 15 f.).
26. Gerhard Paul, '"Kämpfende Verwaltung". Das Amt IV des Reichssicherheitshauptamtes als Führungsinstanz der Gestapo', in Paul and Mallmann, *Gestapo im Zweiten Weltkrieg*, 42–81 (p. 43).
27. Paul, '"Kämpfende Verwaltung"', 50–6.
28. Bruno Freiberg, Ernst Eichler, and Theodor Mommsen (eds), *Dienstaltersliste der höheren Kriminalbeamten der staatlichen Polizeiverwaltungen und der Geheimen Staatspolizei Preußens, des Saarlandes und des Freistaates Danzig, nach dem Stande vom 1. Juni 1935*, 55–66.
29. Address list of the State Police head offices and stations, as of 1 September 1939, in HStAD, RW 36/6.
30. Berschel, *Bürokratie und Terror*, 19, 73, 86 f.
31. Banach, *Heydrichs Elite*, 174 ff.
32. Reinhard Heydrich to Kurt Daluege, 30 October 1941, in BA NS 19/2807.
33. Banach, *Heydrichs Elite*, 191 f.
34. Thomas Köhler, 'Himmlers verlängerter Arm in Rheinland und Westfalen—Die Höheren SS- und Polizeiführer', in Carsten Dams, Klaus Dönecke, and Thomas Köhler (eds), *'Dienst am Volk'? Düsseldorfer Polizisten zwischen Demokratie und Diktatur* (Frankfurt am Main, 2007), 203–33.
35. Ruth Bettina Birn, *Die Höheren SS- und Polizeiführer. Himmlers Vertreter im Reich und in den besetzten Gebieten* (Düsseldorf, 1986).
36. Jan Erik Schulte, *Zwangsarbeit und Vernichtung, Das Wirtschaftsimperium der SS. Oswald Pohl und das SS-Wirtschafts-Verwaltungshauptamt* (Paderborn, 2001).
37. Karin Orth, *Das System der nationalsozialistischen Konzentrationslager. Eine politische Organisationsgeschichte* (Hamburg, 1999), 44 f.
38. Johannes Tuchel, *Konzentrationslager. Organisationsgeschichte und Funktion der 'Inspektion der Konzentrationslager' 1934–1938* (Boppard, 1991), 159 ff.
39. Aleksander Lasik, 'Organisationsstruktur des KL Auschwitz', in Wacław Długoborski and Franciszek Piper (eds), *Auschwitz 1940–1945. Studien zur Geschichte des Konzentrations- und Vernichtungslagers Auschwitz*, Vol. 1: *Aufbau und Struktur des Lagers* (Oświęcim, 1999), 165–320 (pp. 200 f.), who refers to Grabner and Schurz as 'Kriminalsekretär'; Johannes Tuchel, 'Registrierung, Misshandlung und Exekution. Die "Politischen Abteilungen" in den Konzentrationslagern', in Paul and Mallmann, *Gestapo im Zweiten Weltkrieg*, 127–40 (p. 131), who describes Schurz as a 'Kriminalassistent'.
40. Günter Morsch, 'Organisations- und Verwaltungsstruktur der Konzentrationslager', in Wolfgang Benz and Barbara Distel (eds), *Der Ort des Terrors. Geschichte der Nationalsozialistischen Konzentrationslager*, Vol. 1: *Die Organisation des Terrors* (Munich, 2005), 58–75 (p. 65).
41. Gabriele Lotfi, *KZ der Gestapo. Arbeitserziehungslager im Dritten Reich* (Frankfurt am Main, 2003), 58–128.

42. Gabriele Lotfi, 'Stätten des Terrors. Die "Arbeitserziehungslager" der Gestapo', in Paul and Mallmann, *Gestapo im zweiten Weltkrieg*, 255–69 (p. 260).
43. Nikolaus Wachsmann, *Hitler's Prisons: Legal Terror in Nazi Germany* (New Haven and London, 2004).
44. Elisabeth Thalhofer, *Neue Bremm—Terrorstätte der Gestapo. Ein Erweitertes Polizeigefängnis und seine Täter 1943–1944* (St Ingbert, 2003), 70–100.
45. Reinhard Heydrich, 'Die Bekämpfung der Staatsfeinde', in *Deutsches Recht* 6 (1936), 121–3 (p. 121).
46. Herbert, *Best*, 163–8.
47. Schwegel, *Polizeibegriff*, 280–370.
48. Werner Best: 'Die Geheime Staatspolizei', *Deutsches Recht* 6 (1936), 125–8 (pp. 126 f.).
49. Heinrich Himmler, 'Aufbau und Aufgaben der Polizei im Dritten Reich', in Hans Pfundtner (ed.), *Dr Wilhelm Frick und sein Ministerium* (Munich, 1937), 125–30 (p. 128); cf. Longerich, *Himmler*, 202–51.
50. Reinhard Heydrich, 'Aufgaben und Aufbau der Sicherheitspolizei im Dritten Reich', in Pfundtner, *Dr Wilhelm Frick*, 149–53 (p. 149).
51. Wildt, *An Uncompromising Generation*, 137–40.
52. Himmler's instruction regarding ideological training in the SS, 28 June 1937, in Jürgen Matthäus et al., *Ausbildungsziel Judenmord? 'Weltanschauliche Erziehung' von SS, Polizei und Waffen-SS im Rahmen der 'Endlösung'* (Frankfurt am Main, 2003), 177 f.
53. George C. Browder, *Hitler's Enforcers: The Gestapo and the SS Security Service in the Nazi Revolution* (New York, 1996), 49–52.
54. Banach, *Heydrichs Elite*, 106–21.
55. Richard Breitman, '"Gegner Nummer Eins". Antisemitische Indoktrination in Himmlers Weltanschauung', in Matthäus et al., *Ausbildungsziel Judenmord?*, 21–34.
56. Jürgen Matthäus: 'Die "Judenfrage" als Schulungsthema von SS und Polizei. "Inneres Erlebnis" und Handlungslegitimation', in Matthäus et al., *Ausbildungsziel Judenmord?*, 35–86 (pp. 72 f.).

3. Gestapo Employees

1. Dams, *Staatsschutz*, 50.
2. Elisabeth Kohlhaas, 'Die Mitarbeiter der regionalen Staatspolizeistellen. Quantitative und qualitative Befunde zur Personalausstattung der Gestapo', in Paul and Mallmann, *Die Gestapo*, 219–35 (pp. 222 f.).
3. Eiber, *Unter Führung*, 104, 107 f.
4. Gerhard Wysocki, *Die Geheime Staatspolizei im Land Braunschweig. Polizeirecht und Polizeipraxis im Nationalsozialismus* (Frankfurt am Main, 1997), 80.
5. Stolle, *Geheime Staatspolizei*, 94, 111.
6. Faatz, *Gestapoterror*, 400.

7. Hans-Dieter Schmid, *Gestapo Leipzig. Politische Abteilung des Polizeipräsidiums und Staatspolizeistelle Leipzig* (Beucha, 1997), 17 f.

8. Andreas Theo Schneider, *Die Geheime Staatspolizei im NS-Gau Thüringen. Geschichte, Struktur, Personal und Wirkungsfelder* (Frankfurt am Main, 2008), 78.

9. Kohlhaas, *Mitarbeiter*, 223.

10. Address list of the State Police head offices and stations, as of 1 September 1939, in HStAD, RW 36/6.

11. Stolle, *Geheime Staatspolizei*, 130 f.

12. Graf, *Politische Polizei*, 317–29.

13. Shlomo Aronson, *Reinhard Heydrich und die Frühgeschichte von Gestapo und SD* (Stuttgart, 1971); Günther Deschner, *Reinhard Heydrich. Statthalter der totalen Macht* (Esslingen, 1977); Robert Gerwarth, *Reinhard Heydrich, Biographie* (Munich, 2011).

14. Charles Sydnor, 'Reinhard Heydrich. Der "ideale Nationalsozialist"', in Smelser and Syring, *Die SS*, 208–19.

15. On Best see the biography by Herbert, *Best*.

16. Wildt, *An Uncompromising Generation*, 154–60.

17. Andreas Seeger, *'Gestapo-Müller'. Die Karriere eines Schreibtischtäters* (Berlin, 1996).

18. Peter R. Black, *Ernst Kaltenbrunner: Ideological Soldier of the Third Reich* (Princeton, 1984).

19. Wildt, *An Uncompromising Generation*, 172–8.

20. Graf, *Politische Polizei*, 353.

21. Wildt, *An Uncompromising Generation*, 191–6.

22. For the most recent studies in the extensive writings on Eichmann, see David Cesarani, *Eichmann: His Life and Crimes* (London, 2005); Yaacov Lozowick, *Hitler's Bureaucrats: The Nazi Security Police and the Banality of Evil* (London, 2003); Hans Safrian, *Eichmann's Men* (Cambridge, 2010); Irmtraud Wojak, *Eichmanns Memoiren. Ein kritischer Essay* (Frankfurt am Main, 2001). Also Hannah Arendt's classic study, *Eichmann in Jerusalem: A Report on the Banality of Evil* (London, 1977).

23. Claudia Steur, *Theodor Dannecker. Ein Funktionär der Endlösung* (Essen, 1997).

24. Wildt, *An Uncompromising Generation*, 429.

25. Freiberg, Eichler, and Mommsen, *Dienstalterliste 1935*, 61; Severin Roeseling, 'Konkurrenz, Arbeitsteilung, Kollegialität—Zum Verhältnis von Polizei und Gestapo in Köln', in Harald Buhlan and Werner Jung (eds), *Wessen Freund und wessen Helfer? Die Kölner Polizei im Nationalsozialismus* (Cologne, 2000), 198–229 (p. 208).

26. Personnel file Theodor Bilo, in HStAD, PA 153 415.

27. Gerhard Paul, *Staatlicher Terror und gesellschaftliche Verrohung. Die Gestapo in Schleswig-Holstein* (Hamburg, 1996), 96.

28. Gerhard Paul, 'Ganz normale Akademiker. Eine Fallstudie zur regionalen staatspolizeilichen Funktionselite', in Paul and Mallmann, *Die Gestapo*, 236–54.
29. Freiberg, Eichler, and Mommsen, *Dienstaltersliste 1935*, 54–66.
30. Banach, *Heydrichs Elite*, 302–11.
31. Banach, *Heydrichs Elite*, 242 f.
32. Herbert, *Best*, 196.
33. Wagner, *Hitlers Kriminalisten*, 116.
34. Carsten Dams and Klaus Dönecke, 'Eine Erstklassige Truppe? Die Offiziere der Düsseldorfer Schutzpolizei im Nationalsozialismus', in Dams, Dönecke, and Köhler, *'Dienst am Volk'?*, 235–58 (p. 247).
35. The Chief of the Security Police and SD to all Security Police, Criminal Police and SD stations, 31 July 1941, in BA R 58/259, Bl. 231.
36. Jens Banach, 'Heydrichs Vertreter im Feld. Die Inspekteure, Kommandeure und Befehlshaber der Sicherheitspolizei und des SD', in Paul and Mallmann, *Gestapo im Zweiten Weltkrieg*, 82–99.
37. Thomas Mang, 'Gestapo-Leitstelle Wien—Mein Name ist Huber'. Wer trug die lokale Verantwortung für den Mord an den Juden Wiens? (Münster, 2004).
38. Browder, *Hitler's Enforcers*, 56; Stolle, *Geheime Staatspolizei*, 131; Helmut Fangmann, Udo Reifner, and Norbert Steinborn, *'Parteisoldaten'. Die Hamburger Polizei im 'Dritten Reich'* (Hamburg, 1987), 51 f.
39. Overview of the careers of Secret State Police detectives (around 1937), in GLA 345/G2026.
40. Stolle, *Geheime Staatspolizei*, 169 f.
41. Kohlhaas, *Mitarbeiter*, 233.
42. Hans-Dieter Schmid, '"Anständige Beamte" und "üble Schläger". Die Staatspolizeistelle Hannover', in Paul and Mallmann, *Die Gestapo*, 133–60 (pp. 159 f.).
43. Berschel, *Bürokratie und Terror*, 118–20 (p. 141).
44. Zygmunt Bauman, *Dialectic of Modernity* (London, 2000), 96.
45. Raul Hilberg, *Die Quellen des Holocaust. Entschlüsseln und Interpretieren* (Frankfurt am Main, 2003), 132 f.
46. Wildt, *An Uncompromising Generation*, 7–8 f.
47. Browder, *Hitler's Enforcers*, 34.
48. Herbert, *Best*, 190.
49. International Military Tribunal Nuremberg, *Trial of the Major War Criminals before the International Military Tribunal, Nuremberg 14 November 1945–1 October 1946*, vol. 29 (Nuremberg, 1948), 145.
50. Harald Welzer, *Täter. Wie aus ganz normalen Menschen Massenmörder werden* (Frankfurt am Main, 2005), 18–75, who expressly emphasizes this. On Himmler's motivation, see Longerich, *Himmler*, 689 f.
51. *IMT*, vol. 29, 146.

4. The Modus Operandi

1. Klaus-Michael Mallmann and Gerhard Paul, 'Allwissend, allmächtig, allgegenwärtig? Gestapo, Gesellschaft und Widerstand', *Zeitschrift für Geschichtswissenschaft* 41 (1993), 984–99.
2. Wildt, *An Uncompromising Generation*, 350–1 ff.
3. Lothar Gruchmann, *Justiz im Dritten Reich 1933–1940. Anpassung und Unterwerfung in der Ära Gürtner* (Munich, 1988), 583–632.
4. Michael Burleigh, *The Third Reich: A New History* (London, 2000), 178.
5. Tuchel, *Konzentrationslager*.
6. Wachsmann, *Gefangen unter Hitler*, 167–94.
7. Circulars from the Chief of the Security Police and SD of 6 October 1941 and 12 June 1942, in BA R 58/243.
8. Cornelia Schmitz-Berning, *Vokabular des Nationalsozialismus* (Berlin and New York, 2000), 584–7.
9. Johannes Tuchel and Reinold Schattenfroh, *Zentrale des Terrors. Prinz-Albrecht-Straße 8, Hauptquartier der Gestapo* (Berlin, 1987), 134.
10. Berschel, *Bürokratie und Terror*.
11. BA R 58/248, fo. 30 f.
12. BA R 58/775, fos. 1 f., 5.
13. Johannes Tuchel, 'Die Gestapo-Sonderkommission "Rote Kapelle"', in Hans Coppi, Jürgen Danyel, and Johannes Tuchel (eds), *Die Rote Kapelle im Widerstand gegen den Nationalsozialismus* (Berlin, 1994), 145–59.
14. *Das 'Hausgefängnis' der Gestapo-Zentrale in Berlin. Terror und Widerstand 1933–1945*, ed. by the Stiftung Topographie des Terrors (Berlin, 2005), 112–19.
15. Heinz Boberach (ed.), *Regimekritik, Widerstand und Verfolgung in Deutschland und den besetzten Gebieten. Meldungen aus dem Geheimen Staatspolizeiamt, dem SD-Hauptamt der SS und dem Reichssicherheitshauptamt 1933–1945*. Guide to the Microfiche Edition (Munich, 2003).
16. Rainer Eckert, 'Gestapo-Berichte. Abbildungen der Realität oder reine Spekulation?', in Paul and Mallmann, *Die Gestapo*, 200–15.
17. Klaus-Michael Mallmann, 'Die V-Leute der Gestapo. Umrisse einer kollektiven Biographie', in Paul and Mallmann, *Die Gestapo*, 268–87 (p. 271).
18. Interrogation record of Adolf Gerst, 10 September 1945, in STALB El 903/4, 268.
19. Wilhelm Mensing, 'Vertrauensleute kommunistischer Herkunft bei Gestapo und NS-Nachrichtendiensten am Beispiel von Rhein und Ruhr', *Jahrbuch für historische Kommunismusforschung* (2004), 111–30; Franz Weisz, *Die Geheime Staatspolizei. Staatspolizeileitstelle Wien 1938–1945* (Vienna, 1991), 414.
20. Carsten Schreiber, ' "Eine verschworene Gemeinschaft". Regionale Verfolgungsnetzwerke des SD in Sachsen', in Wildt, *Nachrichtendienst, politische Elite, Mordeinheit*, 57–85.

21. Hans Schafranek, 'V-Leute und "Verräter". Die Unterwanderung kommunistischer Widerstandsgruppen durch Konfi denten der Wiener Gestapo', *IWK* (2000), 300–49.
22. Mallmann, *Die V-Leute der Gestapo*, 268 ff.
23. Stolle, *Geheime Staatspolizei*, 266 f.
24. Mallmann, *Die V-Leute der Gestapo*, 277.
25. *'Betrifft, Nachrichtenzentrale des Erzbischofs Gröber in Freiburg'. Die Ermittlungsakten der Geheimen Staatspolizei gegen Gertrud Luckner 1942–1944*, ed. and with commentary by H.-J. Wollasch (Constance, 1999), 70 ff., 106 ff.
26. RSHA decree of 12.4.1941, printed in *IMT*, vol. 28, 439–41.
27. Essential: Doris Tausendfreund, *Erzwungener Verrat. Jüdische 'Greifer' im Dienste der Gestapo 1943–1945* (Berlin, 2006).
28. Christian Dirks, '"Greifer". Der Fahndungsdienst der Berliner Gestapo', in Beate Meyer and Hermann Simon, *Juden in Berlin 1938–1945*. Companion volume to the exhibition of the same name in the foundation Neue Synagoge Berlin—Centrum Judaicum, May–August 2000 (Berlin, 2000), 233–57.
29. Berschel, *Bürokratie und Terror*, 439.
30. Ulla Kuespert, 'Das alltägliche Gesicht des Bösen', in *taz*, 15 November 1997, 17.
31. Ralph Jessen, 'Polizei und Gesellschaft. Zum Paradigmenwechsel in der Polizeigeschichtsforschung', in Paul and Mallmann, *Die Gestapo*, 19–43 (p. 42).
32. Barbara Engelking, '"Sehr geehrter Herr Gestapo". Denunziationen im deutsch besetzten Polen 1940 und 41', in Klaus-Michael Mallmann and Bogdan Musial (eds), *Genesis des Genozids. Polen 1939–1941* (Darmstadt, 2004), 206–20; André Halimi, *La Délation sous l'Occupation* (Paris, 1983).
33. Friso Ross and Achim Landwehr (eds), *Denunziation und Justiz. Historische Dimensionen eines sozialen Phänomens* (Tübingen, 2000).
34. Eric A. Johnson, *Nazi Terror, the Gestapo, Jews and Ordinary Germans* (London, 2000), 368 ff.
35. Robert Musil, *The Man without Qualities* (London, 2002), 465.
36. Robert Gellately, *Backing Hitler: Consent and Coercion in Nazi Germany* (Oxford, 2002), 156, 161, 167; Burkhard Jellonnek, *Homosexuelle unter dem Hakenkreuz. Die Verfolgung von Homosexuellen im Dritten Reich* (Paderborn, 1990); Michael Stolle, '"Betrifft: Ernste Bibelforscher". Zeugen Jehovas im Visier der badischen Gestapo', in Hubert Roser (ed.), *Widerstand als Bekenntnis. Die Zeugen Jehovas und das NS-Regime in Baden und Württemberg* (Constance, 1999), 89–146 (pp. 104 ff.).
37. Stephanie Abke, *Sichtbare Zeichen unsichtbarer Kräfte. Denunziationsmuster und Denunziationsverhalten 1939–1949* (Tübingen, 2003), 21–8.
38. Gellately, *The Gestapo*, 129–252; Mallmann and Paul, *Allwissend*, 993 f.
39. *Der Führer* Nr. 282 of 12 October 1933, in GLA 343/784; *Karlsruher Zeitung* Nr. 245 of 20 October 1933, in GLA 343/784.

40. On the reception of Heydrich's circulars, see Gisela Diewald-Kerkmann, 'Denunziantentum und Gestapo. Die freiwilligen "Helfer" aus der Bevölkerung', in Paul and Mallmann, *Die Gestapo*, 288–305 (pp. 295 ff.).

41. Bernward Dörner, *'Heimtücke'. Das Gesetz als Waffe. Kontrolle, Abschreckung und Verfolgung in Deutschland 1933–1945* (Paderborn, 1998), 322 f.

42. Circular from the RFSS, 28 December 1936; cf. Heydrich's decree of 3 September 1939, in BA R 58/243.

43. Michael P. Hensle, 'Nichts hören und nichts reden—Die Verfolgung von "Rundfunkverbrechen" und "Heimtücke-Rednern" durch NS-Justiz und geheime Staatspolizei', in Sibylle Quack (ed.), *Dimensionen der Verfolgung. Opfer und Opfergruppen im Nationalsozialismus* (Munich, 2003), 81–120 (pp. 91 f).

44. Partially published in Manfred Bosch, *Als die Freiheit unterging. Eine Dokumentation über Verweigerung, Widerstand und Verfolgung im Dritten Reich in Südbaden* (Constance, 1985), 124 f.

45. Bosch, *Als die Freiheit unterging*, 125.

46. See the guidelines for prosecution according to the Treachery Act of 28 December 1936, in BA R 58/243.

47. Meike Wöhlert, *Der politische Witz in der NS-Zeit am Beispiel ausgesuchter SD-Berichte und Gestapo-Akten* (Frankfurt am Main, 1997), 150.

48. Cited in Michael P. Hensle, *Rundfunkverbrechen. Das Hören von 'Feindsendern' im Nationalsozialismus* (Berlin, 2003).

49. Hensle, *Rundfunkverbrechen*, 76.

50. Johnson, *Nazi Terror*, 303–51.

51. Jan Ruckenbiel, *Soziale Kontrolle im NS-Regime. Protest, Denunziation und Verfolgung. Zur Praxis alltäglicher Unterdrückung im Wechselspiel von Bevölkerung und Gestapo* (Cologne, 2003), 237.

52. Richard J. Evans, *The Third Reich in Power, 1933–1939* (London, 2005), 114.

53. Herbert Wagner, *Die Gestapo war nicht allein. . . . Politische Sozialkontrolle und Staatsterror im deutsch-niederländischen Grenzgebiet 1929–1945* (Münster, 2004).

54. Wagner, *Die Gestapo war nicht allein*.

55. Wolfgang Seibel, 'Verfolgungsnetzwerke. Zur Messung von Arbeitsteilung und Machtdifferenzierung in den Verfolgungsapparaten des Holocaust', *Kölner Zeitschrift für Soziologie und Sozialpsychologie* 55 (2003), 197–230; cf. Eberhard Kolb, 'Die Maschinerie des Terrors. Zum Funktionieren des Unterdrückungs- und Verfolgungsapparates im NS-System', in Karl-Dietrich Bracher, Manfred Funke, and Hans-Adolf Jacobsen (eds), *Nationalsozialistische Diktatur 1933–1945. Eine Bilanz* (Düsseldorf, 1983), 270–84.

56. See the correspondence between Reinhard Heydrich and Kurt Daluege of October 1941, in BA NS 19/2807.

57. Report by the Walldorf Gendarmerie, 12 June 1934, in GLA 388/1084.

58. Interrogation report by the Walldorf Gendarmerie station from 12 to 14 June 1934, in GLA 388/1084.

59. Baden-Baden Gestapo field office to the district administrator [Landrat] in Bühl, 6 September 1940, in GLA 346, 1991/49, 2637.
60. Statement by the head of the Villingen Kripo station, 5 November 1959, in GLA 309, 1995/8, 2327.
61. Report by the Special Commission—Central Office—of 11 January 1960, in GLA 309, 1995/8, 2333.
62. Statement by the female defendant, 16 March 1961, in GLA 309, 1995/8, 2324.
63. Berschel, *Bürokratie und Terror*.
64. Herbert, *Best*, 190.
65. Martin Broszat, *Resistenz und Widerstand. Eine Zwischenbilanz des Forschungsprojektes*, in Broszat (ed.), *Bayern in der NS-Zeit*, vol. 4 (Munich, 1981), 691–709 (p. 694).
66. Ian Kershaw, *Hitler: Profiles in Power* (Harlow, 1991), 83–4.

5. The Practice of Persecution in the Reich

1. Johnson, *Nazi Terror*, 253–301.
2. Wolfgang Benz and Barbara Distel (eds), *Terror ohne System. Die ersten Konzentrationslager im Nationalsozialismus 1933–1935* (Berlin, 2001).
3. Werner Best, *Die deutsche Polizei* (Darmstadt, 1941), 29.
4. Evans, *The Third Reich in Power*, 113–14.
5. Fraenkel, *The Dual State*, 3.
6. Tuchel, *Konzentrationslager*, 100 f.
7. Hermann Weber, 'Die Ambivalenz der kommunistischen Widerstandsstrategie bis zur "Brüsseler Parteikonferenz"', in Jörg Schmädecke and Peter Steinbach (eds), *Der Widerstand gegen den Nationalsozialismus. Die deutsche Gesellschaft und der Widerstand gegen Hitler* (Munich, 1985), 73–85 (p. 79).
8. Klaus Drobisch and Günther Wieland, *System der NS-Konzentrationslager* (Berlin, 1993), 11–182.
9. Gellately, *Backing Hitler*.
10. Cited in Gruchmann, *Justiz*, 320.
11. BA R 58/2461.
12. Field report Nordbaden-Pfalz, mid-April 1936, in SAPMO RY 1/I 3/25, 49.
13. BA R 58/3271.
14. BA R 58/264, fo. 142.
15. Decree by Heinrich Müller of 22 April 1937, in BA R 58/264.
16. On the critical treatment of Gestapo reports as source material, see Bernd A. Rusinek, '"Wir haben sehr schöne Methoden..." Zur Interpretation von Vernehmungsprotokollen', in Bernd A. Rusinek, Volker Ackermann, and Jörg Engelbrecht (eds), *Einführung in die Interpretation historischer Quellen. Schwerpunkt, Neuzeit* (Paderborn, 1992), 111–31.
17. The self-abnegation that it took to refuse to give evidence is demonstrated in the (literary) example of the communist character Wallau in Anna

Seghers' novel *The Seventh Cross* (New York, 1942). Cf. Seghers, *Das siebte Kreuz. Ein Roman aus Hitlerdeutschland* (Berlin, 1995), 188–94.

18. An anthology of accounts of such victims can be found in Tuchel and Schattenfroh, *Zentrale des Terrors*, 183–287.
19. Cf. the 'Meldungen wichtiger Staatspolizeilicher Ereignisse', in BA R 58/ 195–213.
20. Detlef Garbe, *Zwischen Widerstand und Martyrium. Die Zeugen Jehovas im 'Dritten Reich'* (Munich, 1999).
21. Klaus-Michael Mallmann, 'Die unübersichtliche Konfrontation. Geheime Staatspolizei, Sicherheitsdienst und Kirchen', in Gerhard Besier (ed.), *Zwischen 'nationaler Revolution' und militärischer Aggression. Transformationen in Kirche und Gesellschaft während der konsolidierten NS-Gewaltherrschaft* (Munich, 2001), 121–36.
22. Decree by the Chief of the Security Main Office and the Chief of the Security Police of 1 July 1937, reprinted in Rürup, *Topographie des Terrors*, 64.
23. Hans Günter Hockerts, *Die Sittlichkeitsprozesse gegen katholische Ordensangehörige und Priester 1936/37. Eine Studie zur nationalsozialistischen Herrschaftstechnik und zum Kirchenkampf* (Mainz, 1971).
24. Banach, *Heydrichs Elite*, 141 ff.
25. Statement by Adolf Gerst in Ludwigsburg internment camp, 10 September 1945, in STALB El 903/4, 268.
26. Decree by Chief of the Security Police of 17.8.1941, in BA R 58/1027.
27. Ulrich von Hehl et al. (eds), *Priester unter Hitlers Terror. Eine biografische und statistische Erhebung* (Paderborn, 1998), 122 ff.
28. For a general study of the gradual disenfranchising of the Jews, see Wolfgang Benz (ed.), *Die Juden in Deutschland 1933–1945. Leben unter nationalsozialistischer Herrschaft* (Munich, 1988). The role of the Gestapo in this process has been described in detail in Johnson, *Nazi Terror*; and in Saul Friedlander, *Nazi Germany and the Jews*, vol. 1, *The Years of Persecution, 1933–1939* (London, 1997), vol. 2, *The Years of Persecution, 1939–1945* (London, 2008).
29. Berschel, *Bürokratie und Terror*, 62.
30. Johnson, *Nazi Terror*, 149.
31. Gellately, *The Gestapo*, 162 ff.
32. Alfons Kenkmann and Bernd A. Ruseinek (eds), *Verfolgung und Verwaltung. Die wirtschaftliche Ausplünderung der Juden und die westfälischen Finanzbehörden* (Münster, 1999).
33. Holger Berschel, 'Polizeiroutiniers und Judenverfolgung. Die Bearbeitung von "Judenangelegenheiten" bei der Stapo-Leitstelle Düsseldorf', in Paul and Mallmann, *Die Gestapo im Zweiten Weltkrieg*, 155–78 (p. 157).
34. Herbert, *Best*, 211; Paul, *Staatlicher Terror*, 180.
35. Jerzy Tomaszewski, *Auftakt zur Vernichtung. Die Vertreibung polnischer Juden aus Deutschland im Jahre 1938* (Osnabrück, 2002).

36. SSD radio broadcast to all Gestapo stations in Baden, 27 October 1938, in GLA 357/33 108.
37. Johnson, *Nazi Terror*, 126.
38. Joseph Walk (ed.), *Das Sonderrecht für die Juden im NS-Staat. Eine Sammlung der gesetzlichen Maßnahmen und Richtlinien—Inhalt und Bedeutung* (Heidelberg, 1981).
39. Berschel, *Bürokratie und Terror*, 340-4.
40. Hans Günther Adler, *Der verwaltete Mensch. Studien zur Deportation der Juden aus Deutschland* (Tübingen, 1974), 392.
41. Hans-Dieter Schmid, '"Finanztod". Die Zusammenarbeit von Gestapo und Finanzverwaltung bei der Ausplünderung der Juden in Deutschland', in Paul and Mallmann, *Die Gestapo im Zweiten Weltkrieg*, 141-54.
42. Witness statement by Herbert Titze on 28.11.1968, cited in Tausendfreund, *Erzwungener Verrat*, 65.
43. Tuchel and Schattenfroh, *Zentrale des Terrors*, 146.
44. Burkhard Jellonnek, 'Staatspolizeiliche Fahndungs- und Ermittlungsmethoden gegen Homosexuelle', in Burkhard Jellonnek and Rüdiger Lautmann (eds), *Nationalsozialistischer Terror gegen Homosexuelle. Verdrängt und ungesühnt* (Paderborn, 2002), 149-61.
45. Patrick Wagner, '"Vernichtung der Berufsverbrecher". Die vorbeugende Verbrechensbekämpfung der Kriminalpolizei bis 1937', in Ulrich Herbert, Karin Orth, and Christoph Dieckmann (eds), *Die nationalsozialistischen Konzentrationslager. Entwicklung und Struktur*, vol. 1 (Frankfurt am Main, 2002), 87-110.
46. For the seminal works on this subject, see: Ulrich Herbert, *Hitler's Foreign Workers: Enforced Foreign Labour in Germany under the Third Reich* (Cambridge, 1997); Ulrich Herbert (ed.), *Europa und der Reichseinsatz. Ausländische Zivilarbeiter, Kriegsgefangene und KZ-Häftlinge in Deutschland 1938-1945* (Essen, 1991).
47. GLA 309, 1995/8, 2341.
48. Reinhard Otto, *Wehrmacht, Gestapo und sowjetische Krieggefangene im deutschen Reichsgebiet 1941/42* (Munich, 1998).
49. Herbert, *Hitler's Foreign Workers*, 231.
50. Lotfi, *KZ der Gestapo*, 317.
51. Decree by the Reichsführer-SS and Chief of the German Police of 28.5.1941, in BA R 58/1027.
52. Lotfi, *KZ der Gestapo*, 311 ff.
53. Circular of 4 August 1941, in GLA 371, 1991/49, 224 a.
54. Herbert, *Hitler's Foreign Workers*, 131.

6. The Gestapo in Europe

1. The Reich Minister of the Interior to the Head of the Civil Administration in Alsace, 25 March 1943, in GLA 330/1991/34/194.

2. Klaus-Michael Mallmann, 'Menschenjagd und Massenmord. Das neue Instrument der Einsatzgruppen und -kommandos 1938–1945', in Paul and Mallmann, *Gestapo im Zweiten Weltkrieg*, 291–316.

3. Ruth Bettina Birn, 'Kollaboration und Mittäterschaft. Die Inkorporierung von einheimischem Personal in die Sicherheitspolizei in den besetzten Ostgebieten', in Wildt, *Nachrichtendienst, politische Elite und Mordeinheit*, 303–23.

4. Christoph Dieckmann, Babette Quinkert, and Tatjana Tönsmeyer (eds), *Kooperation und Verbrechen. Formen der Kollaboration im östlichen Europa 1939–1945* (Göttingen 2003).

5. Dieter Pohl, *Verfolgung und Massenmord in der NS-Zeit 1933–1945* (Darmstadt, 2003), 48.

6. Klaus-Michael Mallmann, 'Die Türöffner der "Endlösung". Zur Genesis des Genozids', in Paul and Mallmann, *Gestapo im Zweiten Weltkrieg*, 437–63 (p. 456).

7. Włodzimierz Borodziej, *Terror und Politik. Die deutsche Polizei und die polnische Widerstandsbewegung im Generalgouvernement 1939–1944* (Mainz, 1999), 50. On corruption in general, see Frank Bajohr, *Parvenüs und Profiteure. Korruption in der NS-Zeit* (Frankfurt am Main, 2001).

8. Robert Seidel, *Deutsche Besatzungspolitik in Polen. Der Distrikt Radom 1939–1945* (Paderborn, 2006), 68.

9. Chief of the Security Police and the SD to all Security Police, Criminal Police and SD stations, 31 July 1941, in BA R 58/259, Bl. 231.

10. Christopher R. Browning, *Ordinary Men: Reserve Police Battalion 101 and the Final Solution in Poland* (London, 2001); Daniel Jonah Goldhagen, *Hitler's Willing Executioners* (London, 1996); Wolf Kaiser (ed.), *Täter im Vernichtungskrieg. Der Überfall auf die Sowjetunion und der Völkermord an den Juden* (Berlin and Munich, 2002); Klaus-Michael Mallmann and Gerhard Paul (eds), *Karrieren der Gewalt. Nationalsozialistische Täterbiographien* (Darmstadt, 2004); Michael Mann, *Die dunkle Seite der Demokratie. Eine Theorie der ethnischen Säuberung* (Hamburg, 2007), 263–409; Gerhard Paul (ed.), *Die Täter der Shoah. Fanatische Nationalsozialisten oder ganz normale Deutsche?* (Göttingen, 2003); Welzer, *Täter*.

11. Raul Hilberg, *Perpetrators, Victims, Bystanders: The Jewish Catastrophe 1933–1945* (London, 1995), 51.

12. The state of research for the various countries is very inconsistent, both for the Gestapo and for general questions. In what follows, mainly new titles concerning the Security Police and SD are mentioned. For additional and older sources, see Michael Ruck, *Bibliographie zum Nationalsozialismus*, 2 vols (Darmstadt, 2000).

13. Franz Weisz, 'Die Machtergreifung im Polizeipräsidium am Schottenring in Wien am 11. März 1938 und die Anfänge der Gestapo', *Archiv für Polizeigeschichte* 10 (1999), 74–82; Weisz, 'Die Machtergreifung im österreichischen Innenministerium in Wien im März 1938 und der Aufbau der Gestapo', *Archiv für Polizeigeschichte* 13 (2002), 2–8.

14. Franz Weisz, 'Personell vor allem ein "ständestaatlicher" Polizeikörper. Die Gestapo in Österreich', in Paul and Mallmann, *Die Gestapo*, 439–62 (p. 441).

15. Mang, *Gestapo-Leitstelle Wien*, 122.

16. Black, *Kaltenbrunner*, 104 ff.

17. Safrian, *Eichmann und seine Männer*, 23–67.

18. Mallmann, 'Menschenjagd und Massenmord', 293.

19. Cited in Helmut Krausnick, *Hitlers Einsatzgruppen. Die Truppe des Weltanschauungskrieges 1938–1942* (Frankfurt am Main, 1998), 18.

20. Jörg Osterloh, *Nationalsozialistische Judenverfolgung im Reichsgau Sudetenland 1938–1945* (Munich, 2006), 192–5.

21. Oldřich Sládek, 'Standrecht und Standgericht. Die Gestapo in Böhmen und Mähren', in Paul and Mallmann, *Gestapo im Zweiten Weltkrieg*, 317–39 (p. 325).

22. Herbert, *Best*, 238 f.

23. Guidelines for the external deployment of the Security Police and the SD, reprinted in Klaus-Michael Mallmann, Jochen Böhler, and Jürgen Matthäus, *Einsatzgruppen in Polen. Darstellung und Dokumentation* (Darmstadt, 2008), 117.

24. Cited in Wildt, *An Uncompromising Generation*, 223.

25. Jochen Böhler, *Auftakt zum Vernichtungskrieg. Die Wehrmacht in Polen 1939* (Frankfurt am Main, 2006), 58.

26. Mallmann, Böhler, and Matthäus, *Einsatzgruppen in Polen*, 18 f.

27. Wildt, *An Uncompromising Generation*, 241.

28. Michael Alberti, *Die Verfolgung und Vernichtung der Juden im Reichsgau Wartheland* (Wiesbaden, 2006), 72.

29. Dieter Schenk, *Hitlers Mann in Danzig. Gauleiter Forster und die NS-Verbrechen in Danzig-Westpreußen* (Bonn, 2000), 221–36.

30. Andrea Löw, *Juden im Getto Litzmannstadt. Lebensbedingungen, Selbstwahrnehmung, Verhalten* (Göttingen, 2006).

31. Götz Aly, *Final Solution: Nazi Population Policy and the Murder of the European Jews* (London, 1999), 70 ff.; Henry Friedlander, *Der Weg zum NS-Genozid. Von der Euthanasie zur Endlösung* (Berlin, 1997), 228 ff.

32. Shmuel Krakoswki, *Das Todeslager Chełmno/Kulmhof. Der Beginn der Endlösung* (Göttingen, 2007).

33. Alberti, *Verfolgung und Vernichtung*, 518.

34. Diemut Majer, *'Fremdvölkische' im Dritten Reich. Ein Beitrag zur nationalsozialistischen Rechtssetzung und Rechtspraxis in Verwaltung und Justiz unter besonderer Berücksichtigung der eingegliederten Ostgebiete und des Generalgouvernements* (Boppard, 1981), 459 ff.

35. Wildt, *An Uncompromising Generation*, 193–6.
36. Borodziej, *Terror und Politik*, 45 f.
37. Seidel, *Deutsche Besatzungspolitik in Polen*, 69 f.
38. Michael Foedrowitz, 'Auf der Suche nach einer besatzungspolitischen Konzeption. Der Befehlshaber der Sicherheitspolizei und des SD im Generalgouvernement', in Paul and Mallmann, *Die Gestapo im Zweiten Weltkrieg*, 340–61 (p. 349).
39. Birn, *Die Höheren SS- und Polizeiführer*, 340.
40. Dieter Schenk, *Hans Frank. Hitlers Kronjurist und Generalgouverneur* (Frankfurt am Main, 2006).
41. Bogdan Musial, *Deutsche Zivilverwaltung und Judenverfolgung im Generalgouvernement. Eine Fallstudie zum Distrikt Lublin 1939–1944* (Wiesbaden, 1999), 341 ff.
42. Sybille Steinbacher, *'Musterstadt' Auschwitz. Germanisierungspolitik und Judenmord in Ostoberschlesien* (Munich, 2000), 178 ff.
43. Borodziej, *Terror und Politik*, 73.
44. Borodziej, *Terror und Politik*, 261 f.
45. Jacek Andrzej Młynarczyk, *Judenmord in Zentralpolen. Der Distrikt Radom im Generalgouvernement 1939–1945* (Darmstadt, 2007), 49–243; Seidel, *Deutsche Besatzungspolitik in Polen*, 227–50.
46. Dieter Pohl, 'The Murder of the Jews in the General Government', in Ulrich Herbert (ed.), *National-Socialist Extermination Policies, Contemporary German Perspectives and Controversies* (New York and Oxford, 2000), 83–103 (pp. 86–90).
47. Christopher R. Browning, *The Origins of the Final Solution: The Evolution of Nazi Jewish Policy, September 1939–March 1942* (London, 2004), 316.
48. Dieter Pohl, *Nationalsozialistische Judenverfolgung in Ostgalizien 1941–1944. Organisation und Durchführung eines staatlichen Massenverbrechens* (Munich, 1997), 139 ff.
49. Schmitz-Berning, *Vokabular des Nationalsozialismus*, 174–6.
50. Mark Roseman, *The Villa, the Lake, the Meeting: Wannsee and the Final Solution* (London, 2002).
51. See Bogdan Musial (ed.), *'Aktion Reinhardt'. Der Völkermord an den Juden im Generalgouvernement 1941–1944* (Osnabrück, 2004), with various essays on the most recent research into the development and implementation of the operation.
52. Yitzhak Arad, *Belzec, Sobibor, Treblinka: The Operation Reinhard Death Camps* (Bloomington, Ind., 1987).
53. Musial, *Deutsche Zivilverwaltung*, 276–8.
54. Peter Black, 'Odilio Globocnik—Himmlers Vorposten im Osten', in Ronald Smelser, Enrico Syring, and Rainer Zitelmann (eds), *Die braune Elite 2. 21 weitere biographische Skizzen* (Darmstadt, 1999), 103–15.
55. Arno Lustiger, 'Der Aufstand im Warschauer Ghetto', in Hans Erler, Arnold Paucker, and Ernst Ludwig Ehrlich (eds), *'Gegen alle Vergeblichkeit'. Jüdischer*

Widerstand gegen den Nationalsozialismus (Frankfurt am Main and New York, 2003), 297–307.

56. Pohl, 'Ermordung der Juden im Generalgouvernement', in Herbert, *Nationalsozialistische Vernichtungspolitik*, 107.

57. Klaus-Michael Mallmann, '"Mensch, ich feiere heut' den tausendsten Genickschuß". Die Sicherheitspolizei und die Shoah in Westgalizien', in Paul, *Die Täter der Shoah*, 109–36.

58. Herbert, *Best*, 323.

59. Robert Bohn, '"Ein solches Spiel kennt keine Regeln." Gestapo und Bevölkerung in Norwegen und Dänemark', in Paul and Mallmann, *Die Gestapo*, 463–81 (p. 480).

60. Robert Bohn, *Reichskommissariat Norwegen. 'Nationalsozialistische Neuordnung' und Kriegswirtschaft* (Munich, 2000), 79.

61. Oskar Mendelsohn, 'Norwegen', in Wolfgang Benz (ed.), *Dimension des Völkermords. Die Zahl der jüdischen Opfer des Nationalsozialismus* (Munich, 1996), 187–97.

62. Konrad Kwiet, *Reichskommissariat Niederlande. Versuch und Scheitern nationalsozialistischer Neuordnung* (Stuttgart, 1968).

63. Guus Meershoek, 'Machtentfaltung und Scheitern. Sicherheitspolizei und SD in den Niederlanden', in Paul and Mallmann, *Gestapo im Zweiten Weltkrieg*, 383–402 (p. 386).

64. Gerhard Hirschfeld, *Fremdherrschaft und Kollaboration. Die Niederlande unter deutscher Besatzung* (Stuttgart, 1984).

65. Raul Hilberg, *The Destruction of the European Jews*, vol. 2 (New Haven and London, 2003), 625–8.

66. Meershoek, 'Machtentfaltung und Scheitern', in Paul and Mallmann, *Gestapo im Zweiten Weltkrieg*, 401 f.

67. Wolfram Weber, *Die innere Sicherheit im besetzten Belgien und Nordfrankreich 1940–1944* (Düsseldorf, 1978), 35, 42.

68. Werner Warmbrunn, *The German Occupation of Belgium 1940–1944* (New York, 1993), 149–71.

69. Birn, *Die Höheren SS- und Polizeiführer*, 304 f.

70. Bernd Kasten, 'Gute Franzosen'. *Die französische Polizei und die deutsche Besatzungsmacht im besetzten Frankreich 1940–1944* (Sigmaringen, 1993), 22–4.

71. Birn, *Die Höheren SS- und Polizeiführer*, 341.

72. Ahlrich Meyer, *Die deutsche Besatzung in Frankreich 1940–1944. Widerstandsbekämpfung und Judenverfolgung* (Darmstadt, 2000), 99.

73. Kasten, 'Gute Franzosen', 245–8.

74. For the seminal work on this subject, see Serge Klarsfeld, *Vichy—Auschwitz. Die 'Endlösung der Judenfrage' in Frankreich*, updated edn (Darmstadt, 2007); Ahlrich Meyer, *Täter im Verhör. Die 'Endlösung der Judenfrage' in Frankreich 1940–1944* (Darmstadt, 2005).

75. Juliane Wetzel, *Frankreich und Belgien*, in Wolfgang Benz (ed.), *Dimension des Völkermords. Die Zahl der jüdischen Opfer des Nationalsozialismus* (Munich 1996), 105–35 (p. 127).
76. Kasten, *'Gute Franzosen'*, 95 ff.
77. Meyer, *Die deutsche Besatzung*, 148.
78. Peter Lieb, *Konventioneller Krieg oder NS-Weltanschauungskrieg? Kriegsführung und Partisanenbekämpfung in Frankreich 1943/44* (Munich, 2007).
79. Hitler's words at a meeting in Berlin on 25 September 1940, cited in Jacob Toury, 'Die Entstehungsgeschichte des Austreibungsbefehls gegen die Juden in der Saarpfalz und Baden (22./23. Oktober 1940)', in *Jahrbuch des Instituts für deutsche Geschichte* 15 (1986), 431–64 (p. 446).
80. Speech by Robert Wagner of 20 October 1940, cited in Franz A. Six (ed.), *Dokumente der deutschen Politik. Das Reich Adolf Hitlers*, vol. 8.2 (Berlin, 1935–44), 527.
81. Activity report of the BdS Strasbourg to the RSHA and the head of the civil administration, in BA R 83 Elsaß/3.
82. Wolfgang Benz (ed.), *Der Ort des Terrors. Geschichte der nationalsozialistischen Konzentrationslager*, vol. 6 (Natzweiler, Groß-Rosen, Stutthof, and Munich, 2007).
83. On the deployment of Police Battalion 64 in Serbia, see Stefan Klemp, *'Nicht Ermittelt'. Polizeibataillone und die Nachkriegsjustiz—Ein Handbuch* (Essen, 2005), 151–66.
84. Walter Manoschek, *'Serbien ist judenfrei'. Militärische Besatzungspolitik und Judenvernichtung in Serbien 1941/42* (Munich, 1995), 40–9.
85. Hilberg, *Destruction*, vol. 2, p. 727.
86. Christopher R. Browning, *Fateful Months: Essays on the Emergence of the Final Solution* (New York and London, 1985), 71–85.
87. For the seminal work on the history of Greece under occupation, see Hagen Fleischer, *Im Kreuzschatten der Mächte. Griechenland 1941–1944* (Frankfurt am Main, 1986).
88. Mark Mazower, *Inside Hitler's Greece: The Experience of Occupation 1941–1944* (New Haven and London, 1993), 219 f.
89. Claudia Steur, 'Eichmanns Emissäre. Die "Judenberater" in Hitlers Europa', in Paul and Mallmann, *Gestapo im Zweiten Weltkrieg*, 403–36 (p. 424).
90. Tatjana Tönsmeyer, *Das Dritte Reich und die Slowakei 1939–1945. Politischer Alltag zwischen Kooperation und Eigensinn* (Paderborn, 2003), 137–62.
91. Safrian, *Eichmann und seine Gehilfen*, 261–75.
92. See in particular: Hamburg Institute for Social Research (ed.), *The German Army and Genocide: Crimes against War Prisoners, Jews and other Civilians in the East, 1939–1944* (New York, 1999); Christan Hartmann, Johannes Hürter, and Ulrike Jureit (eds), *Verbrechen der Wehrmacht. Bilanz einer Debatte* (Munich, 2005); Walter Manoschek (ed.), *Die Wehrmacht im Rassenkrieg. Der Vernichtungskrieg hinter der Front* (Vienna, 1996); Rolf-Dieter Müller, *Der letzte deutsche*

Krieg 1939–1945 (Stuttgart, 2005); Rolf-Dieter Müller, *An der Seite der Wehrmacht. Hitlers ausländische Helfer beim 'Kreuzzug gegen den Bolschewismus' 1941–1945* (Berlin, 2007).

93. Wolfram Wette, *The Wehrmacht: History, Myth, Reality* (Cambridge, Mass. and London, 2007), 93.

94. Andrej Angrick, *Besatzungspolitik und Massenmord. Die Einsatzgruppe D in der südlichen Sowjetunion 1941–1943* (Hamburg, 2003); Ronald Headland, *Messages of Murder: A Study of the Reports of the Einsatzgruppen of the Security Police and the Security Service 1941–1943* (London and Toronto, 1992); Peter Klein (ed.), *Die Einsatzgruppen in der besetzten Sowjetunion 1941/42. Die Tätigkeits- und Lageberichte des Chef der Sicherheitspolizei und des SD* (Berlin, 1997); Helmut Krausnick and Hans-Heinrich Wilhelm, *Die Truppe des Weltanschauungskrieges. Die Einsatzgruppen der Sicherheitspolizei und des SD* (Stuttgart, 1981); Krausnick, *Hitlers Einsatzgruppen*; Yaacow Lozowick, 'Rollbahn Mord. The Early Activities of Einsatzgruppe C', *HGS* 2 (1987), 221–42; Ralf Ogorreck, *Die Einsatzgruppen und die 'Genesis der Endlösung'* (Berlin, 1996); Richard Rhodes, *Die deutschen Mörder. Die SS-Einsatzgruppen und der Holocaust* (Bergisch Gladbach, 2004); Hans-Heinrich Wilhelm, *Die Einsatzgruppe A der Sicherheitspolizei und des SD 1941/42* (Frankfurt am Main, 1996). See also Hilberg, *Destruction*; Peter Longerich, *Holocaust: The Nazi Persecution and Murder of the Jews* (Oxford, 2012).

95. For the seminal work on this co-operation, see Martin Cüppers, *Wegbereiter der Shoah. Die Waffen-SS, der Kommandostab Reichsführer-SS und die Judenvernichtung 1939–1945* (Darmstadt, 2005), 125 ff.; Wolfgang Curilla, *Die deutsche Ordnungspolizei und der Holocaust im Baltikum und in Weißrußland 1941–1944* (Paderborn, 2006); Klemp, '"Nicht ermittelt"'; Dieter Pohl, Die Kooperation zwischen Heer, SS und Polizei in den besetzten sowjetischen Gebieten', in Hartmann, Hürter, and Jureit, *Verbrechen der Wehrmacht*, 107–16; Bernd Wegner, *The Waffen-SS: Organization, Ideology and Function* (Oxford, 1990); Edward B. Westermann, *Hitler's Police Battalions: Enforcing Racial War in the East* (Lawrence, Kan., 2005).

96. Christian Streit, *Keine Kameraden. Die Wehrmacht und die sowjetischen Kriegsgefangenen 1941–1945* (Bonn, 1997).

97. Mallmann, 'Menschenjagd und Massenmord', in Paul and Mallmann, *Gestapo im Zweiten Weltkrieg*, 304 f.; Mallmann, 'Die Türöffner der Endlösung', in Paul and Mallmann, *Gestapo im Zweiten Weltkrieg*, 456–9.

98. Krausnick, *Hitlers Einsatzgruppen*, 155.

99. Wolfgang Scheffler, 'Die Einsatzgruppe A', in Klein, *Einsatzgruppen*, 29–51 (p. 32); Knut Stang, *Kollaboration und Massenmord. Die litauische Hilfspolizei, das Rollkommando Hamann und die Ermordung der litauischen Juden* (Frankfurt am Main, 1997).

100. Ruth Bettina Birn, *Die Sicherheitspolizei in Estland 1941–1944. Eine Studie zur Kollaboration im Osten* (Paderborn, 2006), 261 f.

101. Andrej Angrick and Peter Klein, *The 'Final Solution' in Riga: Exploitation and Annihilation, 1941–1944* (New York and Oxford, 2009).
102. Christan Gerlach, *Kalkulierte Morde. Die Deutsche Wirtschafts- und Vernichtungspolitik in Weißrußland 1941 bis 1944* (Hamburg, 1999), 185.
103. Andrej Angrick et al., '"Da hätte man schon ein Tagebuch führen müssen." Das Polizeibataillon 322 und die Judenmord im Bereich der Heeresgruppe Mitte während des Sommers und Herbstes 1941', in Helga Grabitz, Klaus Bästlein, and Johannes Tuchel (eds), *Die Normalität des Verbrechens. Bilanz und Perspektiven der Forschung zu den nationalsozialistischen Gewaltverbrechen* (Berlin, 1994), 325–85; Martin Hölzl, 'Buer und Belzec. Die Polizeibataillone 65 und 316 und der Mord an den Juden während des Zweiten Weltkrieges', in Stefan Goch (ed.), *Städtische Gesellschaft und Polizei. Beiträge zur Sozialgeschichte der Polizei in Gelsenkirchen* (Essen, 2005), 260–85; Klemp, 'Nicht ermittelt', 225–6, 279–82, 289–94.
104. Lutz Hachmeister, *Der Gegnerforscher. Die Karriere des SS-Führers Franz Alfred Six* (Munich, 1998), 233–8.
105. Christan Gerlach, 'Die Einsatzgruppe B 1941/42', in Klein, *Einsatzgruppen*, 52–70 (p. 62).
106. Dieter Pohl, 'Die Einsatzgruppe C 1941/42', in Klein, *Einsatzgruppen*, 71–87 (pp. 71–4).
107. Martin Dean, *Collaboration in the Holocaust: Crimes of the Local Police in Belorussia and Ukraine 1941–1944* (New York, 2000).
108. Angrick, *Besatzungspolitik und Massenmord*.
109. *Der Dienstkalender Heinrich Himmlers*, 4 October 1941, p. 225. For an overview, see Longerich, *Himmler*, 541–74.
110. Cited in Andrej Angrick, 'Im Windschatten der 11. Armee. Die Einsatzgruppe D', in Paul and Mallmann, *Die Gestapo im Zweiten Weltkrieg*, 481–502 (p. 495).
111. Klaus-Michael Mallman and Martin Cüppers, *Nazi Palestine: The Plans for the Extermination of the Jews in Palestine* (New York, 2010), 116–25.
112. Carlo Gentile and Lutz Klinkhammer, 'Gegen die Verbündeten von einst. Die Gestapo in Italien', in Paul and Mallmann, *Gestapo im Zweiten Weltkrieg*, 521–40 (p. 522 ff.).
113. Steur, *Dannecker*, 113–28.
114. Liliana Picciotto Fargion, 'Italien', in Benz, *Dimension des Völkermords*, 199–227 (p. 216).
115. Gentile and Klinkhammer, 'Gegen die Verbündeten', in Paul and Mallmann, *Gestapo im Zweiten Weltkrieg*, 537 f.
116. Christian Gerlach and Götz Aly, *Das letzte Kapitel. Der Mord an den ungarischen Juden 1941–1945* (Frankfurt am Main, 2004), 98–107.
117. Safrian, *Eichmann und seine Gehilfen*, 295.
118. Gerlach and Aly, *Das letzte Kapitel*, 132 ff.

119. Randolph L. Braham, *The Politics of Genocide: The Holocaust in Hungary*, vol. 2 (New York, 1994), 872–81.
120. Margit Szöllösi-Janze, *Die Pfeilkreuzerbewegung in Ungarn. Historischer Kontext, Entwicklung und Herrschaft* (Munich, 1989).
121. Mallmann, 'Menschenjagd und Massenmord', in Paul and Mallmann, *Gestapo in Europa*, 310–13.
122. Jörg Friedrich, *The Fire: The Bombing of Germany, 1940–1945* (New York and Chichester, 2008); Friedrich, *Brandstätten. Der Anblick des Bombenkriegs* (Munich, 2003).
123. Neumann, *Behemoth*, p. xii.
124. Bernd-A. Rusinek, *Gesellschaft in der Katastrophe. Terror, Illegalität, Widerstand. Köln 1944/45* (Essen, 1989).
125. Sven Keller, 'Verbrechen in der Endphase des Zweiten Weltkrieges. Überlegungen zu Abgrenzung, Methodik und Quellenkritik', in Cord Arens, Edgar Wolfrum, and Jörg Zedler (eds), *Terror nach Innen. Verbrechen am Ende des Zweiten Weltkrieges* (Göttingen, 2006), 25–50 (p. 28).
126. Perry Biddiscombe, *Werwolf! The History of the National Socialist Guerilla Movement, 1944–1946* (Toronto and Buffalo, 1998); Cord Arens, 'Schrecken aus dem Untergrund, Endphasenverbrechen des "Werwolf"', in Arens, Wolfrum, and Zedler, *Terror nach Innen*, 149–71; Andreas Kunz, *Wehrmacht und Niederlage. Die bewaffnete Macht in der Endphase der nationalsozialistischen Herrschaft 1944 bis 1945* (Munich, 2007).
127. Elisabeth Kohlhaas, '"Aus einem Haus, aus dem eine weiße Fahne erscheint, sind alle männlichen Personen zu erschießen", Durchhalteterror und Gewalt gegen Zivilisten am Kriegsende 1945', in Arens, Wolfrum, and Zedler, *Terror nach Innen*, 51–79 (p. 63).
128. Bernd-A. Rusinek, '"Wat denkste, wat mir objerümt han." Massenmord und Spurenbeseitigung am Beispiel der Staatspolizeistelle Köln 1944/45', in Paul and Mallmann, *Die Gestapo*, 402–16 (p. 415).
129. Herbert, *Fremdarbeiter*, 339.
130. Herbert, *Fremdarbeiter*, 320.
131. Marc Spoerer, *Zwangsarbeit unter dem Hakenkreuz. Ausländische Zivilarbeiter, Kriegsgefangene und Häftlinge im Deutschen Reich und im besetzten Europa 1939–1945* (Stuttgart and Munich, 2001), 171 f.
132. HStAD, RW 34/10.
133. Gerhard Paul, '"Diese Erschießungen haben mich innerlich gar nicht mehr berührt." Die Kriegsendphasenverbrechen der Gestapo 1944/45', in Paul and Mallmann, *Gestapo im Zweiten Weltkrieg*, 543–68 (p. 552); Ulrich Sander, *Mörderisches Finale. NS-Verbrechen bei Kriegsende* (Cologne, 2008).
134. Wildt, *An Uncompromising Generation*, 357.
135. Stephan Linck, *Der Ordnung verpflichtet. Deutsche Polizei 1933–1949. Der Fall Flensburg* (Paderborn, 2000), 147–50.

7. The Gestapo after 1945

1. Wagner, *Hitlers Kriminalisten*, 153.
2. Pohl, 'Einsatzgruppe C', in Klein, *Einsatzgruppen*, 82. Cf. Klaus-Michael Mallmann and Andrej Angrick (eds), *Die Gestapo nach 1945. Karrieren, Konflikte, Konstruktionen* (Darmstadt, 2009).
3. Gerhard Paul, 'Zwischen Selbstmord, Illegalität und neuer Karriere. Ehemalige Gestapo-Bedienstete im Nachkriegsdeutschland', in Paul and Mallmann, *Die Gestapo*, 529–47 (p. 534). Cf. Gerald Steinacher, 'Berufsangabe, Mechaniker. Die Flucht von Gestapo-Angehörigen nach Übersee', in Mallmann and Angrick, *Die Gestapo*, 56–70.
4. Paul, *Staatlicher Terror*, 241 f.
5. Adalbert Rückerl, *Die Strafverfolgung von NS-Verbrechen 1945–1978. Eine Dokumentation* (Heidelberg and Karlsruhe, 1979), 25–32.
6. *IMT*, vol. 1, pp. 28–30.
7. Commencement of action against the Gestapo, 20.12.1945, *IMT*, vol. 4, pp. 360–1.
8. Peter Steinbach, 'Der Nürnberger Hauptkriegsverbrecherprozess', in Gerd R. Ueberschär (ed.), *Der Nationalsozialismus vor Gericht. Die alliierten Prozesse gegen Kriegsverbrecher und Soldaten 1943–1952* (Frankfurt am Main, 1999), 32–44.
9. *IMT*, vol. 1, p. 264.
10. *IMT*, vol. 1, pp. 264–5.
11. Kurt Hinrichsen, 'Befehlsnotstand', in Adalbert Rückerl (ed.), *NS-Prozesse. Nach 25 Jahren Strafverfolgung, Möglichkeiten, Grenzen, Ergebnisse* (Karlsruhe, 1971), 131–62.
12. Cited in Peter Black, 'Ernst Kaltenbrunner. Der Nachfolger Heydrichs', in Smelser and Syring, *Die SS*, 289–304 (p. 301).
13. Bengt von zur Mühlen and Andreas von Klewitz (eds), *Die 12 Nürnberger Nachfolgeprozesse* (Berlin, 2000).
14. Ralf Ogorreck and Volker Rieß, 'Fall 9, Der Einsatzgruppenprozess (gegen Otto Ohlendorf und andere)', in Ueberschär, *Der Nationalsozialismus vor Gericht*, 164–75.
15. Sebastian Römer, *Mitglieder verbrecherischer Organisationen nach 1945. Die Ahndung des Organisationsverbrechens in der britischen Zone durch die Spruchgerichte* (Frankfurt am Main, 2005).
16. Justus Fürstenau, *Entnazifizierung. Ein Kapitel deutscher Nachkriegspolitik* (Neuwied and Berlin, 1969), 53–147; Clemens Vollnhals (ed.), *Politische Säuberung und Rehabilitierung in den vier Besatzungszonen 1945–1949* (Munich, 1991).
17. Lutz Niethammer, *Die Mitläuferfabrik. Die Entnazifizierung am Beispiel Bayerns* (Bonn and Berlin, 1982), 540–50.
18. 'Leitheft für die Verteidigung der betroffenen Beamten der Gestapo im Spruchkammer- und Strafverfahren von Dr. Rudolf Merkel und Dr. Joseph Weisgerber in Zusammenarbeit mit dem Arbeitsausschuss für Verteidiger

im Spruchgerichtsverfahren mit Ermächtigung der Vereinigung der Vorstände der Anwaltskammern der Britischen Zone, Nürnberg 1947', in GLA 309, 1995/8, 2347. On Werner Best's influence on Merkel, see Herbert, *Best*, 415.

19. Angela Borgstedt, *Entnazifizierung in Karlsruhe 1946 bis 1951. Politische Säuberung im Spannungsfeld von Besatzungspolitik und lokalem Neuanfang* (Constance, 2001), 22.

20. Niethammer, *Mitläuferfabrik*, 653; Herbert, *Best*, 437.

21. Norbert Frei, *Adenauer's Germany and the Nazi Past: The Politics of Amnesty and Integration* (New York and Chichester, 2002).

22. Fürstenau, *Entnazifizierung*, 238–59.

23. Frei, *Adenauer's Germany*, p. xiii.

24. Herbert, *Best*, 435 f.; Paul, *Staatlicher Terror*, 240; Klaus-Dietmar Henke, 'Die Trennung vom Nationalsozialismus. Selbstzerstörung, politische Säuberung, Entnazifizierung, Strafverfolgung', in Klaus-Dietmar Henke and Hans Woller (eds), *Politische Säuberung in Europa. Die Abrechnung mit Faschismus und Kollaboration nach dem Zweiten Weltkrieg* (Munich 1991), 21–83 (pp. 64 ff.).

25. Heiner Wember, *Umerziehung im Lager. Internierung und Bestrafung von Nationalsozialisten in der britischen Besatzungszone Deutschlands* (Essen, 1991), 8.

26. Paul, *Zwischen Selbstmord*, 534.

27. Michael Wildt, 'Der Hamburger Gestapochef Bruno Streckenbach. Eine nationalsozialistische Karriere', in Frank Bajohr and Joachim Szodrzynski (eds), *Hamburg in der NS-Zeit* (Hamburg, 1995), 93–123.

28. The *Institut für Zeitgeschichte* compiled contemporary reports for the Frankfurt Auschwitz Trial, which were later published: Helmut Krausnick and Martin Broszat, *Anatomy of the SS State* (London, 1970).

29. *Justiz und NS-Verbrechen, Sammlung deutscher Strafurteile wegen nationalsozialistischer Tötungsverbrechen 1945–1999*, ed. Adelheid L. Rüter-Ehlermann and Christaan F. Rüter, vol. 4: *Die vom 30. Januar 1949 bis zum 3. Juni 1949 ergangenen Strafurteile* (Amsterdam, 1970), Nr. 147.

30. Dirk Lukaßen, 'Menschenkinder vor dem Richter'. *Kölner Gestapo und die Nachkriegsjustiz. Der 'Hoegen-Prozess' vor dem Kölner Schwurgericht im Jahr 1949 und seine Rezeption in den lokalen Tageszeitungen* (Siegburg, 2006).

31. Marc von Miquel, *Ahnden oder amnestieren? Westdeutsche Justiz und Vergangenheitspolitik in den sechziger Jahren* (Göttingen, 2004), 146.

32. Herbert, *Best*, 451 ff.; Frei, *Adenauer's Germany*, 67 ff.

33. Johnson, *Nazi Terror*, 3 f.

34. Henry Leide, *NS-Verbrecher und Staatssicherheit. Die geheime Vergangenheitspolitik der DDR* (Göttingen, 2005); Hermann Wentker, 'Die juristische Ahndung von NS-Verbrechen in der Sowjetischen Besatzungszone und in der DDR', *Kritische Justiz* 35 (2002), 1, pp. 60–78.

35. Wolfgang Eisert, *Die Waldheimer Prozesse. Der stalinistische Terror 1950. Ein dunkles Kapitel der DDR-Justiz* (Munich, 1993), 309 f.

36. Leide, *NS-Verbrecher und Staatssicherheit*, 416 f.
37. Beate Meyer, 'Der "Eichmann von Dresden". "Justizielle Bewältigung" von NS-Verbrechen in der DDR am Beispiel des Verfahrens gegen Henry Schmidt', in Matthäus and Mallmann (eds), *Deutsche, Juden, Völkermord*, 275–91.
38. Annette Weinke, *Die Verfolgung von NS-Tätern im geteilten Deutschland. Vergangenheitsbewältigungen 1949–1969 oder: Eine deutsch deutsche Beziehungsgeschichte im Kalten Krieg* (Paderborn, 2002), 355.
39. Handwritten curriculum vitae, undated [presumably early 1950], in GLA 465 a, Ztr.Spr.K. B/Sv/1948.
40. Weinke, *Verfolgung von NS-Tätern*, 59.
41. Reinhard Henkys, *Die nationalsozialistischen Gewaltverbrechen. Geschichte und Gericht* (Stuttgart and Berlin, 1964), 220–38; Martin Broszat, 'Siegerjustiz oder strafrechtliche "Selbstreinigung". Aspekte der Ver gangenheitsbewältigung der deutschen Justiz während der Besatzungszeit 1945–1949', in *Vierteljahreshefte für Zeitgeschichte* 29 (1981), 477–544 (pp. 542 f.).
42. Herbert, *Best*, 508 ff.
43. von Miquel, *Ahnden oder Amnestieren?*, 363–9.
44. Andreas Zielcke, 'Gnade vor Recht?', *Kritische Justiz* (1990), 460 ff.
45. Hermann Lübbe, 'Der Nationalsozialismus im deutschen Nachkriegsbewusstsein', *Historische Zeitschrift* 236 (1983), 579–99.
46. Adalbert Rückerl, *NS-Verbrechen vor Gericht, Versuch einer Vergangenheitsbewältigung* (Heidelberg, 1984), 142; Harald Schmid, 'Eine Vergangenheit, drei Geschichten. Zur Auseinandersetzung mit der NS-Diktatur in der Bundesrepublik Deutschland, der DDR und in Österreich', in Angela Borgstedt, Siegfried Frech, and Michael Stolle (eds), *Lange Schatten. Bewältigung von Diktaturen* (Schwalbach, 2007), 89–119.
47. Hans Pöschko (ed.), *Die Ermittler von Ludwigsburg. Deutschland und die Aufklärung nationalsozialistischer Verbrechen* (Berlin, 2008).
48. Wildt, *An Uncompromising Generation*, 446.
49. Peter Steinbach, *Nationalsozialistische Gewaltverbrechen. Die Diskussion in der deutschen Öffentlichkeit nach 1945* (Berlin, 1981); Jürgen Weber and Peter Steinbach (eds), *Vergangenheitsbewältigung durch Strafverfahren? NS-Prozesse in der Bundesrepublik Deutschland* (Munich, 1984); Norbert Frei, Dirk van Laak, and Michael Stolleis (eds), *Geschichte vor Gericht. Historiker, Richter und die Suche nach Gerechtigkeit* (Munich, 2000).
50. Fritz Bauer Institut (ed.), *'Gerichtstag halten über uns selbst...'. Geschichte und Wirkung des ersten Frankfurter Auschwitz-Prozesses* (Frankfurt am Main and New York, 2001).
51. Wildt, *An Uncompromising Generation*, 410–11; cf. Annette Weinke, 'Amnestie für Schreibtischtäter. Das verhinderte Verfahren gegen die Bediensteten des Reichssicherheitshauptamtes', in Mallmann and Angrick, *Die Gestapo*, 200–20.

52. Akim Jah, '"Unschuldige Mordgehilfen". Das Bovensiepen-Verfahren gegen ehemalige Mitarbeiter der Stapo-Stelle Berlin', in Sabine Moller et al. (eds), *Abgeschlossene Kapitel? Zur Geschichte der Konzentrationslager und der NS-Prozesse* (Tübingen, 2002), 187–99 (p. 199).

53. Herbert, *Best*, 511–18.

54. Guthermuth and Netzbandt, *Die Gestapo*, 207 ff.

55. Jörg Friedrich, *Kalte Amnestie. NS-Täter in der Bundesrepublik* (Munich, 2007).

56. Bernhard Brunner, 'Lebenswege der deutschen Sipo-Chefs in Frankreich nach 1945', in Ulrich Herbert (ed.), *Wandlungsprozesse in Westdeutschland. Belastung, Integration, Liberalisierung 1945–1980* (Göttingen, 2003), 214–42 (p. 241).

57. Sibylle Steinbacher, '"...nichts weiter als Mord." Der Gestapo-Chef von Auschwitz und die bundesdeutsche Nachkriegsjustiz', in Norbert Frei, Sybille Steinbacher, and Bernd C. Wagner (eds), *Ausbeutung, Vernichtung, Öffentlichkeit. Neue Studien zur nationalsozialistischen Lagerpolitik* (Munich, 2000), 265–98.

58. Herbert, *Best*, 436.

59. Leide, *NS-Verbrecher und Staatssicherheit*, 272 ff. Cf. Andrej Angrick, 'Im Fadenkreuz des Todfeindes? Das Ministerium für Staatsicherheit und die Gestapo', in Mallmann and Angrick, *Die Gestapo*, 270–90.

60. Paul, *Zwischen Selbstmord*, 546; Leide, *NS-Verbrecher und Staatssicherheit*, 191 ff.

61. Cited in Dieter Hesselberger, *Das Grundgesetz. Kommentar für die politische Bildung* (Bonn 1996), 364.

62. Curt Garner, 'Schlussfolgerungen aus der Vergangenheit? Die Auseinandersetzung um die Zukunft des deutschen Berufsbeamtentums nach dem Ende des Zweiten Weltkriegs', in Hans-Erich Volkmann (ed.), *Ende des Dritten Reiches—Ende des Zweiten Weltkriegs. Eine perspektivische Rückschau* (Munich and Zurich, 1995), 607–74; Udo Wengst, *Beamtentum zwischen Reform und Tradition. Beamtengesetzgebung in der Gründungsphase der Bundesrepublik Deutschland 1948–1953* (Düsseldorf, 1988), 152–252; Frei, *Vergangenheitspolitik*, 69–100.

63. Law on the regulation of the legal conditions of those falling under Article 131 of the Basic Law of 11 May 1951, BGBl. I, pp. 307–22.

64. Paul, *Staatlicher Terror*, 258.

65. Curt Garner, 'Der öffentliche Dienst in den 50er Jahren. Politische Weichenstellungen und ihre sozialgeschichtlichen Folgen', in Axel Schildt and Arnold Sywottek (eds), *Modernisierung im Wiederaufbau. Die westdeutsche Gesellschaft der 50er Jahre* (Bonn, 1993), 759–90 (pp. 773 f.).

66. Frei, *Adenauer's Germany*, pp. xiv f., 50–1; Garner calculated that at least 100,000 of those charged in the denazification trials could benefit from the '131' regulation: Garner, *Der öffentliche Dienst*, 771.

67. First law on changing the law regulating the legal conditions of those falling under Article 131 of the Basic Law of 19 August 1953, BGBl. I, pp. 980–95, here p. 988. Second law on changing the law regulating the legal conditions

of those falling under Article 131 of the Basic Law of 11 September 1957, BGBl. I, pp. 1275–96, here p. 1287.

68. Legal clarity was only achieved with a judgment by the Federal Administrative Court of 11 September 1958, which allowed the subject's service in the Gestapo to be taken into account only in the exceptional case that 'the subject transferred ex officio to the Secret State Police had taken no part in the organisation's illegal activities'. See GLA 527, 1983/82, 2367.
69. Paul, Zwischen Selbstmord, 545.
70. Cf. in this context also the judgment of the Federal Administrative Court of 11 September 1958, in Entscheidungen des Bundesverwaltungsgerichts, vol. 8, ed. by the members of the court (Berlin, 1959), 26–8.
71. Steinbacher, '. . . nichts weiter als Mord', 284 f.
72. Leide, NS-Verbrecher und Staatssicherheit, 191–331; Angrick, Im Fadenkreuz, 276 ff.
73. Wildt, An Uncompromising Generation, 363 f. (p. 379).
74. Wolfgang Kraushaar, 'Karriere eines Boxers. Johannes Clemens: Vom Dresdner Gestapo-Schläger zum Doppelagenten des KGB im BND', in Hannes Heer (ed.), Im Herzen der Finsternis. Victor Klemperer als Chronist der NS-Zeit (Berlin, 1997), 152–69.

Conclusion: What Remains of the Gestapo?

1. Stolle, Geheime Staatspolizei, 29 f.
2. Frei, Adenauer's Germany, 170 f.
3. For the seminal work on this subject, see Paul and Mallmann, Die Gestapo.
4. Wolfgang Buschfort, Geheime Hüter der Verfassung. Von der Düsseldorfer Informationsstelle zum ersten Verfassungsschutz der Bundesrepublik (1947–1961) (Paderborn, 2004).
5. Wolfgang Reinhard, Geschichte der Staatsgewalt. Eine vergleichende Verfassungsgeschichte Europas von den Anfängen bis zur Gegenwart (Munich, 2002), 363.
6. David Garland, The Culture of Control: Crime and Social Order in Contemporary Society (Oxford and New York, 2002).

SELECT BIBLIOGRAPHY

Abke, Stephanie, *Sichtbare Zeichen unsichtbarer Kräfte. Denunziationsmuster und Denunziationsverhalten 1939–1949* (Tübingen, 2003).

Alberti, Michael, *Die Verfolgung und Vernichtung der Juden im Reichsgau Wartheland* (Wiesbaden, 2006).

Aly, Götz, *Final Solution: Nazi Population Policy and the Murder of the European Jews* (London, 1999).

Angrick, Andrej and Klein, Peter, *The 'Final Solution' in Riga: Exploitation and Annihilation, 1941–1944* (New York and Oxford, 2009) [Angrick, Andrej and Klein, Peter, *Die 'Endlösung' in Riga. Ausbeutung und Vernichtung 1941–1944* (Darmstadt, 2006)].

Arendt, Hannah, *Eichmann in Jerusalem: A Report on the Banality of Evil* (Penguin, 1977).

Arens, Cord, Wolfrum, Edgar and Zedler, Jörg (eds), *Terror nach innen. Verbrechen am Ende des Zweiten Weltkrieges* (Göttingen, 2006).

Aronson, Shlomo, *Reinhard Heydrich und die Frühgeschichte von Gestapo und SD* (Stuttgart, 1971).

Banach, Jens, *Heydrichs Elite. Das Führerkorps der Sicherheitspolizei und des SD 1936–1945* (Paderborn, 2002).

Bauman, Zygmunt, *Dialectic of Modernity* (London, 2000).

Benz, Wolfgang (ed.), *Die Juden in Deutschland 1933–1945. Leben unter nationalsozialistischer Herrschaft* (Munich, 1988).

Benz, Wolfgang (ed.), *Dimension des Völkermords. Die Zahl der jüdischen Opfer des Nationalsozialismus* (Munich, 1996).

Benz, Wolfgang, *Geschichte des Dritten Reiches* (Munich, 2000).

Benz, Wolfgang and Distel, Barbara (eds), *Terror ohne System. Die ersten Konzentrationslager im Nationalsozialismus 1933–1935* (Berlin, 2001).

Benz, Wolfgang and Distel, Barbara (eds), *Der Ort des Terrors. Geschichte der nationalsozialistischen Konzentrationslager*, vol. 1, *Die Organisation des Terrors* (Munich, 2005).

Berschel, Holger, *Bürokratie und Terror. Das Judenreferat der Gestapo Düsseldorf, 1935–1945* (Essen, 2001).

Birn, Ruth Bettina, *Die Höheren SS- und Polizeiführer. Himmlers Vertreter im Reich und in den besetzten Gebieten* (Düsseldorf, 1986).

Birn, Ruth Bettina, *Die Sicherheitspolizei in Estland 1941–1944. Eine Studie zur Kolla-boration im Osten* (Paderborn etc., 2006).

Black, Peter R., *Ernst Kaltenbrunner: Ideological Soldier of the Third Reich* (Princeton, 1984).

Boberach, Heinz (ed.), *Regimekritik, Widerstand und Verfolgung in Deutschland und den besetzten Gebieten. Meldungen aus dem Geheimen Staatspolizeiamt, dem SD-Hauptamt der SS und dem Reichssicherheitshauptamt 1933–1945.* Index volume for the micro-fiche edition (Munich, 2003).

Borgstedt, Angela, Frech, Siegfried and Stolle, Michael (eds), *Lange Schatten. Bewältigung von Diktaturen* (Schwalbach, 2007).

Borodziej, Włodzimierz, *Terror und Politik. Die deutsche Polizei und die polnische Widerstandsbewegung im Generalgouvernement 1939–1944* (Mainz, 1999).

Bracher, Karl-Dietrich, Funke, Manfred and Jacobsen, Hans-Adolf (eds), *National-alsozialistische Diktatur 1933–1945. Eine Bilanz* (Düsseldorf, 1983).

Bracher, Karl-Dietrich, Funke, Manfred and Jacobsen, Hans-Adolf (eds), *Deutschland 1933–1945. Neue Studien zur nationalsozialistischen Herrschaft* (Düsseldorf, 1992).

Broszat, Martin, *The Hitler State: The Foundation and Development of the Internal Structure of the Third Reich* (London, 1981) [Broszat, Martin, *Der Staat Hitlers. Grundlegung und Entwicklung seiner inneren Verfassung* (Munich, 1969)].

Broszat, Martin, 'Siegerjustiz oder strafrechtliche "Selbstreinigung". Aspekte der Vergangenheitsbewältigung der deutschen Justiz während der Besatzungszeit 1945–1949', *Vierteljahreshefte für Zeitgeschichte*, 29 (1981), 477–544.

Browder, George C., *Foundations of the Nazi Police State: The Formation of Sipo and SD* (Lexington, 1990).

Browder, George C., *Hitler's Enforcers: The Gestapo and the SS Security Service in the Nazi Revolution* (New York, 1996).

Browning, Christopher R., *Fateful Months: Essays on the Emergence of the Final Solution* (New York and London, 1985).

Browning, Christopher R., *Ordinary Men: Reserve Police Battalion 101 and the Final Solution in Poland* (London, 1998).

Browning, Christopher R., *The Origins of the Final Solution: The Evolution of Nazi Jewish Policy, September 1939–March 1942* (Lincoln, Neb., 2007).

Buchheim, Hans, Broszat, Martin, Jacobsen, Hans-Adolf and Krausnick, Helmut, *Anatomie des SS-Staates* (Olten, 1965).

Buhlan, Harald and Jung, Werner (eds), *Wessen Freund und wessen Helfer? Die Kölner Polizei im Nationalsozialismus* (Cologne, 2000).

Burleigh, Michael, *The Third Reich: A New History* (London, 2000).

Buschfort, Wolfgang, *Geheime Hüter der Verfassung. Von der Düsseldorfer Informa-tionsstelle zum ersten Verfassungsschutz der Bundesrepublik (1947–1961)* (Paderborn etc., 2004).

Cesarani, David, *Eichmann: His Life and Crimes* (London, 2005) [Cesarani, David, *Adolf Eichmann. Bürokrat und Massenmörder, Biografie* (Berlin, 2004)].

Coppi, Hans, Danyel, Jürgen and Tuchel, Johannes (eds), *Die Rote Kapelle im Widerstand gegen den Nationalsozialismus* (Berlin, 1994).

Crankshaw, Edward, *Gestapo* (London, 1956).

Cüppers, Martin, *Wegbereiter der Shoa. Die Waffen-SS, der Kommandostab Reichsführer-SS und die Judenvernichtung 1939–1945* (Darmstadt, 2005).

Curilla, Wolfgang, *Die deutsche Ordnungspolizei und der Holocaust im Baltikum und in Weißrußland 1941–1944* (Paderborn etc., 2006).

Dams, Carsten, *Staatsschutz in der Weimarer Republik. Die Überwachung und Bekämpfung der NSDAP durch die preußische politische Polizei von 1928 bis 1932* (Marburg, 2002).

Dams, Carsten, 'Kontinuitäten und Brüche. Die höheren preußischen Kriminalbeamten im Übergang von der Weimarer Republik zum Nationalsozialismus', *Kriminalistik*, 58 (2004), 478–83.

Dams, Carsten, Dönecke, Klaus and Köhler, Thomas (eds), *'Dienst am Volk'? Düsseldorfer Polizisten zwischen Demokratie und Diktatur* (Frankfurt am Main, 2007).

Das 'Hausgefängnis' der Gestapo-Zentrale in Berlin. Terror und Widerstand 1933–1945, published by the Stiftung Topographie des Terrors (Berlin, 2005), 112–19.

Delarue, Jacques, *The Gestapo: A History of Horror* (London, 2008) [first published as Delarue, Jacques, *The History of the Gestapo* (London, 1964)].

Der Dienstkalender Heinrich Himmlers 1941/42, ed. with commentary and introduction by Peter Witte et al. (Hamburg, 1999).

Dieckmann, Christoph, Quinkert, Babette and Tönsmeyer, Tatjana (eds), *Kooperation und Verbrechen. Formen der Kollaboration im östlichen Europa 1939–1945* (Göttingen, 2003).

Dierl, Florian, et al. (eds), *Ordnung und Vernichtung. Die Polizei im NS-Staat* (Dresden, 2011).

Dörner, Bernward, *'Heimtücke'. Das Gesetz als Waffe. Kontrolle, Abschreckung und Verfolgung in Deutschland 1933–1945* (Paderborn etc., 1998).

Eisert, Wolfgang, *Die Waldheimer Prozesse. Der stalinistische Terror 1950. Ein dunkles Kapitel der DDR-Justiz* (Munich, 1993).

Evans, Richard J., *The Coming of the Third Reich* (London, 2004).

Evans, Richard J., *The Third Reich in Power, 1933–1939* (London, 2005).

Evans, Richard J., *The Third Reich at War 1939–1945* (London, 2008).

Faatz, Martin, *Vom Staatsschutz zum Gestapo-Terror. Politische Polizei in Bayern in der Endphase der Weimarer Republik und der Anfangsphase der nationalsozialistischen Diktatur* (Würzburg, 1995).

Fraenkel, Ernst, *The Dual State: A Contribution to the Theory of Dictatorship* (Clark, NJ, 2006).

Frei, Norbert, *Adenauer's Germany and the Nazi Past: The Politics of Amnesty and Integration* (New York and Chichester, 2002) [Frei, Norbert, *Vergangenheitspolitik. Die Anfänge der Bundesrepublik und die NS-Vergangenheit* (Munich, 1996)].

Frei, Norbert, 'Zwischen Terror und Integration. Zur Funktion der politischen Polizei im Nationalsozialismus', in C. Dipper, R. Hudemann, and J. Petersen (eds), *Faschismus und Faschismen im Vergleich. Wolfgang Schieder zum 60. Geburtstag* (Cologne, 1998), 217–28.

Frei, Norbert, Steinbacher, Sybille and Wagner, Bernd C. (eds), *Ausbeutung, Vernichtung, Öffentlichkeit. Neue Studien zur nationalsozialistischen Lagerpolitik* (Munich, 2000).

Frei, Norbert, van Laak, Dirk and Stolleis, Michael (eds), *Geschichte vor Gericht. Historiker, Richter und die Suche nach Gerechtigkeit* (Munich, 2000).

Friedlander, Henry, *Der Weg zum NS-Genozid. Von der Euthanasie zur Endlösung* (Berlin, 1997).

Friedlander, Saul, *Nazi Germany and the Jews*, vol. 1, *The Years of Persecution, 1933–1939* (London, 1997).

Friedlander, Saul, *Nazi Germany and the Jews*, vol. 2, *The Years of Extermination, 1939–1945* (London, 2008).

Friedrich, Jörg, *The Fire: The Bombing of Germany, 1940–1945* (New York and Chichester, 2008) [Friedrich, Jörg, *Der Brand. Deutschland im Bombenkrieg 1940–1945* (Munich, 2002)].

Friedrich, Jörg, *Kalte Amnestie. NS-Täter in der Bundesrepublik* (Munich, 2007).

Fritz Bauer Institut (ed.), *'Gerichtstag halten über uns selbst...' Geschichte und Wirkung des ersten Frankfurter Auschwitz-Prozesses* (Frankfurt am Main and New York, 2001).

Fürstenau, Justus, *Entnazifizierung. Ein Kapitel deutscher Nachkriegspolitik* (Neuwied and Berlin, 1969).

Garbe, Detlef, *Zwischen Widerstand und Martyrium. Die Zeugen Jehovas im 'Dritten Reich'* (Munich, 1999).

Garland, David, *The Culture of Control: Crime and Social Order in Contemporary Society* (Oxford and New York, 2002).

Gebauer, Thomas, *Das KPD-Dezernat der Gestapo Düsseldorf* (Hamburg, 2011).

Gellately, Robert, *The Gestapo and German Society: Enforcing Racial Policy 1933–1945* (Oxford, 1990).

Gellately, Robert, 'Rethinking the Nazi Terror System. A Historiographical Analysis', *German Studies Review*, 14 (1991), 23 f.

Gellately, Robert, *Backing Hitler: Consent and Coercion in Nazi Germany* (Oxford, 2002).

Gerlach, Christian, *Kalkulierte Morde. Die deutsche Wirtschafts- und Vernichtungspolitik in Weißrußland 1941 bis 1944* (Hamburg, 1999).

Gerlach, Christian and Aly, Götz, *Das letzte Kapitel. Der Mord an den ungarischen Juden 1941–1945* (Frankfurt am Main, 2004).

Gerwarth, Robert, *Reinhard Heydrich. Biographie* (Munich, 2011).

Gestapo Oldenburg meldet... Berichte der Geheimen Staatspolizei und des Innenministers aus dem Freistaat und Land Oldenburg 1933–1936, ed. with an introduction by Albrecht Eckhardt und Katharina Hoffmann (Hanover, 2002).

Goebbels, Joseph, *Die Tagebücher von Joseph Goebbels. Sämtliche Fragmente*, ed. Elke Fröhlich, Part I. *Aufzeichnungen 1924–1941* (Munich etc., 1987).

Goldhagen, Daniel Jonah, *Hitler's Willing Executioners* (London, 1996).

Graf, Christoph, *Politische Polizei zwischen Demokratie und Diktatur. Die Entwicklung der preußischen Politischen Polizei vom Staatsschutzorgan der Weimarer Republik zum Geheimen Staatspolizeiamt des Dritten Reiches* (Berlin, 1983).

Gruchmann, Lothar, *Justiz im Dritten Reich 1933–1940. Anpassung und Unterwerfung in der Ära Gürtner* (Munich, 1988).

Grundmann, Siegfried, *Der Geheimapparat der KPD im Visier der Gestapo. Das BB-Ressort, Funktionäre, Beamte, Spitzel und Spione* (Berlin, 2007).

Gusy, Christoph, *Weimar—die wehrlose Republik? Verfassungsschutzrecht und Verfassungsschutz in der Weimarer Republik* (Tübingen, 1991).

Gutermuth, Frank and Netzbandt, Arno, *Die Gestapo* (Berlin, 2005).

Hachmeister, Lutz, *Der Gegnerforscher. Die Karriere des SS-Führers Franz Alfred Six* (Munich, 1998).

Halimi, Andrè, *La Délation sous l'Occupation* (Paris, 1983).

Hamburg Institute for Social Research (ed.), *The German Army and Genocide: Crimes against War Prisoners, Jews and other Civilians in the East, 1939–1944* (New York, 1999) [Hamburger Institut für Sozialforschung (ed.), *Verbrechen der Wehrmacht. Dimensionen des Vernichtungskrieges 1941–1944* (Hamburg, 2002)].

Heer, Hannes (ed.), *Im Herzen der Finsternis. Victor Klemperer als Chronist der NS-Zeit* (Berlin, 1997).

Hehl, Ulrich von, *Nationalsozialistische Herrschaft* (Munich, 1996).

Hehl, Ulrich von, et al. (eds), *Priester unter Hitlers Terror. Eine biografische und statistische Erhebung* (Paderborn etc., 1998).

Heinemann, Isabel, *'Rasse, Siedlung, deutsches Blut'. Das Rasse- und Siedlungshauptamt der SS und die rassenpolitische Neuordnung Europas* (Göttingen, 2003).

Henke, Klaus-Dietmar and Woller, Hans (eds), *Politische Säuberung in Europa. Die Abrechnung mit Faschismus und Kollaboration nach dem Zweiten Weltkrieg* (Munich, 1991).

Henkys, Reinhard, *Die nationalsozialistischen Gewaltverbrechen. Geschichte und Gericht* (Stuttgart and Berlin, 1964).

Hensle, Michael P, *Rundfunkverbrechen. Das Hören von 'Feindsendern' im Nationalsozialismus* (Berlin, 2003).

Herbert, Ulrich, *Hitler's Foreign Workers: Enforced Foreign Labor in Germany under the Third Reich* (Cambridge, 1997) [Herbert, Ulrich, *Fremdarbeiter. Politik und Praxis des 'Ausländer-Einsatzes' in der Kriegswirtschaft des Dritten Reiches* (Bonn, 1985)].

Herbert, Ulrich (ed.), *Europa und der Reichseinsatz. Ausländische Zivilarbeiter, Kriegsgefangene und KZ-Häftlinge in Deutschland 1938–1945* (Essen, 1991).

Herbert, Ulrich (ed.), *National-Socialist Extermination Policies: Contemporary German Perspectives and Controversies* (New York and Oxford, 2000).

Herbert, Ulrich, *Best. Biographische Studien über Radikalismus, Weltanschauung und Vernunft 1903–1989* (Bonn, 2001).

Herbert, Ulrich (ed.), *Wandlungsprozesse in Westdeutschland. Belastung, Integration, Liberalisierung 1945–1980* (Göttingen, 2003).

Herbert, Ulrich, Orth, Karin and Dieckmann, Christoph (eds), *Die nationalsozialistischen Konzentrationslager. Entwicklung und Struktur*, vol. 1 (Frankfurt am Main, 2002).

Hilberg, Raul, *Perpetrators, Victims, Bystanders: The Jewish Catastrophe 1933–1945* (London, 1995).

Hilberg, Raul, *Täter, Opfer, Zuschauer. Die Vernichtung der Juden 1933–1945* (Frankfurt am Main, 1997).

Hilberg, Raul, *The Destruction of the European Jews* (New Haven and London, 2003) [Hilberg, Raul, *Die Vernichtung der europäischen Juden*, 3 vols (Frankfurt am Main, 1999)].

Hilberg, Raul, *Die Quellen des Holocaust. Entschlüsseln und Interpretieren* (Frankfurt am Main, 2003).

Hildebrand, Klaus, *Das Dritte Reich*, 6th edn (Munich, 2003).

Hirschfeld, Gerhard, *Fremdherrschaft und Kollaboration. Die Niederlande unter deutscher Besatzung* (Stuttgart, 1984).

Hockerts, Hans Günter, *Die Sittlichkeitsprozesse gegen katholische Ordensangehörige und Priester 1936/37. Eine Studie zur nationalsozialistischen Herrschaftstechnik und zum Kirchenkampf* (Mainz, 1971).

Ibel, Johannes (ed.), *Einvernehmliche Zusammenarbeit? Wehrmacht, Gestapo, SS und sowjetische Kriegsgefangene* (Berlin, 2007).

Jellonnek, Burkhard, *Homosexuelle unter dem Hakenkreuz. Die Verfolgung von Homosexuellen im Dritten Reich* (Paderborn etc., 1990).

Jellonnek, Burkhard, 'Staatspolizeiliche Fahndungs- und Ermittlungsmethoden gegen Homosexuelle', in Burkhard Jellonnek and Rüdiger Lautmann (eds), *Nationalsozialistischer Terror gegen Homosexuelle. Verdrängt und ungesühnt* (Paderborn, 2002), 149–61.

Johnson, Eric A., *Nazi Terror: The Gestapo, Jews and Ordinary Germans* (London, 2000).

Justiz und NS-Verbrechen: Sammlung deutscher Strafurteile wegen nationalsozialistischer Tötungsverbrechen 1945–1999, ed. Adelheid L. Rüter-Ehlermann and Christaan F. Rüter, 37 vols so far (Amsterdam, 1968–2007).

Kaiser, Wolf (ed.), *Täter im Vernichtungskrieg. Der Überfall auf die Sowjetunion und der Völkermord an den Juden* (Berlin and Munich, 2002).

Kenkmann, Alfons and Rusinek, Bernd A., *Verfolgung und Verwaltung. Die wirtschaftliche Ausplünderung der Juden und die westfälischen Finanzbehörden* (Münster, 1999).

Kershaw, Ian, *Hitler: Profiles in Power* (Harlow, 1991).

Kershaw, Ian, *Hitler 1889–1936: Hubris* (Harmondsworth, 1998).

Kißener, Michael, *Das Dritte Reich* (Darmstadt, 2005).

Klarsfeld, Serge, *Vichy—Auschwitz. Die 'Endlösung der Judenfrage' in Frankreich*, aktualisierte Neuausgabe (Darmstadt, 2007).

Klein, Peter (ed.), *Die Einsatzgruppen in der besetzten Sowjetunion 1941/42. Die Tätigkeits- und Lageberichte des Chefs der Sicherheitspolizei und des SD* (Berlin, 1997).

Klemp, Stefan, *'Nicht ermittelt'. Polizeibataillone und die Nachkriegsjustiz—Ein Handbuch* (Essen, 2005).

Koehl, Robert L., *The Black Corps: The Structure and Power Struggle of the Nazi SS* (Madison, Wisconsin, 1983).

Krakoswki, Shmuel, *Das Todeslager Chełmo and Kulmhof. Der Beginn der Endlösung* (Göttingen, 2007).

Krausnick, Helmut, *Hitlers Einsatzgruppen. Die Truppe des Weltanschauungskrieges 1938–1942* (Frankfurt am Main, 1998).

Krausnick, Helmut and Broszat, Martin, *Anatomy of the SS State* (London, 1970).

Kunz, Andreas, *Wehrmacht und Niederlage. Die bewaffnete Macht in der Endphase der nationalsozialistischen Herrschaft 1944 bis 1945* (Munich, 2007).

Lang, Jochen von, *Die Gestapo. Instrument des Terrors* (Hamburg, 1990).

Leide, Henry, *NS-Verbrecher und Staatsicherheit. Die geheime Vergangenheitspolitik der DDR* (Göttingen, 2005).

Lieb, Peter, *Konventioneller Krieg oder NS-Weltanschauungskrieg? Kriegsführung und Partisanenbekämpfung in Frankreich 1943/44* (Munich, 2007).

Linck, Stephan, *Der Ordnung verpflichtet. Deutsche Polizei 1933–1949. Der Fall Flensburg* (Paderborn etc., 2000).

Longerich, Peter, *Holocaust: The Nazi Persecution and Murder of the Jews* (Oxford, 2012) [Longerich, Peter, *Politik der Vernichtung. Eine Gesamtdarstellung der nationalsozialistischen Judenverfolgung* (Munich and Zürich, 1998)].

Longerich, Peter, *Geschichte der SA* (Munich, 2003).

Longerich, Peter, *Heinrich Himmler: A Life* (Oxford, 2012) [Longerich, Peter, *Heinrich Himmler. Eine Biographie* (Munich, 2009)].

Lotfi, Gabriele, *KZ der Gestapo. Arbeitserziehungslager im Dritten Reich* (Frankfurt am Main, 2003).

Lozowick, Yaacov, *Hitler's Bureaucrats: The Nazi Security Police and the Banality of Evil* (London, 2003) [Lozowick, Yaacov, *Hitlers Bürokraten. Eichmann, seine willigen Vollstrecker und die Banalität des Bösen* (Zurich, 2000)].

Lübbe, Hermann, 'Der Nationalsozialismus im deutschen Nachkriegsbewusstsein', *Historische Zeitschrift*, 236 (1983), 579–99.

Lukaßen, Dirk, 'Menschenkinder vor dem Richter'. Kölner Gestapo und die Nachkriegsjustiz. Der 'Hoegen-Prozess' vor dem Kölner Schwurgericht im Jahr 1949 und seine Rezeption in den lokalen Tageszeitungen (Siegburg, 2006).

Majer, Diemut, *'Fremdvölkische' im Dritten Reich. Ein Beitrag zur nationalsozialistischen Rechtssetzung und Rechtspraxis in Verwaltung und Justiz unter besonderer Berücksichtigung der eingegliederten Ostgebiete und des Generalgouvernements* (Boppard, 1981).

Mallmann, Klaus-Michael and Angrick, Andrej (eds), *Die Gestapo nach 1945. Konflikte, Karrieren, Konstruktionen* (Darmstadt, 2009).

Mallman, Klaus-Michael and Cüppers, Martin, *Nazi Palestine: The Plans for the Extermination of the Jews in Palestine* (New York, 2010) [Mallmann, Klaus-

Michael and Cüppers, Martin, *Halbmond und Hakenkreuz. Das Dritte Reich, die Araber und Palästina* (Darmstadt, 2006)].

Mallmann, Klaus-Michael and Musial, Bogdan (eds), *Genesis des Genozids. Polen 1939–1941* (Darmstadt, 2004).

Mallmann, Klaus-Michael and Paul, Gerhard, 'Allwissend, allmächtig, allgegenwärtig? Gestapo, Gesellschaft und Widerstand', *Zeitschrift für Geschichtswissenschaft*, 41 (1993), 984–99.

Mallmann, Klaus-Michael and Paul, Gerhard (eds), *Karrieren der Gewalt. Nationalsozialistische Täterbiographien* (Darmstadt, 2004).

Mallmann, Klaus-Michael, Böhler, Jochen and Matthäus, Jürgen, *Einsatzgruppen in Polen. Darstellung und Dokumentation* (Darmstadt, 2008).

Mann, Michael, *Die dunkle Seite der Demokratie. Eine Theorie der ethnischen Säuberung* (Hamburg, 2007).

Mann, Reinhard, *Protest und Kontrolle im Dritten Reich. Nationalsozialistische Herrschaft im Alltag einer rheinischen Großstadt* (Frankfurt am Main and New York, 1987).

Manoschek, Walter (ed.), *Die Wehrmacht im Rassenkrieg. Der Vernichtungskrieg hinter der Front* (Vienna, 1996).

Matthäus, Jürgen, et al., *Ausbildungsziel Judenmord? 'Weltanschauliche Erziehung' von SS, Polizei und Waffen-SS im Rahmen der 'Endlösung'* (Frankfurt am Main, 2003).

Matthäus, Jürgen and Mallmann, Klaus-Michael (eds), *Deutsche, Juden, Völkermord. Der Holocaust als Geschichte und Gegenwart* (Darmstadt, 2006).

Mazower, Mark, *Inside Hitler's Greece: The Experience of Occupation 1941–1944* (New Haven and London, 1993).

Mensing, Wilhelm, 'Vertrauensleute kommunistischer Herkunft bei Gestapo und NS-Nachrichtendiensten am Beispiel von Rhein und Ruhr', *Jahrbuch für historische Kommunismusforschung* (2004), 111–30.

Meyer, Ahlrich, *Die deutsche Besatzung in Frankreich 1940–1944. Widerstandsbewegung und Judenverfolgung* (Darmstadt, 2000).

Meyer, Ahlrich, *Täter im Verhör. Die 'Endlösung der Judenfrage' in Frankreich 1940–1944* (Darmstadt, 2005).

Miquel, Marc von, *Ahnden oder amnestieren? Westdeutsche Justiz und Vergangenheitspolitik in den sechziger Jahren* (Göttingen, 2004).

Młynarczyk, Jacek Andrzej, *Judenmord in Zentralpolen. Der Distrikt Radom im Generalgouvernement 1939–1945* (Darmstadt, 2007).

Möller, Horst, Wirsching, Andreas and Ziegler, Walter (eds), *Nationalsozialismus in der Region. Beiträge zur regionalen und lokalen Forschung und zum internationalen Vergleich* (Munich, 1996).

Moller, Sabine, et al. (eds), *Abgeschlossene Kapitel? Zur Geschichte der Konzentrationslager und der NS-Prozesse* (Tübingen, 2002).

Mommsen, Hans, *Beamtentum im Dritten Reich. Mit ausgewählten Quellen zur nationalsozialistischen Beamtenpolitik* (Stuttgart, 1966).

Mommsen, Hans, *Der Nationalsozialismus und die deutsche Gesellschaft* (Reinbek, 1991).

Mommsen, Hans, *Alternative zu Hitler—Studien zur Geschichte des deutschen Widerstands* (Munich, 2000).

Mühlen, Bengt von zur and Klewitz, Andreas (eds), *Die 12 Nürnberger Nachfolgeprozesse* (Berlin, 2000).

Müller, Rolf-Dieter, *Der letzte deutsche Krieg 1939–1945* (Stuttgart, 2005).

Müller, Rolf-Dieter, *An der Seite der Wehrmacht. Hitlers ausländische Helfer beim 'Kreuzzug gegen den Bolschewismus' 1941–1945* (Berlin, 2007).

Musial, Bogdan, *'Aktion Reinhard'. Der Völkermord an den Juden im Generalgouvernement 1941–1944* (Osnabrück, 2004).

Musil, Robert, *The Man without Qualities*, trans. Sophie Wilkins and Burton Pike (London, 2002).

Neliba, Günter, *Wilhelm Frick. Der Legalist des Unrechtsstaates. Eine politische Biographie* (Paderborn etc., 1992).

Neumann, Franz, *Behemoth: The Structure and Practice of National Socialism* (New York, 2009) [first published London, 1942].

Niethammer, Lutz, *Die Mitläuferfabrik. Die Entnazifizierung am Beispiel Bayerns* (Bonn and Berlin, 1982).

Ogorreck, Ralf, *Die Einsatzgruppen und die 'Genesis der Endlösung'* (Berlin, 1996).

Orth, Karin, *Das System der nationalsozialistischen Konzentrationslager. Eine politische Organisationsgeschichte* (Hamburg, 1999).

Osterloh, Jörg, *Nationalsozialistische Judenverfolgung im Reichsgau Sudetenland 1938–1945* (Munich, 2006).

Otto, Reinhard, *Wehrmacht, Gestapo und sowjetische Kriegegefangene im deutschen Reichsgebiet 1941 und 42* (Munich, 1998).

Paul, Gerhard, *Staatlicher Terror und gesellschaftliche Verrohung. Die Gestapo in Schleswig-Holstein* (Hamburg, 1996).

Paul, Gerhard (ed.), *Die Täter der Shoa. Fanatische Nationalsozialisten oder ganz normale Deutsche?* (Göttingen, 2003).

Paul, Gerhard and Mallmann, Klaus-Michael (eds), *Die Gestapo. Mythos und Realität* (Darmstadt, 1995).

Paul, Gerhard and Mallmann, Klaus-Michael (eds), *Die Gestapo im Zweiten Weltkrieg. 'Heimatfront' und besetztes Europa* (Darmstadt, 2000).

Pohl, Dieter, *Nationalsozialistische Judenverfolgung in Ostgalizien 1941–1944. Organisation und Durchführung eines staatlichen Massenverbrechens* (Munich, 1997).

Pohl, Dieter, 'The Murder of the Jews in the General Government', in Ulrich Herbert (ed.), *National-Socialist Extermination Policies: Contemporary German Perspectives and Controversies* (New York and Oxford, 2000), 83–103.

Pohl, Dieter, *Verfolgung und Massenmord in der NS-Zeit 1933–1945* (Darmstadt, 2003).

Pöschkö, Hans (ed.), *Die Ermittler von Ludwigsburg. Deutschland und die Aufklärung nationalsozialistischer Verbrechen* (Berlin, 2008).

Quack, Sibylle (ed.), *Dimensionen der Verfolgung. Opfer und Opfergruppen im Nationalsozialismus* (Munich, 2003).

Reichel, Peter, *Vergangenheitsbewältigung in Deutschland. Die Auseinandersetzung mit der NS-Diktatur von 1945 bis heute* (Munich, 2001).

Reichel, Peter, Steinbach, Peter and Schmid, Harald (eds), *Der Nationalsozialismus— die zweite Geschichte, Überwindung, Deutung, Erinnerung* (Munich, 2009).

Römer, Sebastian, *Mitglieder verbrecherischer Organisationen nach 1945. Die Ahndung des Organisationsverbrechens in der britischen Zone durch die Spruchgerichte* (Frankfurt am Main etc., 2005).

Roseman, Mark, *The Villa, the Lake, the Meeting: Wannsee and the Final Solution* (London, 2002).

Ross, Friso and Landwehr, Achim (eds), *Denunziation und Justiz. Historische Dimensionen eines sozialen Phänomens* (Tübingen, 2000).

Ruck, Michael, *Bibliographie zum Nationalsozialismus*, 2 vols (Darmstadt, 2000).

Ruckenbiel, Jan, *Soziale Kontrolle im NS-Regime. Protest, Denunziation und Verfolgung. Zur Praxis alltäglicher Unterdrückung im Wechselspiel von Bevölkerung und Gestapo* (Cologne, 2003).

Rückerl, Adalbert (ed.), *NS-Prozesse. Nach 25 Jahren Strafverfolgung, Möglichkeiten, Grenzen, Ergebnisse* (Karlsruhe, 1971).

Rückerl, Adalbert, *Die Strafverfolgung von NS-Verbrechen 1945–1978. Eine Dokumentation* (Heidelberg and Karlsruhe, 1979).

Rückerl, Adalbert, *NS-Verbrechen vor Gericht, Versuch einer Vergangenheitsbewältigung* (Heidelberg, 1984).

Rürup, Reinhard (ed.), *Topographie des Terrors. Gestapo, SS und Reichssicherheitshauptamt auf dem 'Prinz-Albrecht-Gelände'. Eine Dokumentation* (Berlin, 2005).

Rusinek, Bernd-A., *Gesellschaft in der Katastrophe. Terror, Illegalität, Widerstand. Köln 1944 and 45* (Essen, 1989).

Safrian, Hans, *Eichmann's Men* (Cambridge, 2010) [Safrian, Hans, *Eichmann und seine Gehilfen* (Frankfurt am Main, 1997)].

Schafranek, Hans, 'V-Leute und "Verräter". Die Unterwanderung kommunistischer Widerstandsgruppen durch Konfidenten der Wiener Gestapo', *IWK* (2000), 300–49.

Schildt, Axel and Sywottek, Arnold (eds), *Modernisierung im Wiederaufbau. Die westdeutsche Gesellschaft der 50er Jahre* (Bonn, 1993).

Schmädecke, Jörg and Steinbach, Peter (eds), *Der Widerstand gegen den Nationalsozialismus. Die deutsche Gesellschaft und der Widerstand gegen Hitler* (Munich, 1985).

Schmid, Hans-Dieter, *Gestapo Leipzig. Politische Abteilung des Polizeipräsidiums und Staatspolizeistelle Leipzig* (Beucha, 1997).

Schneider, Andreas Theo, *Die Geheime Staatspolizei im NS-Gau Thüringen. Geschichte, Struktur, Personal und Wirkungsfelder* (Frankfurt am Main, 2008).

Schulte, Jan Erik, *Zwangsarbeit und Vernichtung, Das Wirtschaftsimperium der SS. Oswald Pohl und das SS-Wirtschafts-Verwaltungshauptamt* (Paderborn etc., 2001).

Schulte, Wolfgang (ed.), *Die Polizei im NS-Staat. Beiträge eines internationalen Symposiums an der Deutschen Hochschule der Polizei in Münster* (Frankfurt am Main, 2009).

Schwegel, Andreas, *Der Polizeibegriff im NS-Staat. Polizeirecht, juristische Publizistik und Judikative 1931–1944* (Tübingen, 2005).

Seeger, Andreas, *'Gestapo-Müller'. Die Karriere eines Schreibtischtäters* (Berlin, 1996).

Seibel, Wolfgang, 'Verfolgungsnetzwerke. Zur Messung von Arbeitsteilung und Machtdifferenzierung in den Verfolgungsapparaten des Holocaust', *Kölner Zeitschrift für Soziologie und Sozialpsychologie*, 55 (2003), 197–230.

Seidel, Robert, *Deutsche Besatzungspolitik in Polen. Der Distrikt Radom 1939–1945* (Paderborn etc., 2006).

Smelser, Ronald and Syring, Enrico (eds), *Die SS. Elite unter dem Totenkopf* (Paderborn, 2003).

Spoerer, Marc, *Zwangsarbeit unter dem Hakenkreuz. Ausländische Zivilarbeiter, Kriegsgefangene und Häftlinge im Deutschen Reich und im besetzten Europa 1939–1945* (Stuttgart and Munich, 2001).

Steinbach, Peter, *Nationalsozialistische Gewaltverbrechen. Die Diskussion in der deutschen Öffentlichkeit nach 1945* (Berlin, 1981).

Steinbach, Peter, *Widerstand im Widerstreit. Der Widerstand gegen den Nationalsozialismus in der Erinnerung der Deutschen* (Paderborn etc., 2001).

Steinbach, Peter and Tuchel, Johannes (eds), *Widerstand gegen die nationalsozialistische Diktatur 1933–1945* (Berlin, 2004).

Steinbacher, Sybille, *'Musterstadt' Auschwitz. Germanisierungspolitik und Judenmord in Ostoberschlesien* (Munich, 2000).

Steur, Claudia, *Theodor Dannecker. Ein Funktionär der Endlösung* (Essen, 1997).

Stolle, Michael, *Die Geheime Staatspolizei in Baden. Personal, Organisation, Wirkung und Nachwirken einer regionalen Verfolgungsbehörde im Dritten Reich* (Constance, 2001).

Stolle, Michael, 'Auf dem Weg zu einer Wahrnehmungsgeschichte der Gestapo?', in Peter I. Trummer and Konrad Pflug (eds), *Die Brüder Stauffenberg und der deutsche Widerstand. Eine Bestandsaufnahme aus Sicht der historisch-politischen Bildung* (Stuttgart, 2006), 90–7.

Tausendfreund, Doris, *Erzwungener Verrat. Jüdische 'Greifer' im Dienste der Gestapo 1943–1945* (Berlin, 2006).

Thalhofer, Elisabeth, *Neue Bremm—Terrorstätte der Gestapo. Ein Erweitertes Polizeigefängnis und seine Täter 1943–1944* (St Ingbert, 2003).

Thamer, Hans-Ulrich, *Der Nationalsozialismus* (Stuttgart, 2002).

Tomaszewski, Jerzy, *Auftakt zur Vernichtung. Die Vertreibung polnischer Juden aus Deutschland im Jahre 1938* (Osnabrück 2002).

Tönsmeyer, Tatjana, *Das Dritte Reich und die Slowakei 1939–1945. Politischer Alltag zwischen Kooperation und Eigensinn* (Paderborn etc., 2003).

Tuchel, Johannes, *Konzentrationslager. Organisationsgeschichte und Funktion der 'Inspektion der Konzentrationslager' 1934–1938* (Boppard, 1991).

Tuchel, Johannes and Schattenfroh, Reinhold, *Zentrale des Terrors. Prinz-Albrecht-Straße 8, Hauptquartier der Gestapo* (Berlin, 1987).

Ueberschär, Gerd R. (ed.), *Der Nationalsozialismus vor Gericht. Die alliierten Prozesse gegen Kriegsverbrecher und Soldaten 1943–1952* (Frankfurt am Main, 1999).

Volkmann, Hans-Erich (ed.), *Ende des Dritten Reiches—Ende des Zweiten Weltkriegs. Eine perspektivische Rückschau* (Munich and Zurich, 1995).

Vollnhals, Clemens (ed.), *Politische Säuberung und Rehabilitierung in den vier Besatzungszonen 1945–1949* (Munich, 1991).

Wachsmann, Nikolaus, *Hitler's Prisons: Legal Terror in Nazi Germany* (New Haven and London, 2004) [Wachsmann, Nikolaus, *Gefangen unter Hitler. Justizterror und Strafvollzug im NS-Staat* (Berlin, 2004)].

Wagner, Herbert, *Die Gestapo war nicht allein.... Politische Sozialkontrolle und Staatsterror im deutsch-niederländischen Grenzgebiet 1929–1945* (Münster, 2004).

Wagner, Patrick, *Hitlers Kriminalisten. Die deutsche Kriminalpolizei und der Nationalsozialismus zwischen 1920 und 1960* (Munich, 2002).

Walk, Joseph (ed.), *Das Sonderrecht für die Juden im NS-Staat. Eine Sammlung der gesetzlichen Maßnahmen und Richtlinien—Inhalt und Bedeutung* (Heidelberg, 1981).

Warmbrunn, Werner, *The German Occupation of Belgium 1940–1944* (New York etc., 1993).

Weber, Jürgen and Steinbach, Peter (eds), *Vergangenheitsbewältigung durch Strafverfahren? NS-Prozesse in der Bundesrepublik Deutschland* (Munich, 1984).

Weber, Wolfram, *Die innere Sicherheit im besetzten Belgien und Nordfrankreich 1940–1944* (Düsseldorf, 1978).

Wegner, Bernd, *The Waffen-SS: Organization, Ideology and Function* (Oxford, 1990).

Weinke, Annette, *Die Verfolgung von NS-Tätern im geteilten Deutschland. Vergangenheitsbewältigungen 1949–1969 oder: Eine deutsch-deutsche Beziehungsgeschichte im Kalten Krieg* (Paderborn etc., 2002).

Weisz, Franz, *Die Geheime Staatspolizei. Staatspolizeileitstelle Wien, 1938–1945* (Vienna, 1991).

Weisz, Franz, 'Die Machtergreifung im österreichischen Innenministerium in-Wien im März 1938 und der Aufbau der Gestapo', in *Archiv für Polizeigeschichte*, 13 (2002), 2–8.

Welzer, Harald, *Täter. Wie aus ganz normalen Menschen Massenmörder werden* (Frankfurt am Main, 2005).

Wember, Heiner, *Umerziehung im Lager. Internierung und Bestrafung von Nationalsozialisten in der britischen Besatzungszone Deutschlands* (Essen, 1991).

Wengst, Udo, *Beamtentum zwischen Reform und Tradition. Beamtengesetzgebung in der Gründungsphase der Bundesrepublik Deutschland 1948–1953* (Düsseldorf, 1988).

Wentker, Hermann, 'Die juristische Ahndung von NS-Verbrechen in der Sowjetischen Besatzungszone und in der DDR', *Kritische Justiz*, 35 (2002), 1, pp. 60–78.

Westermann, Edward B., *Hitler's Police Battalions: Enforcing Racial War in the East* (Lawrence, Kan., 2005).

Wette, Wolfram, *The Wehrmacht: History, Myth, Reality* (Cambridge, Mass. and London, 2007) [Wette, Wolfram, *Die Wehrmacht. Feindbilder, Vernichtungskrieg, Legenden* (Frankfurt am Main, 2002)].

Wildt, Michael, *An Uncompromising Generation: The Nazi Leadership of the Reich Security Main Office* (Madison, 2009) [Wildt, Michael, *Generation des Unbedingten. Das Führungskorps des Reichssicherheitshauptamtes* (Hamburg, 2002)].

Wildt, Michael (ed.), *Nachrichtendienst, politische Elite, Mordeinheit. Der Sicherheitsdienst des Reichsführers SS* (Hamburg, 2003).

Wilhelm, Friedrich, *Die Polizei im NS-Staat. Die Geschichte ihrer Organisation im Überblick* (Paderborn, 1997).

Wilhelm, Hans-Heinrich, *Die Einsatzgruppe A der Sicherheitspolizei und des SD 1941/42* (Frankfurt am Main etc., 1996).

Wöhlert, Meike, *Der politische Witz in der NS-Zeit am Beispiel ausgesuchter SD-Berichte und Gestapo-Akten* (Frankfurt am Main etc., 1997).

Wojak, Irmtraud, *Eichmanns Memoiren. Ein kritischer Essay* (Frankfurt am Main, 2001).

Wysocki, Gerhard, *Die Geheime Staatspolizei im Land Braunschweig. Polizeirecht und Polizeipraxis im Nationalsozialismus* (Frankfurt am Main, 1997).

INDEX